The Safe Sea
of Women

The Safe Sea of Women

LESBIAN FICTION

1969–1989

Bonnie Zimmerman

BEACON PRESS · BOSTON

Beacon Press
25 Beacon Street
Boston, Massachusetts 02108-2800

Beacon Press books
are published under the auspices of
the Unitarian Universalist Association of Congregations.

97 96 95 94 93 92 91 90   8 7 6 5 4 3 2

Text design by Linda Koegel

ISBN 0-8070-7904-9
LCN 89-46057

To the women of Lesbian Nation

. . . and now she and the assistant and all women swam in a field of brilliant green, buoyed up by unbelievable green—gathered in a giant sweep all yellow and blue and scooped it into one untouchable safe sea of women.

—*June Arnold,* SISTER GIN

Contents

Acknowledgments

No one's ideas develop in a vacuum. Many other critics and scholars have influenced this work. I owe a debt of gratitude to the individuals—their names are liberally strewn through the chapters to come—whose ideas about lesbian literature and culture have so clearly left a mark on mine.

I am also deeply grateful to the friends and colleagues who read earlier drafts of part or all of this book. Joan Ariel, Ellen Broidy, Susan Cayleff, Clare Colquitt, Cassandra Magis, and Karen Vierneisel all contributed insights and suggestions that proved invaluable to its many revisions. Pat Huckle, my dear friend these many years, generously nurtured me through my worst bouts of insecurity and anxiety. I also received valuable suggestions from my editor, Joanne Wyckoff, and two anonymous readers of this manuscript. Most of all, my thanks go to Berlene Rice, partner extraordinaire, for her ideas, her criticism, her patience, her insistence that I speak honestly, and her enduring love and support.

I also appreciate the institutional support I have received. This book was written with the help of sabbatical and research funds from San Diego State University. Lauren Wilson provided excellent research assistance in the final stages of manuscript preparation.

I would like to extend my sincere apologies to Cassandra Magis and Namascar Shaktini for misspelling their names in the first printing.

Finally, there can be no criticism without creation. So I conclude by thanking the writers whose works made my own possible.

Preface

As a graduate student in the early 1970s, I discovered a reference work that was to serve me as well as any research tool my professors offered: *The Lesbian in Literature,* a bibliography compiled by Gene Damon, the preliberation pseudonym for writer, editor, and publisher Barbara Grier.[1] For days on end I sequestered myself in the university library, conscientiously looking up every novel assigned the letter "A," for "major lesbian characters, and/or action." Unsatiated, I then moved on to "B," for "minor" lesbian characters, and even to "C," for "latent, repressed lesbianism." To the literary critic growing within me, the category "C" promised the rich territory of subversive textual strategies to be decoded and deconstructed. But the impatient political activist had no time for codes. What she wanted were novels that proclaimed the word "lesbian" from the rooftops.

Only occasionally in those years did I come upon a novel—such as *Desert of the Heart* (1964) by Jane Rule or *The Price of Salt* (1952) by Clare Morgan (pseudonym for Patricia Highsmith)—that projected such a positive and empowering image of lesbians. Primarily, I found dreary portrayals of self-hating "inverts"—like Stephen Gordon in Radclyffe Hall's classic *The Well of Loneliness* (1928)—or snide satires of effete, self-absorbed "sapphists" as in Compton Mackenzie's *Extraordinary Women* (1928). Since then I have come to recognize the historical significance of these novels. But in those days of emerging lesbian feminist consciousness, I, like many other women at the time, wanted a literature that expressed the new truths and visions we were creating for ourselves. And so, a generation of authors began to write us into existence.

One author had already initiated this project. In 1969, novelist Alma

Routsong, under the pseudonym Isabel Miller, wrote *A Place for Us,* a love story about two women that rewrote all the established conventions of such stories: the sinister, half-inhuman creature seducing the innocent maiden; the symbolism of deviance and damnation; the inauthentic ending with each woman safely married or dead, but definitely not together in each other's arms. Her novel was romantic and pastoral, the lovers were equally responsible and involved, and they ended up together on the last page. This was a new plot for the lesbian novel and a new beginning for lesbian literature as a whole: the establishment of a literary and symbolic "place" for lesbian writers and readers.

Isabel Miller could not find a commercial publisher for her gentle tale, since it did not conform to the expectations of publishers or the reading public.[2] In 1969, it was as yet unthinkable that two women could love each other and be rewarded with a home and happiness rather than condemned to marriage or death. So Miller printed the novel herself and peddled it around the newly formed women's organizations in New York City and in the pages of *The Ladder,* newsletter of the Daughters of Bilitis, the sole lesbian organization existing at that time. The book's publishing history was a fitting symbol of the erasure of lesbians from public consciousness in the late 1960s, and its underground success foreshadowed what would become a burgeoning alternative publishing industry.

A Place for Us soon became one of the shuttles weaving the web of lesbian community from woman to woman, group to group, city to city. Dog-eared copies were passed around, greatly multiplying the impact of its modest print run of two thousand copies. I was but one of many women in those early days who entered through its pages into a new world I had barely imagined possible. Like the novel's lovers, thousands of us—some already lesbians, others just coming out—embarked upon a journey of heart, mind, and body: "Oh, we were begun. There would be no way out except through" (33).[3] By 1972, when McGraw-Hill bought the rights to *A Place for Us* and set it on bookstore shelves under the innocuous title of *Patience and Sarah,* lesbians all over the country were enthusiastically turning Isabel Miller's fantasy into reality.

And yet, *Patience and Sarah* might have remained a treasured anomaly, along with a few other grand exceptions, had it not been for the women who put their feminist principles into practice by starting independent women's presses. One of these, Daughters Inc., published some of the most creative and carefully crafted lesbian fiction ever to appear, as well as the representative contemporary lesbian novel, *Rubyfruit Jungle* by Rita Mae Brown (1973). Molly Bolt, the hero of this immensely successful book, was a new kind of lesbian figure—brash and unashamed, exuberantly sexual, and ultimately triumphant. Molly reveled in her outlaw status and set herself above the boring world of ordinary mortals. She represented what we were beginning to feel about ourselves, that to be a lesbian was to be daring, special, unique, and very fortunate.

But Patience and Sarah, and Molly Bolt, take off on their journeys alone and end up in their own private worlds still isolated from other women. In contrast, utopian fictions mapped out the terrain of exclusively female communities. One of these, *Les Guérillères* (1971), an epic prose-poem by French author Monique Wittig, created in a text what feminists were attempting to create through social and political activism: an entirely new way of thinking about women, patriarchy, language, and alternative social structures. This new way of thinking was by no means limited to lesbians, neither in the political nor the literary arena. But lesbians in particular were attracted to the notion of a separate space for women. We eventually named this space "Lesbian Nation" after the title of Jill Johnston's 1973 collection of wildly experimental newspaper columns, a book that laid some of the groundwork for what would become lesbian feminist theory.

At first, we new residents of Lesbian Nation felt ourselves to be united in the warm glow of "sisterhood," sexuality, and community—what June Arnold, in *Sister Gin* (1975), was to romantically label the "safe sea of women." But, as sisters often discover, even the closest relationship can be undermined or destroyed by fear, misunderstanding, and differences. The distinctly different outlooks and needs of women of varying sexualities, races, and classes began to splinter existing feminist and lesbian groups. Arnold's *The Cook and the Carpenter,* published in 1973 along with *Rubyfruit Jungle,* captured both the ideal of sisterhood and the reality of difference that were soon to dominate the theory and practice of the lesbian movement.

After 1973, lesbian activists moved in several different directions. Some of us remained active in various gay, feminist, or progressive organizations. Others left these groups completely to form the political movement of lesbian separatism, which concentrated on creating political theory, living collectives, and alternative institutions. Still others were attracted to what came to be called "cultural feminism," which tried to define a uniquely female nature, vision, and artistic expression. But whatever place we made for ourselves, we were part of the extraordinary phenomenon of creating a lesbian community and lesbian culture.

Since 1971, I have participated in the formation of this lesbian community. I also have been an avid reader of lesbian fiction. Although not a fiction writer myself, I have produced lesbian literary criticism and theory for both academic and lesbian journals, books, and newspapers. It has long been my intention to write a book about lesbian literature for the two groups to which I belong, the academic world of women's studies and the lesbian community.

The result is *The Safe Sea of Women,* an overview of the lesbian fiction published primarily by alternative feminist presses in the 1970s and 1980s. I attempt to read this fiction as the collective voice of what we loosely call "the lesbian community." In doing so, I use the fiction to identify what lesbians of the past two decades believe to be the "truth" about lesbian existence.

I have not written a historical or sociological document, although I do note the historical trends found within the genre and relate these back to the community that shapes and is shaped by them. Nor do I provide a sweeping "objective" analysis of the past twenty years of lesbian publishing. After all, it is still very much in process. Each year since 1984, when I began to develop the ideas that turned into this book, more than twenty new novels have appeared, and there are no signs that this proliferation is abating. Several literary journals, including *Sinister Wisdom, Conditions,* and *Common Lives/Lesbian Lives,* publish short fiction as well. Moreover, the political priorities of the community shift continually. Finally, I have been too involved in the community to take the stance of the detached critic, if such a stance is ever possible.

Instead, I want to echo Michal Brody's introduction to *Are We There Yet?* (the history of "Lavender Woman," a Chicago-based lesbian newspaper on which I worked from 1973 to 1975):

The history that follows is not a matter of record in any national publication. It is written the way I remember it, imperfectly, to be sure, and with personal bias. . . . Other witnesses will no doubt find disagreement between their accounts and mine. That's fine. If a single, concrete Truth were possible, this book wouldn't be interesting or even necessary. Contradiction, and what we do with it, is what it's all about.[4]

The Safe Sea of Women expresses my own individual analysis of lesbian fiction. Its perspective neither defines the genre nor represents "the" lesbian point of view. Of course, such a stance can be ingenuous, since fewer books on this literature are likely to be published than on more mainstream writers and texts. With this in mind, I have tried to be as dispassionate and responsible as possible, while still retaining my own point of view. But I do urge all readers to approach this book as the product of one thoughtful yet necessarily biased mind. The bias in my case is provided by my history as a white, professional academic who "came out" in the context of the women's liberation movement of the early 1970s. I look forward to other lesbian critics providing their own perspectives on contemporary lesbian writing. The "contradictions" between our accounts may well provide the space in which future lesbian fiction flourishes.

The Safe Sea of Women began with a short paper written for a conference on women's culture in 1984. Any piece of literary criticism is in its own way the creation of another story—a meta-story, if you like—and in that original conference paper, I outlined the "plot" of what became this book. As the first chapter explains, I view lesbian fiction as the expression of a collective "myth of origins" with four primary divisions (which have become the four inner chapters): the lesbian self, the lesbian couple, the lesbian community, and community and difference. My methodology was traditional: I began with close readings of every novel, memoir, and short story collection that might be labeled lesbian—close to 225 texts, 167 of which are included in this study. Although my analysis has been influenced and invigorated by various critical theories (some will say too much, some will say too little), I have tried always to give pride of place to the fiction itself. I have also allowed the specific texts, and the questions they raise, to dictate the particular methods and approaches I use.

For over a year, I read, annotated, compared, organized, patterned, and pondered until I felt I had located (or—remembering that criticism is itself invention—created) the most characteristic and prevalent symbols and structures within lesbian fiction. I then began to write my story. It has taken over three years to do so, and often I have felt like Alice and the Red Queen running as hard as they could just to stay in the same place. The beginning point was easy enough to choose—1969 was a watershed year—but what would serve as my end? Although friends advised me to set a cut-off date, I simply couldn't; my too-prolific authors kept writing more novels that perfectly fit, or didn't fit, my analysis. I kept adding new examples to the existing chapters, where they remain, until it became clear that my neat plot would require an epilogue. That has become chapter six, which discusses fiction since 1986. Finally, on New Year's Day 1989 (okay, it wasn't quite that tidy), I had to acknowledge the necessity of completion. Hence, the subtitle: *Lesbian Fiction 1969–1989.*

I want to say something about the audience I had in mind while writing this book. Although I hope it will be read by everyone, I have aimed it at a composite figure who is a feminist academic and a lesbian activist. This has not been an easy task. But I have tried to use the tools of contemporary critical theory, while writing in the language of what Virginia Woolf celebrated as "the common reader."[5] A related challenge has been to define my own voice, particularly in the matter of pronouns. Adrienne Rich has written, in a context to which I will return in chapter five, that "even ordinary pronouns become a political problem."[6] My version of the problem has been when to say "I," when to say "we," and when to say "they." I am not entirely satisfied with my solution, but here it is. When I directly express my own opinion, I use "I." When I am speaking about and from the amorphous and generic lesbian community, or to the representative reader, I use "we." When difference and particularity are the focus of the argument, I use "they" to refer to specific groups to which I do not belong. I hope the context will clarify my choices.

Finally, the hardest part of writing this book has been to silence the internal voices that would keep me from writing at all. These voices have many intonations. One very powerful voice belongs to the archetypal Parent who whispers, "But what will the neighbors think?" An even stronger voice is that of the Lesbian Censor who shouts, "You can't say that: it's _____ "(fill in the blank yourself). At times—many, many times—I have felt like the protagonist of Maxine Hong Kingston's *The Woman Warrior* who "tells" on her people. But I hope that I convey in these pages the strong loyalty and affection I feel for the lesbian community and the respect I have for its written expression. I write not as an outsider looking in, but as an insider looking around.

"It Makes a Great Story": Lesbian Culture and the Lesbian Novel

She was telling some one, who was loving every story that was charming. Some one who was living was almost always listening. Some one who was loving was almost always listening. That one who was loving was almost always listening. That one who was loving was telling about being one then listening. That one being loving was then telling stories having a beginning and a middle and an ending.
—*Gertrude Stein,* ADA

In the Glorious Age, the lesbian peoples call the old storytellers, bearers of fables. The bearers of fables come from everywhere and go everywhere.
—*Monique Wittig,* LESBIAN PEOPLES

{These stories} do what I had hoped stories would do: Provoke, teach, reveal women to other women, arouse strong emotions, redefine—because they are true.
—*Judy Grahn,* TRUE TO LIFE ADVENTURE STORIES I

During the past two decades, more than two hundred novels, memoirs, and short story collections have been written and published by women who align themselves with the lesbian movement. A few of these works have been published by mainstream publishers, but since the mid-seventies the vast majority have been published by alternative, usually feminist or gay, presses.[1] They are advertised through lesbian networks, sold in women's bookstores, and reviewed in lesbian, gay, and feminist newspapers. Like Isabel Miller's *A Place for Us,* they are passed around from friend to friend. Their politics, ideas, and literary quality are hotly debated both privately and publicly. Lesbian fiction, therefore, provides unparalleled source material with which to explore the ideas and beliefs of the lesbian community. If the lesbian novel merely mirrored the political and cultural concerns of lesbians, it still would serve an important historical function. But, I will argue, it has helped shape a lesbian consciousness, community, and culture from the movement's beginning.

Fiction is a particularly useful medium through which to shape a new lesbian consciousness, for fiction, of all literary forms, makes the most complex and detailed use of historical events and social discourse. By incorporating many interacting voices and points of view, novelists give the appearance of reality to a variety of imaginary worlds. Novels can show us as we were, as we are, and as we would like to be. This is a potent combination for a group whose very existence has been either suppressed or distorted. Lesbian novelists, then, have taken on the project of writing us into our own version of reality. To do this, they have revised the fragmented and distorted plots inherited from the past as new and "charming" lesbian stories that possess "a beginning and a middle and an ending." My purpose in this book is to show what these stories are and how the lesbian community endows them with meaning.

This chapter begins with a brief history of lesbian literature and an analysis of how, during the past twenty years, lesbian feminists established a sense of community and cultural identity. Second, it outlines the factors I use to define the contemporary genre of lesbian fiction. Next, it offers an explanation for why this genre is important, and a perspective on the quality of lesbian fiction. Following that, it examines the relationship between myth and reality as it is presented in lesbian fiction. Finally, it presents an introduction to the complex "myth of origins" that lesbian writers have constructed and that the rest of the book explores.

The Roots of Contemporary Lesbian Literature

In a 1976 essay on lesbian literature, novelist Bertha Harris argued that to "make a body of work that can be immediately perceived as a 'literature' . . . there must first exist cultural *identity:* a group or a nation must know that it exists *as a group* and that it shares sets of characteristics that make it distinct from other groups." To have a literature, she continued, lesbians must see themselves as a group with a history and sense of "realness."[2] To understand lesbian literature as a specific genre, therefore, it is necessary to consider how lesbians developed an identity as lesbians.

Prior to the twentieth century, women certainly loved other women, chose them as companions, and expressed erotic longings for them. We can draw this conclusion from Greek myths of virgin goddesses and their female followers, from international tales of female transvestites and amazons, from the Old Testament story of Ruth and Naomi, and especially from the lyric poetry written by Sappho (ca. 612–558 B.C.) on the Mediterranean island of Lesbos. On occasion, woman-to-woman eroticism erupts in works by writers such as the medieval troubador Bieris de Romans, the British restoration playwright Aphra Behn, and the nineteenth-century Chinese poet Wu Tsao.[3]

Moreover, between the seventeenth and twentieth centuries in western Europe and North America, some women experienced loving and supportive (although not necessarily sexual) relationships with other women that literary historian Lillian Faderman has named "romantic friendships."[4] These passionate and spiritual relationships were recorded in letters and diaries, and recreated in numerous novels and poems, including Sarah Scott's *Millenium* [*sic*] *Hall* (1762), Mary Wollstonecraft's *Mary: A Fiction* (1787), Christina Rossetti's "Goblin Market" (1859), Louisa May Alcott's *Work* (1873), George Meredith's *Diana of the Crossroads* (1885), and Sarah Orne Jewett's "Martha's Lady" (1897).

Women in the past, however, lacked the "sense of historical continuity" that Bertha Harris claims is a requirement for an explicit lesbian literature. Few felt themselves to be different from other women of their time, or to have an identity defined by a particular sexuality. Although we can recognize lesbian *behavior* or *feelings* throughout the centuries and across all cultures and nationalities, lesbian *identity* was the creation of the late nineteenth century.

Historians identify a number of factors that account for the rise of modern-day lesbianism in the western world.[5] Among these was the increased participation of women in the workforce that permitted some women sufficient economic independence to choose where to live and with whom. In female enclaves such as boarding schools, colleges, and settlement houses, some middle-class women chose lifelong companionship with other women over conventional marriages.[6] The nineteenth-century women's rights movement, like its counterpart in the 1970s, further stimulated the emergence of lesbian identity by increasing women's self-esteem, criticizing heterosexual norms, and providing another female space in which political passions might be eroticized. Sex-segregated factories may have provided similar opportunities for working-class women, although low wages made independent living difficult. Perhaps because of these economic barriers some of these women chose to live, work, and marry as men, often exposed only at their deaths as women.

Not all the influences on emerging lesbian (and gay) culture and identity were salutary, however. In the late nineteenth century, medical experts, or sexologists, began to define same-sex love and sexuality. At first they proclaimed homosexuality to be a congenital condition, if not defect, characterized primarily by cross-gender identification. In other words, lesbians belonged to a "third sex"; they were male souls trapped in women's bodies. This theory was challenged and displaced by Freud and his followers, who described lesbians as women whose normal sexual development had been arrested at an immature, adolescent stage. Although strikingly different from each other, both congenital and psychoanalytic theories "morbidified," as Lillian Faderman puts it, the love between women that in earlier centuries had been tolerated or even sanctified.[7]

In addition, the public presence and influence of the women's rights movement throughout the second half of the nineteenth century generated an anti-feminist reaction that we today would call lesbian-baiting. Women might write glowingly about living together in eternal bliss when they were economically, politically, and legally dependent upon men, but when suffragists and "new women" took advantage of their hard-won legal rights and economic opportunities to turn fantasy into reality, society drew the line. Sylvia Stevenson's recently rediscovered novel *Surplus* (1924) illustrates how post–World War I literature shifted public attitudes by providing cautionary stereotypes of unnatural, "race suicidal" women who preferred female friendships to heterosexual love and childbearing.[8]

Among these stereotypes was the figure of the sinister monster who preys upon innocent younger women. A lesbian version of the femme fatale, or dangerous woman, the man-hating spinster with her unnatural control over another woman took on mythic proportions in late-nineteenth and twentieth century literature.[9] In Sheridan LeFanu's ghost story, "Carmilla" (1871), she becomes an actual blood-sucking vampire. This unnatural creature inhabits the pages of novels as different in historical era and literary significance as Henry James's *The Bostonians* (1885), Clemence Dane's *Regiment of Women* (1915), D. H. Lawrence's *The Fox* (1922), and Dorothy Baker's *Trio* (1943). Along with the immature child afraid of womanhood and the masculine woman, both inspired by sexology theories, the predatory monster became a common lesbian stereotype persisting to the present day.[10] Hence, as the nineteenth century turned into the twentieth, lesbians began to have a label, an identity, for themselves, but that label was connected to notions of sickness and perversion.

Competing with these anti-feminist and medical discourses, however, was the distinctly lesbian literature and sensibility that arose at the beginning of the twentieth century in Paris. With the growth of urban centers during the nineteenth century, newly independent women could find meeting places, such as bars, social clubs, and salons, which were safely anonymous. For some, the "sexual undergrounds" of New York, Berlin, and Paris—the latter vividly portrayed by Toulouse-Lautrec—offered a welcome respite from the moralism of the dominant culture.

For others, the literary movement of modernism provided new forms through which to express the radical changes occurring in attitudes toward sexuality and gender.[11]

Of particular importance to the development of a self-conscious lesbian literary tradition was the group of economically-privileged and artistically-inclined women centered in Paris around the expatriate authors Natalie Barney and Renée Vivien.[12] From classical mythology, biblical stories, historical examples, and the feminist ideology of their era, Barney and Vivien fashioned an image of lesbians as extraordinary and superior creatures possessing a unique sensitivity to life and literature. In particular, they seized upon Sappho—who had recaptured public imagination in 1892 when archaeologists discovered fragments of previously unknown poems—as their inspiration and model. Barney and Vivien explicitly identified themselves as Sappho's heirs, and, in their lives and their texts, tried to re-establish her circle of women-loving poets. Many of Vivien's erotic poems, which initiated self-defined lesbian writing, are responses to and rewritings of her great precursor, Sappho.

But Renée Vivien (like Djuna Barnes, author of the modernist classic *Nightwood* [1936]), borrowed her image of Sappho and lesbians from the exotic "femme damnée," intoxicated with death and lust, of the Symbolist poets Baudelaire, Swinburne, and Pierre Louÿs. Vivien's version of lesbianism thus oscillates between exquisite damnation (the tone of Colette's depiction of Vivien in *The Pure and the Impure* [1932]) and astonishing feminism, the latter most notable in her philosophical novella, *A Woman Appeared to Me* (1904).

Nonetheless, Vivien was noteworthy for her unambiguous inscriptions of lesbian sexuality and identity. Many other serious writers of that era—such as Gertrude Stein, Virginia Woolf, Angelina Weld Grimké, Amy Lowell, and Willa Cather—relied instead upon codes and subterfuge to express lesbian desire, a strategy that protected them from censure. By suppressing pronouns, changing the gender of characters, inventing a cryptic language for sexuality, or hinting obliquely at relationships between women, these writers could tell, but not quite tell, lesbian stories. Through codes, Woolf could evoke lesbian love ecstatically in *Mrs. Dalloway* (1925) and whimsically in *Orlando* (1928), a fantasy portrait of her lover, author Vita Sackville-West. Stein, a significant role model for contemporary lesbian writers, wrote (but never published) *Q.E.D.* (1903), a realistic novella about a lesbian triangle, and *The Autobiography of Alice B. Toklas* (1933), which clearly portrays the domestic side of her relationship with Toklas. But to write about sexuality and passion, Stein created an elaborate private code in texts like "Lifting Belly" (1915–17) and "A Sonatina Followed By Another" (1921).

Natalie Barney, virtually unique in her era, declined both the damnation of Renée Vivien and the codes of Gertrude Stein. She survives today not through her writing—plays and epigrams which have yet to be translated and published in any significant number—but through the representations of her life by other writers. Her most significant manifestation is as Valerie Seymour in the classic lesbian novel, *The Well of Loneliness* (1928), by Radclyffe Hall. Valerie offers a welcome relief from the tortured self-hatred of the hero, Stephen Gordon, that wounded male soul trapped in a woman's body. It is ironic that Hall, a writer of modest talents compared to her illustrious contemporaries, should have created the novel and hero that have had the most profound and lasting influence on modern-day notions of lesbians. Yet, for all its old-fashioned rhetoric about "inversion" and its stylistic infelicities, *The Well of Loneliness* never obscures its central premise: that homosexuals deserve a place within nature and society. It is, moreover, an old-fashioned, readable novel with a strong plot, a noble and martyred hero, sharply-defined secondary characters, plentiful romance, and a tearjerker ending. It was shocking enough to be condemned by moralists, apologetic enough to be approved by sympathetic liberals, and explicit enough to be eagerly welcomed by lesbians. Hence, for over forty years, *The Well of Loneliness* and Stephen Gordon virtually defined lesbianism.

Shortly after its publication, *The Well of Loneliness* was condemned as obscene and officially banned in Britain until the 1960s. This was but the first sign of the periodic waves of repression that would attempt to wipe lesbians and gay men out of public consciousness and even existence. The Stalinist era in the Soviet Union effectively reversed the liberatory policies enacted during the early years of the Russian Revolution; for example, homosexuality was recriminalized in 1934. The contemporaneous Nazi movement went far further by destroying thriving gay communities throughout Europe, sending myriads of gay men and lesbians into exile or concentration camps.

On the cultural front, the situation was more mixed. Tightening moral standards throughout the 1930s rendered lesbianism so invisible in the mass media that the first film version of Lillian Hellman's famous 1934 play, *The Children's Hour,* eliminated the accusation of lesbianism around which the plot revolves. But lesbianism remained an acceptable, even popular, literary subject. Many novels published during the 1930s deserve a place in literary and lesbian history, among them the aforementioned *The Autobiography of Alice B. Toklas, Nightwood,* and *The Pure and the Impure,* Vita Sackville-West's *The Dark Island* (1934), Dorothy Richardson's *Dawn's Left Hand* (1931), Gale Wilhelm's *We Too Are Drifting* (1935) and *Torchlight to Valhalla* (1938), and Christa Winsloe's *The Child Manuela* (1933; a novel based on her play and film, *Mädchen in Uniform*). Jeannette Foster's 1956 classic, *Sex Variant Women in Literature,* surveys dozens of other novels, plays, and stories by male and heterosexual female writers that depict lesbians at length or in passing. Most of these, however, were strongly laced with the homophobic stereotypes of predatory, masculine, infantile, or hopelessly unhappy lesbians that were the legacy of early twentieth-century writing.

In the United States after World War II, Joseph McCarthy's House Committee on Un-American Activities identified homosexuals, along with communists and liberals, as subversives. The resulting purges of suspected homosexuals from government service inspired similar witch-hunts in virtually every sector of society throughout North America and Europe. Retaliation against known homosexuals was certain, swift, and brutal. Stories of those days record how gay people lost their jobs and homes, suffered incarceration in mental institutions and prisons, and endured violent attacks in the streets and bars. Lesbians and gay men lived double lives, always fearing exposure, except for the few political activists and overt "butches" and "queens" who, by their choice of lifestyle, were forced to the margins of society. Although the 1950s also saw the formation of gay and lesbian organizations, such as the Mattachine Society and The Daughters of Bilitis, the years between *The Well of Loneliness* (1928) and the rise of gay liberation (1969) were bleak ones indeed. Nonetheless, hidden, underground gay communities survived in large urban centers. Centered around bars and private friendship networks, they formed a subculture that, as the language of the time reminds us, existed "in the shadows" or "in the twilight world," but not in the bright, open light of day. [13]

Perhaps because lesbian life was so hidden during those decades, the written word was crucial to sustaining and promoting lesbian identity. More lesbian novels were published in the United States during the 1950s and early 1960s than at any other time in history. Most, however, were pulp paperbacks that depicted lesbians as tragic, maimed creatures trapped in a world of alcohol, violence, and meaningless sex. The plots either doomed them to a cycle of unhappy love affairs or redeemed them through heterosexual marriage. Many of these novels were soft-core pornography written by men for men. Those written by women (whether lesbian or not) seldom challenged the insidious conventions and formulas, although occasionally an author revealed an affirmative and subversive subtext beneath the homophobic surface. Ann Bannon, in her Beebo Brinker series, created several strong lesbian characters, while Valerie Taylor gave her protagonist, Erika Frohmann, surprisingly feminist attitudes. Whatever their quality or perspective, however, the pulp novels were read avidly by lesbians and reviewed seriously in *The Ladder,* the one lesbian journal of that era. [14]

These pulp paperbacks were crucial to the lesbian culture of the 1950s because they offered proof of lesbian existence. Any story that depicted a lesbian world, no matter how deeply submerged in the shadows, was valuable to a woman who otherwise felt herself to be alone. Moreover, the recurrent theme of suffering and sacrifice, as in *The Well of Loneliness,* invested a character with nobility, allowing the reader to feel, if not happy, at least purged and uplifted. The pulp novels also provided some women with welcome representations of lesbian sexuality and relationships. These women may have read against the grain, finding in the excesses and distortions of the text an ironic and amusing affirmation of their membership in a hidden and special subculture. Finally, the best of these stories portrayed lesbians as strong and independent women, and thus indicated the feminist direction that lesbian politics and literature were to take.

Serious and substantial fiction also emerged in the 1950s and 60s, bridging the gap between the great modernist writers of the 1920s and

1930s—Woolf, Barnes, and Stein—and the explicitly feminist literature of the late 1960s and early 1970s. Catharine Stimpson, in her essay
on the twentieth-century lesbian novel, identifies Mary McCarthy's
best-seller, *The Group* (1963), as a turning point in public consciousness
because its appealing lesbian character, Lakey, breaks with the stereotypes of the past.[15] I would point to two other, less mainstream, novels
that have a central place in the development of a lesbian literary tradition. *The Price of Salt* (1952) by Clare Morgan and *Desert of the Heart*
(1964) by Jane Rule, both sensitive and dignified novels in the tradition
of the 1950s romance, demonstrated how lesbian fiction, freed from the
stereotypes and narrative conventions of the past, might determine its
own voice. Unlike the tragic or childish characters in most pulp paperbacks, the lesbian lovers in these novels are complex characters who
make choices for themselves. Although they struggle with their identities and their place in society, they are permitted satisfying and authentic endings. These novels, and a handful of others, such as May Sarton's
Mrs. Stevens Hears the Mermaids Singing (1965) and Maureen Duffy's *The
Microcosm* (1966), signaled the beginning of an entirely different way of
writing about lesbians.

In 1969, Alma Routsong's *A Place for Us,* or *Patience and Sarah* was
published. *A Place for Us* came into the world quietly and would not
have had its current significance had it not been for the political and
social events transforming western societies during the 1960s and
1970s. Lesbian life and literature was never the same after this time.

Lesbian Feminism and Lesbian Culture

In 1969, the hidden gay world exploded into the open when drag
queens and dykes at a Greenwich Village bar, the Stonewall Inn, fought
back against one police raid too many. Gay liberation was born that
night into a political arena already established by the civil rights movement, the new left, the anti-war movement and the emerging women's
liberation movement. Very quickly, lesbians within gay liberation and
women's liberation coalesced into what came to be called lesbian liberation, and later lesbian feminism. Although not the first generation to
openly proclaim their lesbianism, the women who came of age during
the 1960s were able to establish the most dynamic and pervasive sense of

lesbian cultural identity ever recorded. More than any group of lesbians in history, we (for I belong to this generation) insisted upon our right to say who we are, what we think and feel, how we live and love.

Many factors combined to make this transformation possible. The first was the sheer number and variety of women—bar dykes, college students, housewives, working women—who initially sought out lesbian organizations and social events. These numbers provided clear evidence that we were a distinct and potentially powerful group. Furthermore, the example of Black nationalism spurred many groups, lesbians being just one among them, to solidify their cultural identities. The process of separating from women's liberation or gay liberation groups also intensified our perception of ourselves as a group. Political activism, as well, bonded lesbians together. And, perhaps most important of all, feminist ideas, like ripples spreading out on water, eventually touched most lesbian communities and all lesbian creativity.

Those of us who began to identify as lesbian feminists asked anew the simple question, who or what is a lesbian? One answer is that lesbians are women who love and desire women rather than men. For some women that is definition and identity enough, but for lesbian feminists in the early 1970s, it was only a starting point. We argued that when women commit their passion and attention to other women, we defy society's most fundamental expectations and prohibitions for female behavior. Hence, lesbian feminists evolved a political or metaphoric sense of what it means to be a lesbian.

The theory or political position of lesbian feminism combined a commitment to female integrity, bonding, and sexual passion with an uncompromising rejection of male-centered ways of thinking and being. In place of these old ways, lesbian feminism presented a perspective from the margins of patriarchal society, a point of view rooted in women's forbidden love and desire for one another. Lesbian feminists proposed, therefore, that the word "lesbian" *stood for* a specific relationship to the dominant society rather than simply being a name for women who "happen" to make love to other women.

The first such use of "lesbian" can be found in a manifesto written in 1970 by the Radicalesbians collective, "The Woman Identified Woman," which defined the lesbian as "the rage of all women condensed to the point of explosion." To French theorist and writer Monique Wittig, "lesbian" signified that which disrupts western patriarchal and heterosexual dualism. The lesbian does so because she lives outside the rule of the fathers, because she is, as Bertha Harris put it, an outlaw and monster. Critic Mary Carruthers further argued that in lesbian poetry (and, as we shall see, in lesbian fiction as well):

> The word *lesbian* encapsulates a myth of women together and separate from men. . . . *Lesbian* is also the essential outsider, woman alone and integral, who is oppressed and despised by traditional society, yet thereby free to use her position to re-form and remember. . . . *Lesbian* is also erotic connection, the primary energy of the senses which is both physical and intellectual, connecting women, a woman with herself, and women through time. Finally, *lesbian* signifies a change of relationships, radical internal transformation; it is a myth of psychic rebirth, social redemption, and apocalypse.[16]

To all these writers, the word "lesbian" represented a point of view, or mode of interpretation, rather than a sexual behavior or innate identity. In the late 1980s, some lesbians, including a number of novelists, replaced this expansive political definition with the more specific sexual definition of lesbianism. But during the 1970s and early 1980s, the meaning of the word "lesbian" was profoundly influenced by feminist politics and ideology.

In the process of creating this feminist point of view, contemporary lesbians shaped a distinctive lesbian, or lesbian feminist, culture.[17] The term "culture," as I use it, refers to more than literature, music, theater, and art, although the production of these creative forms has been one of the most notable activities of the lesbian community. Culture also encompasses the ideals and ethos of a group, all the intangibles that distinguish it from other groups. In the words of critics Billie Wahlstrom and Caren Deming, culture "limits and organizes human experiences. It does so by providing a version of reality that guarantees the shared meanings necessary for social existence."[18]

Unlike many other social groups, lesbians, as we have seen, have had a difficult time establishing a "version of reality" that makes sense of our experiences *to us*. Lesbian existence has been so shrouded in "lies, secrets, and silence," to borrow Adrienne Rich's phrase, that we have struggled mightily to establish those "shared meanings."[19] The events of 1969 broke the silence surrounding lesbian existence and thus stimulated the creation of the group identity that Bertha Harris, in 1976, named as a requirement for a distinctly lesbian literature. That identity was shaped in accordance with feminist beliefs and further refined by our artistic endeavors.

Feminism, in every historical era, emphasizes the right of women to develop their own voice and speak (or write) about their own reality. Accordingly, the creation of a lesbian feminist identity has gone hand-in-hand with the creation of specific cultural artifacts, such as novels. Between 1969 and 1978 lesbian writers, invigorated by political radicalism and literary experimentation, set out the premises of a new genre. Many of them consciously hearkened back to lesbian writers of earlier decades: Bertha Harris to Djuna Barnes, Monique Wittig to Renée Vivien and Natalie Barney, Jill Johnston to Gertrude Stein, and June Arnold to Virginia Woolf. Elana Nachmann (who later renamed herself Elana Dykewomon) and Sharon Isabell wrestled with the legacy of Radclyffe Hall, while Jane Rule and Isabel Miller emerged from the lesbian romance genre of the 1950s. Some of them fashioned their stories directly out of the materials of their own lives; others created an imaginative and daring language unique to this period in contemporary lesbian literary history. Together, they created an audience for the coming out stories, romances, and utopias that have been the staple forms of lesbian fiction ever since.

These lesbian writers, along with artists, musicians, political theorists, and myriads of unnamed women, deliberately and self-consciously established a sense of continuity with lesbians of the past and community among lesbians in the present. This community—or Lesbian Nation—possesses, in the words of Monique Wittig, "its own literature, its own painting, music, codes of language, codes of social relations, codes of dress, its own mode of work." [20] Wittig goes on to claim that this lesbian community and culture is diverse and international: "Just as they are unlimited by national frontiers (the lesbian nation is everywhere), so lesbians come from all social categories."

While Wittig's claim is theoretically compelling, in reality this lesbian culture has been embraced so far primarily by white western women. Lesbian culture is not delineated by actual geographical boundaries, which may explain why the territorial metaphor of Lesbian Nation is so widely used. We do not have a common language, although lesbian "wimmin" love to play with etymology, creating new words and original spellings.[21] Nor is lesbian identity established through a shared birth heritage; lesbians "come out" rather than being born into a culture as African-Americans or Jews may be. No matter what your desires are at age two or twelve, you still must choose to act upon your feelings and identify with the community.

Lesbian culture is like a philosophical or religious system that provides its adherents with a way of viewing the world anew. A Jew, Christian, or Moslem, for example, finds a ready-made mythology, history, literature, and ethos waiting for her. For the past fifteen to twenty years, lesbians have been constructing a similar cultural identity from existing traditions, lifestyles, myths, and stories. We mix together Sappho, amazons, Gertrude Stein, and Natalie Barney (who herself manipulated and recreated myths and symbols); add bar culture from the fifties; season liberally with new left politics and new age consciousness; strain through traditional literary metaphors; and cover over completely with feminism to produce a lesbian culture. Today when a woman comes out as a lesbian, she has an identity and belief system waiting for her should she choose to embrace it.

Defining Lesbian Fiction

Among the products of lesbian culture is the flourishing genre of lesbian fiction. What defines this genre? What do we mean by "lesbian writing" and "lesbian writer"? Like the category "women's literature," "lesbian literature" is not defined by inherent, static characteristics that can be easily and uniformly identified and agreed upon, but by the perspective of a community of writers and readers. The boundaries of the genre are and always will be fluid, since writers may enter or leave and readers may disagree over its exact perimeters. "Lesbian" is not an ethnic or national designation, nor is it a stylistic or historical one, although it combines elements of each.

Instead, lesbian writing can best be defined through a *cluster* of factors; if a writer or text exhibits enough specific characteristics we can call her or it "lesbian." The factors vary according to historical era; what identifies a lesbian in 1980 may differ from what did so in 1880 or 1930. Keeping in mind that this book covers the period from roughly 1969 to 1989, the following are the factors I use to identify lesbian writing.

The first is the writer herself, for the nature of lesbian fiction makes it impossible to separate the text from the imagination that engenders it. [22] Lesbian writers, unlike those writers who incorporate a lesbian character or lesbian scene in a novel, are women who identify themselves in some way with the lesbian community. [23] They may identify themselves as lesbians in their creative writing (by stressing autobiographical elements, for example) or in biographies or interviews. They may do so through their choice of publisher, since certain presses are exclusively or primarily lesbian or gay. They may publish their works in lesbian journals, give readings at lesbian bookstores and centers, or attend lesbian panels at conferences.

Since writers do not always leave obvious clues to their identity, we next turn to the literary text itself. A lesbian novel has a central, not marginal, lesbian character, one who understands herself to be a lesbian. In fact, it has many or mostly lesbian characters; it revolves primarily around lesbian histories. A lesbian novel also places love between women, including sexual passion, at the center of its story. Fiction that inscribes relationships between women through codes and allusions does not belong in the genre of self-defined lesbian literature. A contemporary lesbian novel very often exhibits lesbian intertextuality; that is, it refers to famous lesbians of the past and present, to lesbian events such as music festivals, and to other lesbian books. It also expresses a women-centered point of view. Unlike heterosexual feminist literature (which also may be very women-centered), a lesbian text places men firmly at the margins of the story.

Third, I include audience reception—who reads the books, and for what purpose—as part of this definition. Lesbian novels are read by lesbians in order to affirm lesbian existence. Conversely, the books a woman reads are what make her a lesbian feminist, or a member of "the lesbian community." Lesbian fictions function like the coming out stories that Julia Penelope Stanley and Susan Wolfe describe; they "are the foundation of our lives as Lesbians, as real to ourselves; as such, our sharing of them defines us as participants in Lesbian culture, as members of a community." [24]

A number of critics have identified a possible fourth factor—lesbian style. Since lesbianism is a disruptive, experimental lifestyle, the argument runs, lesbian writing ought to be radically transformative.[25] Adopting Virginia Woolf's attack on the patriarchal sentence, these critics argue that lesbian writers, like their early twentieth century foremothers, reject conventional language, plot, and structure.[26] We might expect, therefore, to find contemporary writers employing postmodernist techniques (such as self-referentiality, unconventional plot structure, an unstable chronology and narrative voice) to disrupt the illusion that the goings-on in the text simply mirror "real life."

Although this aesthetic theory is intellectually compelling, I see little evidence that lesbians employ a unique style or form. Only a handful of writers—such as Bertha Harris, Monique Wittig, June Arnold, and Elana Nachmann, all of whom published important works between 1973 and 1976—use experimental techniques. June Arnold herself offered a provocative definition of the lesbian novel as a collective form "developing away from plot-time via autobiography, confession, oral tradition into what might finally be a spiral. Experience weaving in upon itself, commenting on itself, *in*clusive, not ending in final victory/defeat but ending with the sense that the community continues."[27] In fact, neither the "disruptive" nor the "spiraling" form survived much beyond the 1970s. Instead, most lesbian novels have become so conservative in style and form that the representational mode reigns virtually unchallenged today.[28]

But if there is no unique lesbian style, there are, finally, subjects and themes characteristic of lesbian fiction, particular ways in which lesbian writers express the visions and beliefs of the lesbian community. Through these, the writers of novels, short stories, and fictionalized memoirs attempt to establish the "real story," the "truth" about lesbian existence. However, truth is not exactly the same thing as objective reality; moreover, reality itself is an elusive concept. I shall argue, therefore, that lesbian writers create a *mythology* for the lesbian community, one that can be both inspirational and stifling. What we present as the truth about lesbians certainly includes representations of real life, but it also includes the myths and fantasies that provide us with a sense of ourselves as what Monique Wittig calls "lesbian peoples."

The Question of Quality

Although the genre I have defined has an avid following of addicted readers, ever-increasing numbers criticize the literature for being naive and unsatisfying in both form and content. This criticism, originating within the community itself, makes it necessary to address the question of whether or not lesbian fiction is "good" enough to merit serious attention from literary critics, or to satisfy the common reader. Julia Penelope, for example, asks, "Why do I usually feel 'ripped off' somehow, as though I expected something from a book that the writer didn't, and couldn't, give to me? What do I want that I'm not getting?" Joanna Russ responds by castigating the existing body of lesbian feminist fiction:

> Oppressed minorities experience a cultural and artistic deprivation which makes any art about our lives precious to us whether it's good, bad or mediocre.
>
>   Nonetheless the literature that gives people a sense of identity and pride in one way can also be clumsy, stupid, anti-sexual, romantic in the bad sense, simple-minded, evasive about such gritty realities as money and power, contemptuous of the old or those who look "funny" or are the "wrong color," snobbish, thin, humanly empty and in all ways disrespectful of the beauty, horror, power and infinite variety of the universe. I find most Lesbian novels (like most other novels) unbearable for the above reasons.[29]

Russ and Penelope join a long line of readers, both scholarly and common, who remain unsatisfied and in gastric distress after heavy meals of lesbian fiction. To an extent this distress arises from the narrow and static definitions some apply to lesbian fiction. If we refer only to those popular romances published by a handful of overtly lesbian presses, we may well characterize the genre as "unbearable." But we overlook many other texts that qualify such pessimism. We also fail to notice the changes that occur over time, such as a striking improvement in style and content. Moreover, to understand why contemporary lesbian fiction only sporadically fulfills our expectations, we must consider aspects of lesbian culture that affect literary quality.

The lesbian feminist culture that dominated the 1970s, and continues as one strong voice among many in the 1980s, was fiercely egalitarian. Unlike the dominant culture, or even mainstream feminist culture, both of which expect artists and writers to possess special talents, lesbian culture operates under the assumption that if any woman can be a lesbian, then any lesbian can (and should) be a writer. The breaking of the long silencing of lesbian speech has led to a flood of intense, immediate, intimate, and sometimes awkward written expression. Writers are more likely to be motivated by politics than by art, as the lesbians who named themselves C.L.I.T. (Collective Lesbian International Terrors) both mandated and predicted:

> We are also training ourselves to respond in writing, to make up for the present lack of Lesbian literature and media. This is a beginning step in demolishing the "creative artist" or "writer" mystique that separates and inhibits us, giving some the role of active "star" while the rest remain the passive audience.[30]

Lesbians often write not because they feel compelled to create art or because they love language, but because lesbians need a literature that is honest and true (or at least true to the image we are creating about ourselves). They begin to write as amateurs (in the original sense of the word, as "lovers"), one reason for the preponderance of autobiographical novels, which may be assumed to be the easiest form for a neophyte to master.[31]

When combined with a characteristic lesbian distrust of all standards perceived to be male, heterosexual, middle class, and elitist, such ultraegalitarianism can produce naive or poor writing. At the same time, it can be an asset. Women who have historically been shut out from the literary establishment are encouraged to tell their stories, thereby adding to the supply of plots, images, and fantasies that constitutes the language of lesbian literature. Lesbian literature, in principle at least, is unusually sensitive to varieties of experience, to the needs of a diverse community, and to the integration of politics and art.

But while the lesbian community has developed alternative standards of *content*—standards based upon honesty and fidelity to the range of lesbian lives—it has yet to redefine artistic quality. Instead, the community holds to a leveling imperative which can lead to "trashing," the lack of support for, or outright condemnation of, expertise (as we see in the quotation from C.L.I.T.). Reviewers may avoid serious criticism in favor of sisterly support, except when political values are in question. When Joanna Russ, for example, demolished the embarrassingly bad fantasy novel, *Retreat,* she herself was attacked by other writers for failing in sisterhood.[32]

If, on the other hand, a writer steps over the line of acceptable political belief—if she is "politically incorrect"—she may be savaged by her more correct critics. Political correctness, a lesbian version of "socialist realism," can be a straightjacket for the lesbian writer.[33] Even though the community began to joke about political correctness in the 1980s, most lesbian writers have internalized a rigid censor. We (for I fight this censor in myself) still write with fetters on, fearing to alienate any segment of the community. As a result, much lesbian fiction exhibits a subtle or not-so-subtle party line, avoids satire and irony, and is ambivalent about the imagination and experimentation.

The dominance of these community standards may account for the fact that novelists abandoned experimental style and form after the 1970s. Since no clearly-defined lesbian audience existed at first, writers wrote for themselves, or for other writers. They certainly felt political responsibility, but not to any established lesbian "truth." This situation has changed dramatically. Writers today write for a community that wants its fiction accessible, entertaining, and just "correct" enough to be a bit bland. Like most readers, this audience is unfamiliar with experimental techniques; hence, lesbian novels are, ironically, "straight" forward—that is, traditional and realistic—in form. We might ponder the question of what lesbian publisher in the 1990s would take a chance with Bertha Harris's complex and difficult novel, *Lover.*

In short, many novels are produced by inexperienced writers who, despite their best intentions, construct conventional plots and flat characters; who are unfamiliar with the varieties of narrative voice; who pay little attention to literary history and theory or to other writers; and who consider style to be the means to an end (the story) and not part of the end itself. Many lesbian writers, like the readers and writers of formula romances that Janice Radway studies in *Reading the Romance,* perceive language as nothing more than "a tool for accomplishing some purpose. In sum, it 'says' things."[34] In lesbian narratives, the "thing" that language "says" is the experience of being a lesbian—and the quicker we get on with it, the better. Few individual writers use language as a complex signifying system, or present multiple and interacting layers of plot, character, or theme. Moreover, even the most skilled and sophisticated writers may be sufficiently receptive to the political and popular demands of the community to avoid experimentation, ambiguity, irony, philosophizing, or controversy. Although readers increasingly call for more complexity and subtlety, many lesbian novels remain disappointingly thin and transparent.

Because so many novels are written within the context of what has become a dominating and forceful lesbian mythos, in certain ways lesbian fiction resembles a popular genre. Like the historical romance or the mystery, it is molded by specific conventions and formulas.[35] To give an obvious example, most lesbian novels require good lesbians, bad men, and happy endings. As a result, too many are a mere cut above potboilers. Even fiction that aims conscientiously at verisimilitude can be obvious and often forgettable. The most realistic texts can be so heavily laced with politically correct ideas and conventional images that their portrayal of reality is compromised by romanticism and sentimentality.

These inadequacies must be attributed in part to the reluctance of critics and publishers to sort out the good from the bad, the effective from the ineffective, the original from the clichéd, and thereby encourage a more complex approach to storytelling. But even were we to do so, junk novels might still prevail because, twenty years after its inception, lesbian fiction is as much a commodity as is its mainstream counterpart. The hungry audience that now exists demands sustenance from a commercially successful alternative publishing industry. Novels that need revising or even abandoning are instead rushed into print; some of our most popular authors publish one or more novels a year.

But to say that much lesbian fiction is conventional is not to say that it is bad. It is to say, rather, that the fiction is bound to the community that engenders and absorbs it. The significance of lesbian fiction lies not so much in the individual text abstracted from its political and social context, but in the genre taken *as a whole,* in its interplay of ideas, symbols, images, and myths. The purpose of this writing—self-aware or not—is to create lesbian identity and culture, to say, *this* is what it means to be a lesbian, *this* is how lesbians are, *this* is what lesbians believe. Whatever their aesthetic value, lesbian texts are "sacred objects" that bind the community together and help express—by which I mean both reflect and create—its ideas about itself.[36]

Mythmaking and Truthtelling

The purpose of lesbian fiction is to "map out the boundaries of female worlds"—of Lesbian Nation—and in this way assist women in coming out, provide models for behavior, and encourage us to feel good about ourselves.[37] Like the coming out story, fiction "continu[es] the process of recreating reality and creating a continuum of wimmin's culture and community; connections are made among wimmin in the present, and a record of the past becomes available to wimmin of the future."[38] Accordingly, lesbian novels are written as much for education and inspiration as for entertainment. Nancy Toder, for example, explains that she wrote *Choices* "to inspire women to be the best that they can be. I wanted to create an autonomous, *whole* female character who is lesbian. The power of such images in helping us create ourselves is tremendous."[39] Other texts, such as Jeannine Allard's *Légende,* with its suggestive title, offer themselves as inspirational tales for contemporary readers so they can live and love and perpetuate the lesbian world.

In short, lesbian fiction incorporates myths. Myths are "sacred stories" (to use Mircea Eliade's terminology) that "illustrate what primarily concerns [a] society . . . [and that] help to explain certain features in that society's religion, laws, social structure, environment, history, or cosmology."[40] Myths tell a people who they are, where they came from, and how they are to act. The myths incorporated in lesbian fiction help us construct the meaning of our lives. They resemble the epic tales of the past: at the same time that Homer entertained, for example, he also instructed far-flung people in what it meant to be Greek. This similarity was noted by Elana Nachmann when she compared her protagonist in *Riverfinger Women* with the "traveling storyseller," Homer (4).

Lesbian mythmaking (like the creation of new words and spellings) is a political project aimed at overturning the patriarchal domination of culture and language. In Noretta Koertge's *Valley of the Amazons,* Helen, a separatist ideologue, offers this argument to the novel's protagonist:

"Don't ever doubt the power of myths, Tretona—I mean womyn's myths, not the bullshit stories we grew up with. We have to build a feminist mythology and recover womyn's herstory. What difference does it really make how the two are intertwined? Both are sources for spiritual growth and political action" (38). Tretona, however, is not impressed by Helen's logic. Myth, in her view, is synonymous with falsehood: "It's phony biology. You're just spinning myths," which, she says, remind her of Nazi and Stalinist lies.

The debate between Helen and Tretona illustrates the complex relationship between mythmaking and truthtelling in lesbian fiction. Are myths simply lies and "bullshit stories"? Or are they the building blocks of lesbian culture? Is the purpose of fiction to tell the truth by reflecting an existing reality? If so, whose reality is being reflected and whose truth is being told?

It is certainly understandable that lesbians would be wary of myth when we remember how negative and harmful existing myths have been. The myths of sin and perversion or of the mannish or vampiric lesbian left their mark on virtually all lesbian literature preceding the current wave of feminist writing. From the sophisticated novels of Djuna Barnes and Radclyffe Hall through the pulp romances of the 1950s, the lesbian character "creates for herself a mythology of darkness, a world in which she moves through dreams and shadows."[41] Paradoxically, this mythic lesbian figure is believed to be both unreal and all too real indeed. A male-centered culture has no place for the woman who lives outside its boundaries. Unable to imagine an actual existence for lesbians, it creates fantasy images, such as the vampire, the monster, or the man-woman. And these are always *negative* images because the dominant culture also fears that such women really may exist; hence, they must be controlled and stigmatized through symbols of perversion.

Given such examples, we can see why the word "myth" connotes falsehood and inauthenticity to Tretona. Helen may exalt the power of mythmaking, but, in real life, many women deflate it. For example, a reviewer in the influential feminist newspaper, *off our backs,* criticizes Monique Wittig's mythic *The Lesbian Body* for neglecting to show the daily life of the island women. This reviewer prefers the written exchanges between jailed radicals Susan Saxe and Jill Raymond as a better "prelude" to the revolutionary world she desires.[42] Similarly, a character in Linnea Due's *Give Me Time* disparages the tribal vision of women telling tales "around the campfire in front of women's hogans in 2040." [43] It is hardly surprising, then, that Judy Grahn—an unparalleled myth-maker in her poetry and theory—titled her two edited collections of fiction, *True To Life Adventure Stories.*

In response to this skepticism, other writers argue that, if the meaning of lesbian existence has already been fashioned out of myth, stories with mythic weight are required to change it. Lesbian feminist writers should, and do, create their own myths to resist and then change the dominant culture. As critic, poet, and novelist Paula Gunn Allen defines it, myth is "a language construct that contains the power to transform something (or someone) from one state or condition to another." [44] An illustration of Allen's point is provided by Audre Lorde's memoir, *Zami: A New Spelling of My Name,* which expands the notion of "real life" beyond fact and "what really happened." Since real life includes myth, legend, fantasy, storytelling, and poetry, as well as events and experiences, Lorde names her work a "bio-mythography." As she explains, *Zami* "has the elements of biography and history of myth. In other words, it's fiction built from many sources." [45] The author shapes this material into a new story (a new spelling of her name) that becomes a myth for other women, particularly Black lesbians who have been bereft of myth and history.

Despite such persuasive arguments, most lesbian novelists write to provide their readers with an authentic portrayal of lesbian life, not a new mythology. In place of mythmaking, lesbian writers and readers often expect fiction to "tell it like it is"—that is, to tell the truth about lesbians in order to replace existing lies and stereotypes.

In the introduction to a recently published British collection of short stories, Alison Hennegan articulates the premises of this "truthtelling" position:

> Fiction offers many delights, fulfills many purposes but one of the oldest and most constant is to teach, inform, show us to ourselves in ways we recognise and acknowledge to be true. . . . But before we can recognize ourselves, we must be drawn true and, for lesbians, truth about us in fiction has proved hard to find. . . .

> People learn from fiction. They look to it for information, re-
> assurance, affirmation about the ways in which other (fictional)
> people feel, believe, act and—most important of all, it sometimes
> seems—love. Some critics may, do, find such a confusion of Life and
> Books maddeningly, even dangerously wrong-headed. Neverthe-
> less, readers (and different critics) doggedly, rightly continue to seek
> in imaginary lives and people values and experience which they re-
> cognise as 'real' and 'true.'[46]

Hennegan claims for "truth" what I have associated with "myth": the
values of "information, reassurance, [and] affirmation." Virtually all lesbian fiction is written to be useful, and to be useful it must be true.
What is in question, then, is the meaning of truth.

In general, lesbian readers and writers equate authenticity and truth
with a clear reflection of reality. Kady Van Deurs, in her memoir, *The
Notebooks that Emma Gave Me,* goes so far as to write, "I throw out The
Novel. I have nothing to give but my life—everything that has ever
happened as I know it. . . . Do think about the novel: is it the best,
most direct, most honest way we have to speak to each other?" (141).
When we read fiction, we expect it to reflect what we know (or believe
we know) to be the "honest" truth about lesbians. Like the young Arden
in Sheila Ortiz Taylor's *Faultline* or Nelly in Bertha Harris's *Lover,* we are
entranced by the presumed stability of "true facts" (4; 89). Many novels,
therefore, are transparently autobiographical, while others are jour-
nalistic slices of life. Their mode of exposition is classic expressive realism and their intention is fidelity to the dynamics of individual lesbian
lives and the collective lesbian community.[47]

It would be a fatal distortion to ignore this intention; indeed, it
would be a political erasure of lesbian literature since the creation of
authentic lesbian images and plots is a deliberate project to displace the
damaging myths and stereotypes of patriarchal culture. Having learned
through consciousness-raising and political activism that the old text is
full of holes, lesbians are constructing a whole new text. This new text is
then presented as the truth about the lesbian self, lesbian relationships,
and the lesbian community. When it is discovered to be inaccurate or
distorted, by racism for example, new texts are written to correct the old
and to reweave the fabric of our culture. As one version of truth is

unraveled, another truth is put in its place. Few lesbian writers or readers would be happy with the idea that we have been mostly telling half-truths—or that there may not be a truth at all.

Nevertheless, I question the notion that literature can simply reflect reality or even that it is possible to tell the truth in any literary form.[48] As the above metaphor reminds us, a novel is a text—a weave of words—not a mirror held up to life. Writers *create* truth and reality as much as they reflect it. This is particularly true of the visionary and experimental lesbian novelists of the 1970s, among them Monique Wittig, Bertha Harris, Elana Nachmann, June Arnold, and Sally Gearhart. But even the more conspicuously realistic texts of the 1980s lace their portrayal of reality with the myths of lesbian culture. Reality surely cannot be reduced to words on a page (as poststructuralist theory may imply), but neither is it a thing in itself that the diligent author can reproduce by close attention to phenomena.

As an example, consider a scene in *Patience and Sarah* in which Patience discovers that fire is yellow, not red (p. 10). This discovery is an important step in Patience's assertion of herself as an artist and a lesbian. She disentangles the fiction of fire by attending to how it appears to her; in other words, she reads the text closely and discovers that her community has been mis-reading it, or seeing only one story in it and naming that the truth. In place of that truth, however, the text constructs another: fire is "really" yellow. Yet fire is no more yellow than it is red. Fire is our perception of a chemical process, which we then name in our own terms.

Similarly, patriarchal culture "reads" the text of a lesbian life and names it deviant or depraved. Contemporary lesbians expose that reading by showing how it turns the lesbian into a fantasy or traps her in a fiction. In its place, however, we are easily tempted to enshrine another reading, equally static and potentially entrapping. In attempting to say *this* is a lesbian identity, *this* is what it means to be a lesbian, we simply call fire yellow instead of red. Rather than reveal the truth about lesbians, we fabricate new myths for old without acknowledging that our stories are exactly that—stories.

In a sense, then, lesbian myths and stories are no more "true" than the old patriarchal literature. But—and this is a crucial point—they do serve lesbians better. Where the old mythology was debilitating, the new is inspiring. As the irreverent protagonist of *The Sophie Horowitz Story* puts it, "it may not be exactly true, but it makes a great story" (54). Moreover, to say that lesbian writers are constructing stories and myths is hardly to criticize them. The task of the writer is precisely that: storytelling.

To create new stories and myths, lesbian fiction writers (some intentionally and some not) draw upon many of the fundamental myths and symbols found in western culture: the quest, the garden, the fall from innocence, the island. These give rise to basic narrative forms, including the *bildungsroman* (novel of development), the romance, and the utopian/dystopian fantasy. All these myths, forms, and symbols are shaped and altered by writers according to the premises of their particular era or culture, and they are transmitted through literary texts from one generation to the next. In other words, a writer inherits her language and stories from other writers, and not from the Great Mother, the female unconscious, or, for that matter, "real life."

To put it another way, lesbian writers revise the "good" (or neutral) myths of our common literary heritage in order to replace the "bad" myths tainted by homophobia and misogyny.[49] Lesbian fiction is not exactly a brand new way "to phrase what has never been," although it does present new versions of the old stories.[50] Nor is it the recovery of a preexisting women's tradition, although lesbian writers enthusiastically honor the women of the past.[51] Rather, lesbian fiction writers "appropriate" both the shared literary heritage and the particular ideas of our historical era, and "endow" them with the "intentions and meanings" of the lesbian community.[52] In the process of doing this, they also create new myths that are specific to the culture we are forming as lesbian feminists. These myths can serve as inspirational tales, or, as we shall see, they can themselves become "lies" that mute the voices of specific members of the community.

In sum, lesbian fiction employs elements of both realism and mythmaking in an attempt to create an "authentic" lesbian consciousness and voice, to express what lesbians feel to be true and important about ourselves.[53] Because lesbian literature is created by individuals who intend to tell the truth, it more closely relates to actual experiences than does a traditional mythology. Nevertheless, interwoven into the fabric of even the most transparently realistic texts are the myths, fantasies, political visions, and cultural ideals—in short, the ideology—cherished by the lesbian feminist community.

The Lesbian Myths

The most important myth for any community is its myth of origins.[54] Accordingly, lesbian writers have created a complex "myth of our own" that explains how the lesbian community became what it is, that describes our situation and condition, that defines us as a people. Myths of origins do not just valorize the past, they also make sense of the present and provide a blueprint for the future. The myth of origins in Genesis, for example, tells the story of the creation of the earth and the human race in the past, explains why there is suffering and death in the present, and teaches us how we are expected to live in the future. The lesbian myth of origins articulates a vision of a world existing before the bonding between woman and woman was disrupted by men and patriarchal power. It then offers this vision as a model for the communities we are creating in the present and for the future.

The most comprehensive of these mythmakers, Monique Wittig, skillfully and imaginatively blends ancient myth and prehistory with contemporary feminist ideology and poststructuralist theory. *Les Gué-rilleres,* for example, can be read as a feminist myth of origins recounting the battle of women against men and the creation of a new women-centered or egalitarian (it isn't clear which) society. Her second narrative, *The Lesbian Body,* reads in part like an epic of the ancient matriarchal past. That Wittig is consciously creating myth is suggested by the witty revisions of patriarchal legends such as those about the holy grail and the golden fleece strewn through her texts.

Lesbian Peoples: Materials for a Dictionary (written with Sande Zweig) presents the most fully-formed myth of origins for lesbians. Wittig pulls apart the floating lore of lesbian culture and the pseudohistory invented by writers like Helen Diner and Elizabeth Gould Davis, and presents the pieces in the form of dictionary entries from which a story can easily be reassembled.[55] Although the *Dictionary* spans a period of time from the prehistoric past to the imaginary future, it is hardly a history supported by "scientific evidence." However, since the lesbian peoples reject both "science" and "evidence," on its own terms her story may be as true as his-[s]tory. Schooled as she is in contemporary philosophy, Wittig suggests that there is no objective, incontrovertible reality to be reproduced by any text, whether fictional, historical, or scientific. What matters is what a group believes and uses to shape its yearnings: in other words, its myths. What the lesbian peoples believe about their origins is as true as a purportedly scientific, but actually patriarchal, history. And what we believe to be our destiny is what we cause to happen.

The myth of origins in *Lesbian Peoples* runs as follows. Once upon a time, in the Golden Age, women lived together in total harmony, undivided by nationality, language, or men (men are completely absent here, a tongue-in-cheek reversal of patriarchal myths in which women are the missing sex). The Golden Age ended when some women grew enamored of their reproductive ability and created the first division, that between the mothers and the amazons (allegorically, the division between heterosexual women and lesbians). The amazons became warriors and outlaws, the mothers became slaves and women.

Patriarchal history records the succeeding eras that intervene between the Golden Age and the second level of Wittig's myth: the Glorious Age, our own future. One day "a small group of companion lovers who called themselves the Red Dykes, in sheer modesty" create "the vanishing powder," and half the population simply walks away: "It therefore caused a double disappearance through which both parties forgot each other, did well and continue to do so" (128). No revolution, no violence; all the lesbians just skip town to create a new utopian world on islands ringed around the equator.

Through this story, Wittig invests the contemporary lesbian lifestyle with the dignity of a culture. As the lesbian peoples create their culture through shared storytelling, so in writing this book, Wittig creates a cosmology from the myths and tales of the past and our hopes for and visions of the future. Like any other myth of origins, *Lesbian Peoples* banishes linear time by merging the past (this is what happened to the amazons), present (this is how we are living now), and future (this is the nation we can create).

Lesbian fictions draw upon a variety of mythic traditions for their myths of origin: Jewish, Judeo-Christian, American Indian, African, Afro-Caribbean, and classical. Some authors, as we will see, revise the edenic imagery found in Genesis. Audre Lorde's *Zami* draws upon African and Afro-Caribbean myths and legends to create a myth of origins both for the author and for Black lesbians as a group. Sally Gearhart, in *The Wanderground,* uses the Greek myth of Demeter and Kore, which relates the rape of the goddess and the separation of mother and daughter by man (although, interestingly enough, it does not incorporate the story of Demeter's subsequent erotic relationship with Baubo, although this would seem indispensable to a lesbian, not merely feminist, myth of origins). In Gearhart's and many other feminist versions of the fall from grace, the snake in the garden is man or, more precisely, male violence. Such retellings invert traditional myths, such as the one in Genesis, in which the agent of the fall is woman. Other texts, like Wittig's *Lesbian Peoples,* assign responsibility to the community of women itself. Common to all, however, is the vision of an original lost time when women were sufficient unto themselves, or, at least, "a nostalgia for a lost Eden, the sense that, given another chance, we could do it differently." [56]

This myth of origins draws upon certain conventional symbols. The garden, for example, symbolizes a primeval memory—or, more likely, projected wish—that women were once together and whole in Paradise until we were exiled and lost our home. Home, a recurring image in the fiction, may be mother's womb or breast recovered through lesbian love, or, in critic Catharine Stimpson's words, "a return to primal origins, to primal loves, when female/female, not male/female, relationships structured the world." [57] Home may also be imagined as a mythical place of origin that is regained when we come together to create our communities of women. In a Marxist framework, this golden age may be identified as the pure communist era predating capitalism; in a Freudian/Lacanian scheme, it is the pre-oedipal phase prior to the separation of mother and child. Those lesbian writers disinclined to use either of these "male" constructs can turn instead to myths of ancient matriarchies or Sappho's fabled island (as did Natalie Barney and her circle, whose lives and texts strikingly resemble those of contemporary lesbian feminists) for images of that golden past. [58] The garden can be found at every level of the lesbian myth: it symbolizes the natural self we search for on our journey back from exile, the enveloping warmth of the lover's arms, and the utopian community of women.

Equally central to the Christian myth of origins—to its story of sin and redemption—is the idea of the fortunate fall. Originally we were created as innocent children, abiding in a womb-like place of peace, fruitfulness, and joy, without knowledge of suffering, pain, or death. But we were also created with free will, the capacity to err, and curiosity. Consequently Eve ate the apple, enticed Adam into joining her, and we became knowing and sinning adults. As a result we were exiled from the Garden and began our sad journey toward death. Christianity added to this Hebrew myth the idea of a savior born to reclaim us from death through his suffering. Because of Christ we will be reborn into immortality, not on the basis of innocence (the prelapsarian condition of Adam and Eve) but of knowledge and free will. Since none of this would have happened had not Adam and Eve sinned—no human community would even exist—the fall was fortunate.

Writers influenced by the Christian ethos continue to be plagued by this myth of sin and redemption. Lesbianism, which both transgresses the biblical injunction against same-sex relationships and signifies female refusal of male authority, casts a woman out of the garden and onto her journey into exile. The classic rendering of this tale is found in that very Catholic novel, Radclyffe Hall's *The Well of Loneliness.* Sinning against both heaven and earth, Stephen Gordon is barred from her ancestral home by the avenging angel, her own mother. She becomes first an exile and wanderer until, through love and suffering, she is redeemed, even becoming a veritable Christ-figure.

As lesbian literature has discovered its feminist voice, however, it has lost patience with the old Christian myths. The hero of M. F. Beal's *Angel Dance,* for example, remarks that the fall was probably engineered by Eve because she was tired of catering to Adam's whims. Jane Rule, in *Desert of the Heart,* "converts" her Eve figure to lesbianism, the very opposite of what conventional Christianity deems the virtuous life. Should an image of hell turn up, as in Elizabeth Lang's *Anna's Country,* a lover's touch strokes it away, just as feminism wipes out sin and remorse in the lesbian novel. Even novels that use evangelicism as part of their backdrop—such as Noretta Koertge's *Who Was That Masked Woman?* or Ann Allen Shockley's *Say Jesus and Come to Me*—banish Christian myth and imagery: there is no fall, fortunate or otherwise, no damnation, no redemption. Feminist writers are more likely to turn to other sources, such as Greek tragedy or American Indian legends, for the metaphor of falling, which they then use to signify the disempowerment of the adolescent lesbian (as in Paula Gunn Allen's *The Woman Who Owned the Shadows* and Michelle Cliff's *Abeng*), the pride and disobedience of the lesbian outlaw (as in Janine Veto's *Iris* and Dodici Azpadu's *Goat Song*) or, as I discuss in chapter five, the vertigo that accompanies growth into a new identity.

In both Judeo-Christian and Greek myth, the fall is followed by a journey into exile. Adam and Eve begin the sad human journey toward death; the tragic hero, such as Oedipus, travels from his high place into obscurity. But the journey may also be triumphant. In the quest myths that we find in all cultures, an exceptional being, the hero, begins a journey symbolizing the human adventure. This journey has been reshaped in the lesbian novel of development, or the coming out novel. The lesbian hero, a stranger in the strange land of heterosexuality, sets out on a difficult adventure that eventually brings her home to her lesbian self and the lesbian community. The community to which the lesbian hero journeys is typically situated on an island or in a pastoral setting. Thus, the island, the journey, the garden, and the fall are fundamental symbols in the stories lesbians tell about our lives.

I have structured this book around the three most prominent and pervasive myths in lesbian fiction: the formation of the lesbian self, the lesbian couple, and the lesbian community. These myths were established by several early novels. *Rubyfruit Jungle* (1973), placed the quest for a lesbian self at the center of the lesbian novel and concluded by creating a new lesbian hero. *Patience and Sarah* (1969) helped to define an ideal lesbian couple, continuing and refocusing both the traditional green world romance and the pulp lesbian love story. *Les Guérillères* (1971), although not explicitly a lesbian novel, inspired the notion of warrior women establishing a new territory—a Lesbian Nation—to which any lesbian might immigrate.

These myths are by no means static. They have been continually questioned and revised in later texts. In particular, the myth of a united, utopian community has been subverted by those texts that introduce the *differences* of politics and identity into lesbian literary expression. Overall, the myths of self (the quest), couple (the green world romance), and

community (the safe sea of women), along with their revisions and sub-
versions, are central to most contemporary lesbian fictions.

In the following chapters, I take the reader on a journey that parallels the
odyssey of the archetypal lesbian hero who populates our literature and
imagination. At first isolated and inchoate, the lesbian discovers herself
and shapes a definition of what it means to be a lesbian. As she moves
through the patriarchal terrain, she spies a possibility incarnate in another woman who may become her lover. Alone or together, these
women journey on to find their place in a new homeland, Lesbian Nation. They initially idealize this new community as a utopian site of
peace and harmony, but soon learn that they must confront the differences of personal identity and political persuasion that exist among
them. The ensuing struggle reshapes and to some extent fragments the
community, so that the hero journeys into herself to heal her wounds
and, in some cases, creates a new identity that is no longer mono-
lithically lesbian. As she pauses in her journey, the lesbian hero, and the
literature and community she represents, stands at a crossroads.

"Amazon Expedition": The Lesbian Self

Annie sighed deeply and leaned her face against Eleanor's hair.
"Tell me a bedtime story, Annie."
"Goldilocks?"
"No, silly, something real. . . ." . . . Eleanor giggled. "Tell me your
come out story. I never heard that."
—Lee Lynch, TOOTHPICK HOUSE

So you just go to any gym class
And you'll be sure to see
One girl who sticks to teacher
Like a leaf sticks to a tree
One girl who runs the errands
And who chases all the balls
One girl who may grow up to be the gayest of all.
—Meg Christian, "Ode to a Gym Teacher"

When lesbians meet—as friends, lovers, or community—we create bonds and trust among ourselves by telling coming out stories. Coming out is the rite of passage through which a lesbian establishes and affirms herself. It is the tale we tell ourselves to state who we are and why we exist, a gift shared between lovers, like Annie and Eleanor in Lee Lynch's *Toothpick House,* and among friends. It is the currency, the means of exchange, within Lesbian Nation. The telling of the coming out story can bind individual lives together, as in Maureen Brady's *Folly,* where, after their initial love-making, Folly and Martha take "to telling the story of that first night over and over, as a ritual" (145). The coming out story explains how we came to be lesbians, how our consciousness formed and our identity developed. It repeats a few basic patterns and defines a collective identity. The coming out story is one of the fundamental lesbian myths of origin, the first basic tale of all lesbian communities.

Coming out is an expression of activity, implying movement from one state of being to another. We come out of the condition or state of heterosexuality (or, in many cases, presexuality) into that of lesbianism. Coming out provides "a point of exit from mainstream heterosexist culture." [1] Further movement may take a lesbian out of the closet of denial, suppression, or passing and into a freer and bolder state of self and public expression. But the first movement is always a personal and interior one, the claiming or discovering of the lesbian within one's self. In lesbian novels, this movement is consistently imagined as a journey. [2]

The journey as a metaphor for personal growth or development of self pervades myth and fiction. We begin our journey at birth and end it only with death. The journey motif shapes the basic quest tale, which follows the extraordinary life adventures of a hero, as well as the fictional forms that derive from it such as the *bildungsroman* and the picaresque. Moreover, the Judeo-Christian myth of origins portrays the human journey as an exile from a superior state of being that once existed in the Garden of Eden and will exist again in Paradise. These literary and religious myths resonate strongly for gay people, who not only journey figuratively from heterosexuality to homosexuality, but may need to travel literally from an oppressive environment to one in which we feel ourselves to be free. The exile from home and the journey to a new and more promising land is central to most lesbian and gay lives.

This chapter explores how lesbian writers draw upon literary, religious, and experiential sources to write the story of the lesbian self. In doing so, they revise and transform the beliefs of the dominant culture into more authentic and validating tales that attempt to answer the question of what makes a woman a lesbian. We will also see some of the ways in which lesbian writers draw upon the archetypal figure of the hero to construct new shapes for the lesbian self.

The Coming Out Novel and Narrative Form

Novels about the lesbian self, or coming out novels, written prior to the onset of the gay liberation and women's liberation movements (ca. 1969) typically conformed to the pattern of the classic *bildungsroman*.[3] In these narratives—such as Radclyffe Hall's *The Well of Loneliness* (1928), Christa Winsloe's *The Child Manuela* (1933), or Dorothy Bussy's *Olivia* (1949)—the lesbian pilgrim progresses through the dangerous territory of heterosexuality, loosening the constraints placed upon her imagination (her lesbianism) by a hostile society (most often her parents, teachers, and employers, although every member of society is her potential enemy). Along her path she is educated socially, sexually, and emotionally; she discovers her "true self," integrates her lesbianism with the rest of her personality, and finally accommodates to the outside world by either rejecting her lesbianism (a rare choice), escaping through death or madness, or enduring a life of loneliness and despair.

Coming out in the prefeminist novel is a process that includes an awareness of sexual feelings for another woman, a realization that society condemns lesbian love, and an acceptance of lesbian identity through either sexual initiation or self-naming. The feminist coming out novels of the past two decades add to this process an affirmation of one's lesbianism to the outside world and a journey toward freedom. By rejecting heterosexuality, the new lesbian hero recreates herself in a different mode. Once she recognizes that coming out "connects us with power," as Adrienne Rich puts it, she can travel through the patriarchal landscape to its point of exit where she unites with other lesbians to create an alternative society.[4]

Some lesbian novels draw upon biblical tales of exile, such as the expulsion from Eden or the wandering of the Israelites in the desert, for their symbolism and narrative form. These stories reverse the patriarchal myth that presents lesbianism as a state of exile from "normal" heterosexuality. *The Well of Loneliness* demonstrates how a lesbian might internalize this latter story: because she transgresses the laws of God and Man, Stephen Gordon is exiled from her edenic birthplace and wanders in a symbolic wilderness. Stephen never comprehends that heterosexuality is a state of exile for many women. To find her "true self," the hero must come "home" to women.

Jane Rule's *Desert of the Heart* illustrates this shift from the patriarchal myth to its lesbian inversion. Published in 1964, this novel came out at the beginning of the organized and self-conscious lesbian feminist movement.[5] Evelyn, one of the two protagonists, journeys to Reno for a divorce and, while there, discovers her true self and true love in the desert, a starkly beautiful terrain lying outside man's law and human society. Her journey from the city to the wilderness resembles the first, archetypal, journey into exile, that of Adam and Eve; in coming to Reno, Evelyn has "been thrown out of the garden" (162). But Rule suggests that Evelyn only thinks she is an outcast when she first comes to the desert. In reality, Evelyn has been in exile in her marriage—heterosexuality is the alien territory—and she has come home at last to her lesbian self.

Feminist fictions of the 1970s make excellent use of these motifs of exile and journeying. For example, Verena Stefan's *Shedding* (written and published in Germany in 1975, then translated and published by Daughters in 1978), presents lesbianism as the final destination toward which the protagonist travels. The novel relates the story of the central character's journey through the "alien territory" of man's world (15). As Verena "sheds" her dependency on men and male judgment, she turns instead to women. Within the text, a myth of origins recounts how the original "circle of women" took a wrong turn and "scattered to the four winds" (9). The archetypal female journey is an interrupted one. In the world of men, Verena feels herself to be at worst a stranger and interloper and at best a guest, but never her own self. By traveling back to women, Verena rediscovers that self.

For Verena, the woman she finds is her childhood friend, Ines, with whom she had started out on the road to adulthood during her "pioneer days" (6). While Verena had been sidetracked into heterosexuality, Ines had continued on the road toward a self-affirming, feminist adulthood. As Verena herself begins to move into female enclaves created by the early women's liberation movement (such as a living collective and a political group) and eventually into an erotic relationship with another woman, she finds that she is "in empty space" (74). No longer living in the fatherland, she is not yet fully in Lesbian Nation: "A year ago, shortly before I left for America, the venture with Fenna began to take shape. We came upon regions of human affection which had lain fallow until then. . . . we even had to learn how to speak. We were at one and the same time helpless and grateful in barren, unmapped territory" (83). Verena's venture into this "unmapped territory," women's space, leaves her finally her own woman, whole and self-defined, with a vision of lesbian eroticism and female community at the end.

Shedding is an example of a "novel of awakening" in which a heterosexual woman falls in love and subsequently awakens to lesbian identity.[6] The protagonist of Elizabeth Lang's *Anna's Country,* another example, experiences coming out as a journey across the border into a new territory: Anna's country, or lovers' country. *To the Cleveland Station,* by Carol Anne Douglas, incorporates the journey motif in its very title. The protagonist, Brenda, oscillates between Washington, the location of her heterosexual life, and Cleveland, where her lesbian lover lives, as she wavers about coming out. Exiled from both places, adrift in no-woman's land, Brenda is lost in "the void" (27). She no longer wishes to inhabit the world of heterosexuality but she cannot reside in Lesbian Nation, the new world, because her lover forbids her to visit. Cleveland, for perhaps the first time, represents the promised land: "I am not allowed to go to Cleveland. You might wonder why I care. How many people would consider themselves in exile if Cleveland were their Eden, their Jerusalem?" (1).

Lesbian novels that follow a hero from childhood to adulthood adopt elements of the picaresque, another classic fictional form derived from the quest tale.[7] Molly Bolt, the hero of *Rubyfruit Jungle,* is a quintessential *picaro,* a bastard and orphan of unknown origins who is adopted by working class people. Leaving home at an early age to find herself and make her fortune, she undergoes a series of loosely-strung adventures that reveal her energy and cleverness. She indulges in love affairs along the way, but never finds her one true love. She gets in trouble, but always triumphs over adversity. After making her way to the lesbian paradise, Greenwich Village, Molly undertakes a final journey home, or at least back to her adoptive mother, to reconcile herself with her roots. As in the classic picaresque, she returns at last to the big city ready to conquer a prejudiced world.

Rubyfruit Jungle may be the best-known lesbian picaresque, but it is not unique. *Yesterday's Lessons,* by Sharon Isabell, although subdued and depressed in contrast to the more traditionally comic and spirited picaresque, also follows the fortunes of a working class hero. Unlike Molly Bolt, Sharon is unable to triumph over her poverty or society's hatred. Rather, she is beaten down by both. Her wandering appears aimless. Feeling hopeless and defeated much of the time, she never consolidates her lessons nor, as a result of them, becomes a better player at the game of life. She is definitely "a young [wo]man from the provinces" who can't find her way to the promised land.[8] Nevertheless, although Sharon is still "confused" and mired in the oppression that has plagued her throughout her pilgrimage, the last image of the book is one of buoyancy and defiance. Sharon gets on her motorcycle and flies: "I was flying and I was free and when I was on that bike I was happy. I begin to feel as long as I had that bike I had hope. No matter how many people laughed at me or no matter what anyone said they couldn't take that away from me. My Freedom!" (206). We don't know where Sharon lands, but we suspect that her defiance may aid her on her difficult journey.

The Existential Discovery: "I Am Not the Only One"

Whether it conforms to the *bildungsroman,* the religious tale of exile, the novel of awakening, or the picaresque, the lesbian coming out novel takes its pilgrim on a progress toward wholeness. The lesbian begins her journey—or "amazon expedition," to quote the title of the first lesbian anthology—alone and unguided.[9] The protagonist may comment metaphorically that there are no rules for being a lesbian, no maps to guide her along her journey. "I had no words for what I was. I had no models," writes the narrator of one "real life" coming out story.[10] The lesbian hero must overcome this invisibility, a metaphysical dilemma unique to homosexuals. The dominant culture suppresses her existence so thoroughly that she may not even know she exists.

As she proceeds, however, the hero may notice herself in a text. If these texts are patriarchal, as they usually are, she is presented with an unappealing or shameful image of lesbians. The text may not necessarily be written; in *Rubyfruit Jungle* and *Riverfinger Women,* the images are passed down through the jokes and innuendos of friends or schoolmates. But the act of reading, because it is private and personal, generates a particularly complex encounter with both shame and affirmation. When Sharon, in *Yesterday's Lessons,* discovers her first lesbian in a "true confessions" magazine, she feels "scared and happy at the same time" (50). To be sure, this image of the lesbian is so debilitating that it takes Sharon years to free herself of the fear the story awakens. And yet, even a contemptible image of a lesbian is proof that lesbians exist.

Ultimately, the lesbian character must find some way of exorcising fear and shame while holding on to the existential discovery: I exist. When Tretona, in Noretta Koertge's *Who Was That Masked Woman?,* learns about homosexuality in her therapy session, she heads immediately for the books in the HQ section of the library—an archetypal journey for the emerging lesbian. There she reads social science research informing her that, although lesbians exist in significant numbers, they are sick, maladjusted, or depraved. Tretona puts her graduate school training to good use by rejecting the shoddy methodology of these studies; as a result, she is able to claim a lesbian identity while ignoring the damaging conclusions of the experts. She is much luckier than the prototypical lesbian, Stephen Gordon, who subscribes to the image of the invert drawn from the pages of nineteenth-century sexologists. Since Stephen is unable to unravel the texts that create her identity, she remains trapped within their portrayal of the lesbian as a maimed creature.

Su, in *Sister Gin,* is also trapped within a web of words. When she finally comes out to her mother, she equivocates as best she can: "'I want to tell you something. I'm a lesbian, you know.' The last two words were included as buffer, so *lesbian* would be surrounded with palatable monosyllables" (77). Whenever Su is confronted by the angry, lesbian side of herself (whom she names "Sister Gin"), she immediately makes a date with a male friend, who acts as a buffer, like the words, "you know." When Sister Gin accuses her of hating the word lesbian (and thus herself), Su responds to her in a note, "*Lesbianism*. I hope I never *hear* that word again" (102−3). So powerful is the word, however, that Su crosses it out, rendering herself invisible, before she throws away the piece of paper. Only at the end of the novel can Su put away the lies and the gin, and proclaim her lesbianism to the world.

Sister Gin is a good example of how lesbian literature employs two competing "languages": the language of struggle and pain, and the language of celebration and joy. Catharine Stimpson, in her analysis of classic lesbian fiction, identifies these as the "narrative patterns" of the "dying fall" (struggle) and "the enabling escape" (celebration).[11] I use "language" here to refer not only to the specific words, symbols, metaphors, myths, and narrative forms an author uses to tell a tale, but also to the general concepts that shape the ideas and actions of individuals and groups: what we might call a "discourse" or an "ideology." As Stimpson points out, the language of struggle defines early twentieth-century texts, although the language of celebration seeps through the cracks as well. With the rise of women's liberation and gay liberation, however, lesbian literature abandoned the old language of struggle and pain for the powerful new discourse of celebration and joy.

Lesbian feminist novels are written, in part, to be counter-texts, stories in which isolated or unenlightened women can find images of strength and sanity. We establish lesbian community through shared experience and shared stories that overcome "our geographical and social isolation."[12] In many novels, a character discovers a feminist text with a positive image of lesbians. Elisheva, in Alice Bloch's *The Law of Return,* is at first inhibited by the texts of orthodox Judaism from expressing herself as a lesbian or an intellectual. Later she recognizes herself in the feminist books she finds in a Women's Center: "'Of course,' she says to herself. 'Of course. It's so simple. This book is about me. I am one of these women. I am a lesbian'" (214).

A few writers cast a skeptical eye at the convention that texts or stories create lesbian lives. Jane Rule, who often smashes the icons of lesbian orthodoxy, has her lesbian character Alma in *Contract with the World* reject all textual models. After comparing herself to Kate Millett, Violette Leduc, Rita Mae Brown, and Adrienne Rich, Alma concludes that as a writer she in no way resembles them. She particularly distances herself from mainstream feminists by insisting that for her and most women, "loving another woman is nothing but that, with no redeeming politics or transforming art" (154).

Although Alma rejects the idea of the text as a transforming model, inspiration, or vision, most lesbian feminist writers claim exactly the opposite. The author of *Légende,* for example, defines her novel as just such an inspirational text: "What I have tried to do is envision the lives of several people who, each in her own way, lived out a destiny with authenticity, faithfulness, courage, and hope—the potential for which resides in all of us. I hope that, like me, it gives you dreams and visions, and courage to make them true" (10). Not surprisingly, the texts themselves are replete with writers writing texts. A major motivation for lesbian writers, both of and within texts, is the imagining of a new literature that creates new stories and new images for lesbians. These new stories express how lesbians live and feel—or, at least, how we believe we live and feel. As Inez Riverfingers says, these writers are forming us "into identifiable shapes" (*Riverfinger Women,* 7).

Nature, Normality, and Lesbian Existence

In order to create new shapes for the lesbian self, the lesbian writer must challenge and eventually transform the language, or ideology, of the dominant society. Specifically, she must dispel its conviction—and her own internalization of it—that lesbianism is unnatural or abnormal, that it is a sin or illness. The gay and women's liberation movements countered this conviction with the claim that lesbianism is healthy, normal, and natural. The lesbian novel takes up this debate in a complex fashion. While some novelists argue fervently that lesbianism is gloriously normal and natural, others call into question the concept of normality itself.

The religious definition of homosexuality as a sin is nowhere evident in lesbian feminist literature. Patience and Sarah, for example, discover their lesbian love in a calvinist New England community without ever experiencing the judgment of religious law. At worst, Patience's sister-in-law quotes St. Paul only to be flustered when his condemnation turns against those who condemn others.

Other narratives demonstrate that life is not so smooth and comfortable for the lesbian hero. She may still find herself trapped within the modern dichotomies of "natural" and "unnatural," or "normal" and "abnormal." As lesbians of earlier generations questioned whether or not homosexuality was part of God's plan, so contemporary lesbians may ask if Nature has a place for us. Society responds with a resounding no, citing either religious texts or pseudoscientific literature that link sexuality to reproduction. Nature, it is assumed, is only concerned with reproducing itself.

In *The Well of Loneliness*, Radclyffe Hall intermingles both religious and psychological terminology as she leads Stephen Gordon on her quest to prove that God and Nature make a place for inverts. Stephen resolves her dilemma—for she is extremely conventional and believes that nature is a grand reproductive machine—by differentiating between two meanings of "nature": first, the natural world or Mother Nature, and second, human nature or the inclinations of the self. Since Stephen feels her nature to be homosexual, and since her own nature must be part of Mother Nature, she concludes that there must be a place for homosexuals in God's scheme.

Maricla Moyano's *BeginningBook*, written in 1962 but not published until a decade later, is virtually obsessed with a similar question about the normality of lesbianism.[13] Her protagonist, Calvert, cannot accept herself as a lesbian because she thoroughly associates heterosexuality with a normal, healthy life aimed at reproduction, or the "life-purpose." Love between women, on the other hand, is "utter frivolity and irresponsibility" (24). Since heterosexuals are capable of reproducing themselves, they connect with the ongoing time-stream, while lesbians live only in the moment. Calvert's dilemma resembles Stephen Gordon's and so does her solution. She too transforms the metaphor of nature from biological to psychological. Having once perceived love between women as unhealthy because it did not fit with natural law, she later sees it as moral and orderly because it is consistent with her own nature. Society, she decides, not nature, deems homosexuality unnatural. Acting in accordance with one's own desires constitutes the healthy life. Life with a woman restores the wholeness she had lost by trying to live a so-called normal life with a man.

There is a noticeable element of special pleading in *The Well of Loneliness* and *BeginningBook,* resting as they do upon the assertion that whatever an individual wants to do is "natural." Many readers might prefer the position suggested by the clever title of Anna Livia's *Relatively Norma:* all concepts of normality are relative, not because homosexuality is normal and natural, but because heterosexuality itself is weird and crazy. Who among us, gay or straight, is capable of defining what is or is not normal?

Some contemporary writers tackle head-on the question of the naturalness of lesbianism. Jane Rule sets the stage for this by dismantling the very concept of nature in *Desert of the Heart.* On the surface, nature is not always fecund and blooming. The desert appears sterile and empty, as homosexuality may to ignorant onlookers, but in fact the desert is a natural landscape bursting with life. Ann and Evelyn fall in love in the desert, and make love there by a desolate lake. By redefining nature, Rule appropriates it for lesbian use, a solution not unlike that of Stephen and Calvert. In another way, however, she asserts that the desert is "antinatural," a landscape in which life must fight to survive. Like the gambling casino, the desert symbolizes free will and choice—the characteristics that make us fully human. Lesbianism is in its way antinatural; that is, it disrupts the biological "imperative" linking sex and reproduction. The casino rising in the desert, love blooming between two women: both are representations of the human will creating life in any landscape.

Rule suggests one particularly intriguing direction in contemporary lesbian theory: since lesbianism exists outside the realm of nature, it represents the most fully human existence. This position permeates novels of the 1970s, such as M. F. Beal's *Angel Dance* (1977). Her hero contrasts a domestic reality constrained by the biological rhythm of birth, sex, reproduction, and death, to a nocturnal world inhabited by "all the rest of us socio-politico-sexual-intellectual deviants" (117). According to proponents of this view, the unnaturalness of the lesbian makes her a shatterer of conventions, and, as we will see, an outlaw, monster, or warrior within patriarchy.

Bertha Harris, in *Confessions of Cherubino* (1972), extols this romantic image (in her case, derived from Renée Vivien and Djuna Barnes) of the lesbian as a decadent creature of the night who shuns fertility and daylight. At first, Ellen yearns for a "normal" life embodied in a pleasant little home like that of her parents; later, she decides that to live in such a way would result in the loss of her extraordinary self. Similarly, Inez Riverfingers at first wants to "make a movie about Inez and Abby, so that people would see that lesbians are beautiful, there is nothing, nothing at all unnatural about them, they too can have weddings and be in the movies" (*Riverfinger Women* [1974], 13). Like Ellen in *Confessions of Cherubino,* she abandons that fantasy for one of lesbians as "tough street women" (4). Both novels associate the normal and natural with the ordinary, with heterosexuality. Lesbianism, by contrast, is antinatural and antinormal and hence extraordinary.

Bertha Harris embellishes this position in *Lover* (1976), although here she abandons her fascination with nocturnal decadence. The family of women in *Lover* is utterly unnatural, super-normal, extra-ordinary— and healthy and flourishing. There isn't even a "normal" world with which to contrast them. They *are* the world; *they* define its terms and its limits. Theirs is a world that "inverts" all expected terms (perhaps Harris's backhanded tribute to Radclyffe Hall), a world in which false is true and abnormal normal, where mothers bear daughters with no men around and all women are lovers. By banishing the category "women," Harris eliminates the conventional categories of nature. She suggests that we define ourselves by our activity, loving, and not by our reproductive function. Like Jane Rule and M. F. Beal, Harris proposes that "lesbian" is a more profoundly human definition than "woman" because it disrupts the inevitable connection between sex and reproduction.

But as the dreams of Ellen in *Confessions of Cherubino* and Inez in *Riverfinger Women* indicate, lesbian feminists also insist that lesbianism is gloriously normal and natural, perhaps more natural for women than heterosexuality. Because our first love is for our mother, the argument runs, society must force daughters on an unnatural path away from other women and toward men. Heterosexuality may be the norm, but it is not natural, or at least no more natural than lesbianism. This insistence upon the naturalness of lesbianism is certainly one reason why so many love scenes and relationships in lesbian novels are consummated outdoors, in the arms of Mother Nature.[14] Stephen Gordon is never so gloriously at one with her own nature as on her honeymoon with Mary Llewellyn in the lush gardens of Tenerife. Lesbian novelists also affirm the naturalness of lesbianism by claiming, as in *The Wanderground* and other utopian novels, that women have a special tie with nature. Lesbians love to pick up information about lesbian seagulls and parthenogenic lizards: any trivia supporting the notion that lesbianism is part of Mother Nature.[15] We may become archivists like Donna, in *The Cruise,* who "maintained a large scrapbook with clippings of articles from newspapers and magazines that showed homosexuality to be quite within the order of things; or where gay men and women were written up favorably as brave, law-abiding, upstanding citizens of a community" (127).

Finally, some writers—all in the 1980s—assert the natural, normal status of lesbianism by celebrating the lesbian mother. If sterility and nonprocreativity "proves" that lesbianism is unnatural, then the lesbian mother represents a contradiction. Malthus, a character in *Faultline* (1982) calls the lesbian mother an oxymoron. He is proven wrong, however, by Arden, an ardent lesbian and a terrific mother of six. Not surprisingly, as the normality of lesbian existence has become a dominant discourse within the lesbian community, many other novels—such as *Between Friends* (1982), *Triangles* (1984), *Spring Forward, Fall Back* (1985), *Sinking/Stealing* (1985), and *Look Under the Hawthorne* (1987)—feature lesbians as mothers.

The Woman with a Difference

Whether an author places lesbianism in nature or against it, she is likely to associate lesbianism with difference from social norms. Djuna Barnes, in her 1928 satire, *The Ladies Almanack,* first described the lesbian as a "Woman born with a Difference."[16] Like Barnes, contemporary feminist authors change the connotation of this difference from *stigma* to *superiority*—a rhetorical move that sociologist Barbara Ponse labels the "aristocratization" and "radical destigmatization" of lesbianism.[17] The fictional lesbian-to-be knows herself to be alien, other, outsider, weird, or queer—although she may have no idea that this difference is connected with sexuality. At first she experiences her difference as a stigma, a sign that she has been rejected by and exiled from her community. After ascribing new meaning to this difference, however, she claims her lesbianism as a sign of superiority, or at least of her place in an alternative community previously hidden from her. The terms of her difference may then become codes or metaphors for lesbianism itself.

According to social science research, many lesbians grow up feeling different before recognizing themselves as lesbians.[18] Of equal importance, the quest hero in literature and myth is often marked as different from her or his peers, perhaps by being the offspring of royalty or the gods.[19] In the lesbian coming out novel, this mark is typically connected to strength and intelligence, artistic sensibility, or, in particular, the reversal or rejection of traditional gender roles. Drawing upon both experiential and literary models, lesbian authors transform the stigma of difference into a celebration of otherness.

In *The Well of Loneliness,* to begin with the most notorious example, Stephen feels herself to bear "the mark of Cain," the mark of inversion and damnation. After Cain slays Abel, God "marks" him and sends him into exile. In a parallel fashion, the lesbian, having committed the heinous crime of same-sex love, is exiled from the world of normal heterosexuality and marked by God for all to see. But, reading Genesis more closely, we note that God actually marks Cain to protect him from harm, not to punish him. So it is possible to interpret the mark of Cain as a sign of God's protection, as if lesbians are singled out for a unique role in society. Stephen learns that "inverts" are often creative artists and that she bears a special gift and responsibility. In this way, she eventually transforms the mark of Cain from that of the pariah to that of the chosen one.

Jane Rule, without succumbing to Radclyffe Hall's tortured self-pity, also portrays difference as a source and "mark" of lesbian identity in *Desert of the Heart.* Evelyn (whose last name is Hall) carries "the mark of a strong, intelligent woman like the brand of Cain on her forehead" (50). Her "unfeminine" strength, we learn, is one reason her marriage failed. "Strong, intelligent woman" is one prefeminist code for lesbian. In feminist literature, it serves as one of the claims made for the specialness and superiority of lesbianism: strong women are lesbians, lesbians are strong women.

Molly Bolt, the hero of *Rubyfruit Jungle,* epitomizes this identification between difference and specialness. Molly is unique from birth; she is half-French, traditionally a magic nationality in lesbian culture. Molly decides early in her life that she does not want to be like other women, trapped by the female destiny of marriage and motherhood, nor does she want to grow old or die like her cousin Leroy's mother.[20] She also rejects the only observable alternative to womanhood, being a man, since men aren't particularly enviable either. Her adoptive father's life is hard and short; Leroy is clearly her inferior. Both roles are so undesirable that Molly will have to carve out an adult role radically different from that of either male or female. Molly must become a lesbian.

But this rejection of gender dualism is precisely why the lesbian is stigmatized. In a particularly "true-to-life" experience, Molly learns that the word "queer," the most despised of epithets, refers to someone or something that cannot be assimilated into traditional gender roles, and is, therefore, frighteningly different.[21] Longing to be different, however, Molly embraces her identity as a rule-breaker, outlaw, queer, and lesbian.

The author spares Molly the consequences of her choice. Although a tomboy, she is not masculine. She is smart, popular, and a leader. Her affairs remain secret until she is free of society's clutches. Even getting thrown out of college for her lesbianism becomes a blessing, for it sends her off on her path to adulthood. Homophobia may exist in the world of *Rubyfruit Jungle,* but it leaves no lasting mark on Molly Bolt.

Unlike Molly, Inez in *Riverfinger Women* bears the full burden of social condemnation. She is fat and crazy, and then "queer" on top of that. She gives the world many weapons with which to attack her, and the world (in the form of a male schoolmate and then the Committee, an embodiment of patriarchy) uses them with glee. Inez's adolescence may be a more faithful representation of reality than is Molly's, but the two share a similar understanding of difference. Inez knows herself to be "the *odd person out,*" the one who did not sell out, as she puts it, to Spock and suburbia (5). The price she pays is high: "Think then what it would mean to be a queer. Hey, Lezzie, come over here" (19). At a time when lesbian sexuality "is at best a joke . . . at worst, a weapon," Inez learns how inhibiting it is to be a homosexual in America: "To know inside yourself at seventeen is not the same as saying it out loud" (33, 66).

In contrast to *Riverfinger Women, Patience and Sarah* presents a joyous example of the lesbian difference. Since Patience and Sarah have no model for their love, their ability to fall in love and act upon that love shows how and why certain women, and not others, find themselves as lesbians. Patience and Sarah are not perplexed over the possibility of women loving women. It's easy and natural for women to love and cherish each other, particularly in sex-segregated societies.[22] But they ponder how to connect that love to sexuality and separation from conventional society. The author implies that Patience and Sarah become lovers because each is unique and special. Differing from other women in their community, they acknowledge and accept their feelings for one another. Patience's sister-in-law, on the other hand, is too conventional to act upon her strong feelings for Patience. Other women may be too conventional and obedient to recognize those feelings at all.

Patience is different because she is an artist. She can see things that others cannot, and finds a way in which to express them. She can see what color fire "really" is and not just what it is commonly called. Similarly, she can see who Sarah really is, and that two women could fall in love with each other in defiance of society's rules. Sarah is different because she was raised as a boy. In a farming family of daughters, someone must be "the boy," and Sarah was designated for the role. She wonders if her ability to speak openly of her love for Patience is connected to her ability to use a gun, a classic phallic symbol that in this context signifies potency and activity, not masculinity. Sarah possesses the power of doing and acting that is reserved for men in a patriarchal society.

Both Patience and Sarah are outsiders. Each has a power derived from feeling special, and each is in internal exile from her society's ways and customs. Since Patience and Sarah differ radically from their world— Patience sees, and Sarah acts—they also name a feeling that others have felt but have been unable or unwilling to name for themselves.

As Sarah's story illustrates, the most common indicator of future lesbianism is adolescent tomboyishness.[23] Stephen Gordon and Molly Bolt, Manuela in *The Child Manuela,* Calvert in *BeginningBook,* Sharon in *Yesterday's Lessons,* Tretona in *Who Was That Masked Woman?*—all are tomboys. In prefeminist literature and in contemporary popular culture, lesbians are masculine women. But in feminist coming out novels, tomboy behavior has nothing to do with male hormones or male identification, and everything to do with freedom.[24] It is a sign not only of incipient lesbianism, but also of incipient feminism. These novels associate athletics and preference for boys' activities and boys' clothing with the rejection of the traditional, narrow choices allotted to women. Maleness signifies freedom, comfort, activity, and choice. The schoolgirl protagonist of Maureen Brady's story, "Corsage," for example, wishes "she were a boy so she could wear pants to the assembly. She'd be less vulnerable. So many things could happen to you in a skirt" (*The Question She Put to Herself,* 39). The list of disasters she subsequently conjures up fully justifies her longing for the safety of pants.

Should the protagonist identify too strongly with the masculine role, however, the events of the novel and the influence of other characters teach her that she is following the wrong path. Sarah, for example, at first doesn't do "woman things" (*Patience and Sarah,* 21). Unlike Molly Bolt, she rejects the limitations of femininity without recognizing the equal limitations of masculinity. Although Sarah's boyishness is part of her charm, Patience knows that her attraction to Sarah is lesbian, not pseudo-heterosexual: "Time enough later to teach her that it's better to be a real woman than an imitation man, and that when someone chooses a woman to go away with it's because a woman is what's preferred" (23). In fact, Sarah learns about womanhood not from Patience, but from her own experience passing as a male in the outside world. She realizes that she does not want to be male: "I didn't *like* to fight. I never really knew for sure till then how much I had the feelings of a woman, and not only that but I rated a woman's feelings higher" (79). Sarah returns to Patience no longer a boy, but a lesbian.

Constructing a Lesbian Self

The lesbian coming out novel, drawing upon both experience and the conventions of the quest myth, imagines a lesbian identity structured around a subjective sense of difference. But some readers might object that I am begging an important set of questions. Are these characters different because they are lesbians, or lesbians because they are different? Do Molly, Sarah, or any of the others reject the typical female choices because they are lesbians, or do they become lesbians because they reject these choices? In other words, is one born a lesbian or does one choose to become one? Is there an innate lesbian self that the hero is questing after? If so, what causes or explains it?

There are no simple, "common sense" answers to these questions.[25] Theories about lesbian identity have shifted throughout the centuries in response to the psychological or political ideologies that dominated a particular era. Most western religious traditions define homosexuality as a conscious choice to engage in forbidden sexual behavior. Sexologists in the late nineteenth century, such as Karl Heinrich Ulrichs and Richard von Krafft-Ebing, countered this position with the first "scientific" theory proposing a homosexual identity established at birth. According to this theory, a lesbian is a congenital invert; like Stephen Gordon, she is a man trapped in a woman's body. The "inversion" theory quickly lost ground to the developmental models of Freud and his followers, which located lesbian identity in the failure to make a complete transition from childhood to adult female sexuality (defined as "normal" heterosexuality). Next came the existential theory of choice put forth in Simone de Beauvoir's *The Second Sex,* which led directly to contemporary lesbian feminism. In its emphasis on free will, it proposes an etiology for lesbianism ironically similar to that of the religious notion: to be a lesbian is a choice that any woman can make (or resist). Finally, congenital theories not unlike those of the nineteenth-century sexologists are having a resurgence of popularity within the gay and lesbian communities today.[26]

This brief history suggests that "identity," far from being a given or an essence, is instead *constructed* by the dominant discourse (or discourses) of a particular era. What we find within our selves may very well be what society—either the dominant culture or the gay subculture—says we will find. The assumptions that underlie the various theories we formulate influence the biographies we construct for ourselves and the fictions we create.

The coming out narrative, whether a spoken story or written novel, is a textual re-creation of a past life. An important element of the lesbian story is how-I-got-this-way. This question is of never-ending interest to lesbians, stirring many writers to write in the first place. Lesbians are hardly unique in asking the age-old question of how the past influences the present, but the lesbian experience makes that question particularly compelling. When a woman comes out as a lesbian, she makes such a radical break with her society and her past that the questions *why* and *how* are insistent. She weighs all other events in relation to the central one of coming out, the claiming or discovering of her lesbian identity. As the lesbian writes her coming out story, she reinterprets past happenings, lays different emphases, and draws different conclusions.

Because of this, a writer may fashion a layered narrative, alternating past and present time, either in a pattern or at random, rather than employing an omniscient third-person narrator.[27] This technique allows the writer to contrast a character in the present time (usually the mature, self-accepting lesbian) with the same one in the past, unaware of self yet groping toward her destiny. Critic Mab Segrest draws a useful comparison between coming out stories and slave narratives: both "are told from the vantage point of freedom/the present—the plots move from worse to better, as the narrative starts in a place where the writer can finally afford to begin to remember."[28]

In short, lesbians recreate our past histories to conform to our current identities, which we construct in the face of extreme social condemnation and in conformity with a sometimes rigid community image. To be a good, "real," lesbian, one must (a) have had crushes on teachers (preferably gym) and/or camp counselors; (b) never have had any interest in boys; (c) have pined after one's best friend in high school or after a college roommate, and so on. Women of different ages, classes, or races may tell somewhat different stories, but one is pressured to shape one's personal story in accordance with the communal tale, or myth. This does not mean that the communal story is necessarily untrue. A lesbian life pattern may indeed exist, and conformity to it is how a woman knows she is a lesbian. There is, after all, a fairly conventional life pattern for heterosexuals. Nevertheless, lesbian stories blend real happenings and selective memory, and even a bit of invention, into a relatively limited variety of patterns in conformity with the prevailing ideology of the lesbian community.

BORNS AND BORN-AGAINS

Lesbian writers and readers (like the rest of society) do tend to believe nonetheless in an "essential self" or "core identity." Sociologist Barbara Ponse thus identifies three kinds of lesbians: "primary," "elective," and "idiosyncratic." [29] Sheila Ortiz Taylor, in *Spring Forward, Fall Back,* describes lesbians another way:

> Lane had always loved women, had always known that her life with males would be as comrades and not as lovers. . . .
>
> There was another kind of lesbian, though, another lesbian history, where the woman did not know, or only knew somewhere in the locked attic of her own elusive mind, for years. This woman lived two lives in her lifetime: first the heterosexual, then the homosexual, the second as if by solemn choice and not by chance or chemistry. (146–147)

Both Ponse and Taylor suggest that women enter Lesbian Nation by several paths. Some, the "primary" lesbians, are born that way; using Taylor's words, we might call this "chemistry." Others, women in the women's movement or "elective" lesbians, make the "solemn choice" to come out. "Idiosyncratic" women succumb to "chance" and fall in love, sometimes placing little significance on coming out, but more often seeing the world through radically altered eyes. Since few lesbian feminist novels deny the significance of coming out, I draw a distinction between just two types of lesbians in lesbian fiction: the "born-lesbian" (women who feel they always preferred women) and the "born-again lesbian" (women who make a political choice or who fall in love and then see the world anew).

These two models of identity do not necessarily oppose each other. Instead, in the novels the reader often finds the two models interacting. This is particularly true in Maricla Moyano's *BeginningBook.* The protagonist, Calvert, ruminates over her "beginnings"—specifically, why she is attracted to women—and comes up with several different conclusions, most of which derive from the psychoanalytic concepts that dominated in the 1950s. She first suspects that she is a lesbian because she was always different, an outsider. Or is it because she wanted to be a boy, to have the freedom and mobility attached to the masculine role? Is it due to role-modeling, following the example of her mother's love for her aunt, or the result of fusing with her mother when a child? In the end, Calvert concludes that she is a lesbian because she resents subservience to men, a restatement of Simone de Beauvoir's existentialist theory.

Choices, an enduringly popular novel written (not unexpectedly) by a psychologist, most conscientiously investigates this "$64,000 question": what makes someone gay? (132). Why do some women "choose" women and others men? Why do some choose women and then abandon them? Is sexual orientation a choice at all—or are women subtly coerced into heterosexuality, as Adrienne Rich suggests in her influential essay, "Compulsory Heterosexuality and Lesbian Existence"? [30] *Choices* makes no strong case for a congenital explanation. Nancy Toder, a humanistic psychologist like Sandy, her protagonist, wrote the novel in the late 1970s when biologically-based arguments were extremely suspect. She offers one developmental theory—that Sandy's mother taught her to respect and, thereby, love women—but does so half-humorously. The novel ultimately comes down strongly on the side of the feminist/existentialist theory of choice. Given the right circumstances—the right woman or the women's liberation movement—the heterosexual fog lifts and a woman makes the choice to love women.

Except . . . Sandy wonders if there aren't temperamental or developmental factors at work, if the fog lifts for some women and not others because of an innate lesbian self lying beneath the layers of female heterosexual socialization. Can we truly say that "any woman can be a lesbian" (to quote Alix Dobkin), or must only some women be lesbians in order to be their real selves? [31] Are some women predisposed to choose women, or (as a radical feminist might explain it) would all women prefer women if our culture did not impose heavy sanctions? We are left pondering the possibility that inclination as well as choice may be a factor in lesbian identity. In the best liberal tradition, the novel's concluding message evades the very dilemma it raises: make the options widely known and sufficiently attractive so that all women can freely choose among them. How many would choose lesbianism, and for what reasons, remains an unknown factor.

Certain novels counterpose the born-lesbian and born-again lesbian models in a formal manner, at times recalling the rancor between the "real" lesbians and the "political" lesbians in the early days of lesbian feminism. [32] Gillian Hanscombe's *Between Friends,* for example, explores the relationship between Meg, a born-lesbian, and Jane, a born-again lesbian. Meg points out to Jane that she cannot know what it was like to have been a "natural" lesbian, shunned and alone since girlhood; Jane, the awakened lesbian, has a political consciousness that Meg lacks. What is presented theoretically in *Between Friends* (in the form of obsessively intellectual letters) is presented dramatically in Lee Lynch's *Toothpick House.* The lesbians who gather at the bar seem to be born-lesbians, primarily because they automatically reject conventional feminine roles. In contrast, the feminists at the university consciously reject these roles and choose to become lesbians. We could infer that some women reject feminine roles because they are lesbians and others become lesbians because they reject the roles. Finally, there is the example of Victoria, who doesn't exactly choose to be a lesbian, she "just" falls in love with another woman. It isn't clear whether her moderate feminism or a mild predisposition (she has never been interested in men) allows or causes her to fall in love.

Lesbian novelists of the 1970s are much more likely to propose the born-again or elective model than the primary or born-lesbian model. These writers were among the thousands of women in the early 1970s who, fed up with patriarchy in the bedroom and energized by sisterhood in the women's liberation movement, turned to lesbianism. A character in *The Sophie Horowitz Story* describes this phenomenon ironically: "It's so strange, you know, in the early seventies, one day, half the women's movement came out as lesbians. It was like we were all sitting around and the ice cream truck came and all of a sudden I looked around and everyone ran out for ice cream" (126). It is hardly surprising, then, that such women rejected the "born-lesbian" argument—at least in public. Not only was this model alien to our experience, it also seemed to require that one accept either biological imprinting (a person can only be born gay because of genes or hormones) or some form of psychological determinism (rejecting mother, unresolved oedipal crisis, traumatic early sexual experience, and so on). Neither explanation proved very popular because feminists were wary of both biological determinism and the psychotherapeutic system.

Instead, movement women in the 1970s claimed to be lesbians because we chose to be so. And we chose female partners because, supposedly, women understand each other's bodies, women are more nurturant and sensitive than men, women are exploited by men, and so on. Alienation from patriarchy exiles women; love for women propels us home.[33]

Many women's liberation novels, like Marge Piercy's *Small Changes* or Verena Steffan's *Shedding,* conclude with a woman coming out through her experiences in the women's movement. Liz, in Valerie Miner's *Blood Sisters,* finds her experience of sisterhood eroticized first by her love for her cousin and later by her involvement with lesbians on a feminist journal. Polly, Liz's homophobic mother, sums up the connection between feminism and lesbianism in a delightful observation: "Polly had known this would happen all along. Women's poetry. Women's music. It all led to women's bodies" (126).

The most self-conscious and agonized of women's liberation coming out novels, *To the Cleveland Station,* presents a classic example of a feminist who chooses lesbianism with her head, rather than with her heart or hormones. Although she claims to have long ago recognized herself in a text (*The Children's Hour*), it isn't until the women's movement that the intellectual Brenda finds a rationale for coming out.[34] Brenda is determined to be a lesbian because she is committed to the political ideal of lesbianism, but she won't leave her husband until she has found a home in Lesbian Nation. She feels that you may call yourself a lesbian for a hundred years, but sleeping with a woman really makes you one.

It is already evident from a number of these examples that falling in love is the main road taken toward lesbianism, a much more familiar journey than that of searching out the innate self or sitting down with books of feminist theory. As Pam in Barbara Wilson's *Murder in the Collective* wryly puts it, "I couldn't say I'd always been a lesbian. Some of it definitely had to do with Hadley" (134). Similarly, Sandy is "convinced that having known Jenny was crucial to her development of lesbian feelings" (*Choices,* 200). Falling in love, an important component of the coming out novel, is also the source of a number of its most significant metaphors: awakening, rebirth, conversion, and re-vision.

Novels of lesbian awakening typically center around "ordinary" women, sometimes middle class housewives, sometimes working class women. They may meet an open lesbian or they may just fall in love with the girl next door. It is not uncommon for such a woman to deny being a lesbian, and, like Molly Bolt's first lover, to say instead "I just love Molly" (106). The protagonist of Joanna Russ's *On Strike Against God* fears being "labeled" as a result of loving a woman: "it's got nothing to do with me; I'm not a Lesbian. Lesbians. Lez-bee-yuns. Les beans. Les human beans? I'm a Jean-ist" (70). But the hero of most lesbian awakening novels embraces the label without fear or regret. Once the fog has lifted, she is fully and proudly a lesbian. Her life is completely changed; she has been converted to lesbian identity and lesbian vision.

Arden Benbow, the hero of Sheila Ortiz Taylor's *Faultline,* exemplifies the ordinary housewife who is changed forever when she falls in love with another woman. Although unique from birth, having been born on the San Andreas Fault, Arden is not a born-lesbian. Nor does she choose lesbianism for political reasons. She is literally shocked, propelled, into another woman's arms by an earthquake. With her, it is all "chance." But falling in love radically transforms Arden, as if with this movement she sheds one set of clothing and dons another. For Arden, becoming a lesbian leads to an entirely new way of seeing and being in the world.

Jane Rule, in *Desert of the Heart,* refers to this process as "conversion," the transformation from one belief system to another (129, 158). Novels of awakening propose that lesbianism has less to do with sexual behavior or orientation than with discovering a new perspective on the world. Accordingly, they rely extensively upon metaphors of position and vision. After her beloved has acknowledged her presence, the protagonist of Monique Wittig's *The Opoponax* is transformed: "When Catherine Legrand opens her eyes she decides she must have been asleep because the light has changed" (227). The light also changes for Pam in *Murder in the Collective;* having come out, she notices heterosexism everywhere. Folly, in the novel by the same name, experiences her coming out as a rebirth; when her lover asks her if she is okay, she replies: " 'Okay? More like born. I just realize that I've been dead most of my life.' . . . She knew that her world had shifted and when things settled, she'd be standing on new ground" (*Folly,* 114–115). Like Arden, Folly has felt the earth shift beneath her feet, giving her a new vantage point from which to survey the landscape.

These metaphors of re-vision, awakening, journeys, and rebirth are jumbled together in Elizabeth Lang's *Anna's Country,* once Anna, having slept with Hope, takes a "journey" across the border of Lesbian Nation (76). Like other "sleeping beauty" characters, Anna is swept away by sexual desire without really making a choice. But after making love with a woman, "a film had been washed from her eyes" and Anna sees everything anew: "Details that had been blurred in her mind jumped forward as significant. She could see possibilities, details, questions that had not seemed questions before" (79). She never again can live an unexamined life.

Overall, the lesbian novel, particularly of the 1970s and early 1980s, emphasizes the elective model of lesbian identity. But the theory of the primary lesbian self is also clearly present both in the lesbian novel and in the dialogue of the lesbian community. Many lesbians argue persuasively that we always preferred women to men, always felt different from other girls, always experienced sexuality with women. As Julia Penelope [Stanley] writes in her coming out story: "I am one of those wimmin for whom there was never any doubt about my sexuality: I've always loved wimmin, and my mother was my first womonlove. My first conscious expression of my Lesbianism occurred when I was four or five."[35]

The first novel to articulate this experience of lesbian identity was *Who Was That Masked Woman?* (1981).[36] Tretona spends a good portion of her developmental journey pondering why she is attracted to women and what she should do about it. Who is the essential self, the real woman, beneath the mask? Although Tretona recalls that she learned to rebel against the female role from her mother (born-again lesbians might see her rebellion as her first step toward lesbianism), she ultimately concludes that she has always been "queer," that lesbianism is her "true skin" (107, 108). She is a born-lesbian who has masked herself as straight. Coming out, for Tretona, means coming home to her real self. This is what therapy reveals to her, much to the chagrin of her straight therapist.

Novels published in the latter part of the 1980s continued to develop the discourse of born-lesbianism, even going so far as to substitute it for the dominant feminist ideology. In Antoinette Azolakov's *Cass and the Stone Butch* (1987), for example, a dialogue between the title characters pokes fun at the feminist language of choice:

> "I know it wasn't a choice for me. I was just always a dyke. I always loved women. I didn't *choose* it! It's just how I am!"
>
> I grinned at her in the dark. "Lester," I said, "I could kiss you. You can't imagine how nice it is to hear somebody else say that after all these years of hearing how woman-identified we're all supposed to be."

"Yeah, no shit. I thought I was the only one, until I met you."
"Well, you aren't. And nobody can tell me we're unique, either. I think this lesbian-feminist stuff doesn't account for a lot of what lesbians feel, but most dykes have bought the whole line and just closed their minds to what they really, deep-down know." (92)

Cass and the Stone Butch does not attempt to locate the source of that "deep-down" knowledge, nor why some women have "always loved women." But a number of other novels propose lesbianism as the most *natural* identity for women. In *Folly,* the title character draws upon the motif of journeying to describe the coming out process: "It's like going down a long, back road winding round and round, getting so used to going on and on, winding along, that you don't even know you're still looking for something; then all of a sudden you're not exactly looking but you found something, you're home where you wanted to be" (174). For a character in Kathleen Fleming's *Lovers in the Present Afternoon,* that journey leads to "a vast cavern with beautifully grained wood for walls and great windows to let the light flow in" (193). Such copious references to caves and rooms and winding roads inevitably suggest a feminist revision of the psychoanalytic theory that lesbians are trying (inappropriately) to return to mother's womb.

Nancy Chodorow and Adrienne Rich, among others, provide a theoretical framework with which to examine this trend in lesbian fiction. They suggest that, since women in most cultures are the primary custodians of children, the first love object for all children is a woman.[37] Freudians argue that a woman must then shift her attention from her mother to her father, a shift that if interrupted leads to lesbianism. Rich, in her prose and poetry, turns this argument around by pointing out that, if a woman's original love is for another woman, society must violently wrench her away from her true nature, her "birthright," and define her "homesickness for a woman" as "unnatural."[38] Lesbianism, in this context, provides a way for a woman to come home again.

Writers before 1980—Maricla Moyano in *BeginningBook* and Jane Chambers in *Burning,* for example—occasionally adopt this idea that coming out is a journey back to the mother. But it is more noticeable in the literature of women of color and Jewish women written in the first half of the 1980s, in part because the idea had become commonplace in lesbian discourse and in part because of the close connection between mother and daughter that is (or is argued to be) characteristic of these cultures. In Audre Lorde's *Zami,* for example, Audre's journey to her lesbian self is symbolized by the journey to Carriacou, the home of her foremothers and her actual mother. Moreover, several erotic childhood scenes in this elegantly written memoir convey the child's passionate desire to fuse with her mother. So too, in *Abeng,* Michelle Cliff partially ascribes Clare's inclination toward women to her desire for her mother: "At twelve Clare wanted to suck her mother's breasts again and again— to close her eyes in the sunlight and have Kitty close her eyes also and together they would enter some dream Clare imagined mothers and children shared" (54). In Paula Gunn Allen's *The Woman Who Owned the Shadows* and Alice Bloch's *The Law of Return,* the return to the mother is symbolic rather than erotic. In each novel, the protagonist's journey to selfhood and women takes her back to a spiritual encounter with mythic or historic foremothers.

These various examples—lesbian-from-birth, lesbian-by-choice, lesbian-through-love—indicate to what extent we construct our lives and our fictions in accordance with the standards and myths of our cultural contexts. At one time it was *de rigeur* to claim, in Jill Johnston's words, that "all women are lesbians except those who don't know it."[39] Philosopher Marilyn Frye later pointed out how newly "out" lesbians insist that they never had any interest in men, whether this is true or not.[40] In the late 1980s it seemed equally fashionable to claim a lesbian identity virtually from conception, an idea parodied by a cartoon in which a midwife, presenting a woman with her newborn child, pro-claims, "Congratulations. It's a lesbian."[41] The recent popularity of the born-lesbian model, as *Cass and the Stone Butch* suggests, may signal an end to the feminist hegemony over lesbian ideology; it may also reflect the secret admiration elective (or "political") lesbians feel for primary, or "real" lesbians. It is certainly used as a defense against the increasing conservatism and hostility of the dominant culture, because, if we are born that way, we are not responsible for our sexuality and hence less vulnerable to attack.

The language through which we characterize lesbian identity has shifted from the existentialism ("I chose to be a lesbian") that dominated the lesbian myth of personal origins in the 1970s, to the growing essentialism ("it's just how I am") of the 1980s. The next step may be to develop a more complex theory and model of lesbian origins that incorporates elements of both. After all, our sense of self (whether lesbian or otherwise) is no more shaped exclusively by blind determinism than it is by fully conscious motivations. Ultimately, the "truth" of one model or another is of less significance than what the interplay among various voices teaches us about the values and beliefs held at different historical times by different groups within the lesbian community. That interplay may allow us to construct a myth large enough to include all the individual realities of lesbian lives.

The Lesbian Hero

The coming out novel uses the conventions of the quest, the picaresque, and the *bildungsroman* to imagine the origins of the lesbian self. The lesbian, therefore, is a quest hero who, like all heroes, is marked as special from birth, undergoes journeys and adventures, sometimes conquers and performs good deeds. The mythic hero may be a warrior or a prophet; in modern fiction, the quintessential hero is an artist or writer. As the quest myth was incorporated into contemporary popular culture, the hero became a cowboy, detective, or spy. Adapting these conventional figures to the particular realities of lesbian life, lesbian writers give them new shape and meaning. In so doing, they also create powerful and evocative new codes for the lesbian self.

The lesbian hero may be one of the conventional heroic types. There are many artists and writers, for example, increasing numbers of detectives, and even a few cowgirls. Noretta Koertge, for one, considers the spy to be an archetype for the lesbian: "Being queer is like being on lifetime assignment as a secret agent in some foreign country. No matter how careful you are, no matter how practiced you are at emulating the natives, you know that at any minute you may be uncovered" (*Who Was That Masked Woman?*, 232). Lesbian utopian or speculative fiction sometimes presents heroes as leaders of new worlds. A few very recent novels draw upon real life by presenting the athlete or "jock" as a heroic type.[42] The political reality of lesbian custody cases provides yet another image for the lesbian hero: she may be a mother, like Arden Benbow or the protagonist of *Sinking, Stealing* who escapes and travels west with the daughter of her dead lover. As a fighter against the prejudices of patriarchal society, the lesbian mother is similar to the warrior or outlaw. These last two figures, as well as the witch and magician, the androgyne, and the artist, are among the many forms given to the lesbian archetypal hero.

OUTLAWS, WITCHES, AND MAGICIANS

The hero as outlaw archetype is closely allied with, indeed an outgrowth of, the motifs of journeying and exile. The woman who journeys through patriarchy and exits it for Lesbian Nation places herself outside the laws and customs of the old world. Adrienne Rich, for example, in one of her "Twenty-One Love Poems," imagines two women traveling beyond the recognized boundaries of patriarchy to a new "country that has no language/no laws. . . ."[43] Not only an exile, the lesbian is also an outlaw. Lesbian Nation is an uncharted territory, or frontier, and as such resembles the old west. It is not surprising that in a number of novels—such as *Patience and Sarah* or *The Journey*—the lesbian or lesbian couple leaves civilization for the western wilderness. According to lesbian mythology, when a woman loves another woman, she breaks a fundamental rule of patriarchal society and puts herself beyond the pale.

In prefeminist literature the lesbian hero often mourned this loss of legitimacy and longed for acceptance into the community from which she had been exiled. At the same time, different examples written by both lesbians and nonlesbians fixed upon the *otherness* of the lesbian, primarily in the shape of the glamorous and dangerous vampire. After the 1871 publication of Sheridan LeFanu's ghost story, "Carmilla," the lesbian vampire became a popular icon in art, literature, and film.[44] She might be a romantic, *fin-de-siècle* alien (like a Djuna Barnes character or the figure of Renée Vivien in Colette's *The Pure and the Impure*), or an evil, spirit-sucking monster like characters in the novels of Clemence Dane or Dorothy Baker. In either case, she inhabited the lifeless, nocturnal world that dominated the vision of prefeminist lesbian literature.

Feminist literature reverses the signs attached to the lesbian outlaw or monster. Although many lesbian writers fervently claim normal status for the lesbian, a revised version of the romantic lesbian outlaw or monster takes shape in the fiction of the 1970s. This revised version does not refer back to the stereotype of the decadent lesbian vampire, however. References to vampires are typically hurled only as an insult by a threatened male against a woman he perceives as a rival. Few positive reclamations of the lesbian vampire have yet been written, such as Jewelle Gomez's elegant story, "No Day Too Long."[45] Instead, the lesbian outlaw archetype is rooted in the anti-authoritarianism of the 1960s, the decade during which a significant number of lesbian writers came to adulthood. Belonging to a generation that learned a profound disrespect for the law and social convention, we took to heart Dylan's words, "to live outside the law you must be honest," sometimes reversing them to mean that to be honest you must live outside the law.[46] Our skepticism began with the civil rights movement and the Vietnam war, with our realization that the law upheld the wrong side. Then, as feminists, we concluded that the law enforced male privilege and authority.

But it is as lesbians, perhaps, that we have felt our strongest alienation from the law, since we are legislated against in civil, criminal, religious, and social codes. This alienation is subtler for lesbians than for gay men. As Marilyn Frye argues, lesbians simply don't exist in patriarchal language and consciousness; we are considered to be both naturally and logically impossible.[47] Furthermore, should society acknowledge our existence, its description of us is so alien from what we know ourselves to be that we are faced with a profound and sometimes unbreachable gap between image and reality. In self-defense, if for no other reason, we claim alienation as superiority and specialness, and glorify the status of the outlaw. Bertha Harris established the tone of this glorification when she extolled the lesbian (in fiction at least) as "a creature of tooth and claw, of passion and purpose: unassimilable, awesome, dangerous, outrageous, different: distinguished."[48]

Some lesbians go further by arguing that lesbianism strikes a political blow against the heart of male supremacy: the family and gender roles. The separatist Furies collective insist that lesbians are, or should be, outlaws or criminals within patriarchy.[49] Even a moderate like Jane Rule, through her character, Alma, proposes that lesbianism ought to be an attack on convention and law: "Two women in a ring of flesh, as if they were continually giving birth to each other, may go back as far as Sappho, but as a symbol they have more in common with war than with

peace, fission rather than fusion, destructive of all holy cliches: motherhood, the family, maple syrup, our bacon wrapper flag!" (*Contract with
the World,* 155).

The lesbian outlaw, therefore, is one of the most popular shapes feminist writers throughout the contemporary era give to the archetypal
hero. But since the laws she breaks are patriarchal ones, the lesbian
outlaw is hardly ever vicious or even an ordinary crook. When a lesbian
character breaks the law she does so for high-minded reasons, or the law
she breaks is a wicked one. Novels as diverse as June Arnold's *The Cook
and the Carpenter* (1973), Red Jordan Arobateau's *The Bars across Heaven*
(1975), Gillian Hanscombe's *Between Friends* (1982), Dodici Azpadu's
Goat Song (1984), and Jan Clausen's *Sinking, Stealing* (1985) present
characters who defy the law in their quest for survival or obedience to a
higher moral law. And when Kat, in *The Winged Dancer,* is wrongly
convicted of murder and sent to prison, she and her lover end up solving
the crime.

Kat is by no means the only detective in lesbian fiction. As we shall
see in chapter six, in the 1980s the mystery novel grew to be so popular
with lesbian writers that it threatened to displace even the romantic love
story. Lesbians may be not only secret agents, as Noretta Koertge
claims, but also detectives, because we must constantly read "clues" in
order to decipher another woman's sexual identity, and sometimes even
our own.[50] The lesbian detective invariably resolves a crime against gays
or women, thereby furthering our perception that the patriarchal world
is the true criminal world and the lesbian the ideal purveyor of justice.
A strong vein of optimism and rationality runs through most of these
novels, a belief that society is or can be fundamentally good and orderly
if a few loose (patriarchal and homophobic) ends are tied up. Most lesbian detectives are not in the American hardboiled tradition, where the
detective is almost indistinguishable from the crook; instead, they are
either apple-cheeked amateurs, like Nyla Wade or Stoner McTavish, or,
as in Katherine Forrest's Kate Delafield novels, part of the police force
itself.[51]

Ironically, the lesbian hero may end up resembling a "dutiful daughter," society's housewife as it were, rather than an outlaw.[52] In Ann Allen
Shockley's *Say Jesus and Come to Me,* for example, Myrtle's campaign to
clean up Nashville recalls contemporary feminist campaigns to clean up

pornography and other social evils.[53] Although we romanticize alienation from society, we still wish to remain upstanding citizens of a righteous society.

Many lesbian heroes journey on to the boundaries of that ideal community, the great good place of Lesbian Nation. To establish that place, the lesbian outlaw may mutate into the lesbian warrior, and turn from breaking laws to waging full-scale war against patriarchy. To be sure, it isn't just lesbian (or even women) writers who are drawn to the figure of the woman warrior, but lesbians certainly have adopted the amazon as an inspirational figure. In *Riverfinger Women,* for example, the outlaw and warrior merge in Inez's imagination. At first envisioning herself and Abby as the most normal of women, brides, she later abandons that fantasy for one of lesbians as outlaws, witches, and smashers of icons. Riverfinger women, she says, are "tough, strong, proud: free women" who live outside the law: man's law, the law of the Committee, of Daddy (16). Inez imagines herself and Abby first as Rainbo Woman and Lucy Bear living in a magic forest outside civilization; then the forest becomes the location of guerilla warfare, and the Riverfinger women represent "the first promise of an armed women's nation" (6).

Monique Wittig, more than any other writer, popularized this idea of women withdrawing, turning outlaw and warrior, to create "an armed women's nation." Having been nurtured by nuns on stories of powerful warrior women, the young girls in *The Opoponax,* exchange "carbine five five bullets," and then exit the garden of childhood for the fantasy battlefield of *Les Guérillères* (243). Wittig developed her lesbian mythology further in *Lesbian Peoples: Materials for a Dictionary,* in which the "amazons" remain outlaws and outsiders after the "mothers" destroy the prepatriarchal golden age of women. Contemporary lesbians, Wittig suggests, are reviving the spirit and vision of those ancient amazons.

Novels written in the 1970s, like those of Nachmann and Wittig, more than novels written a decade later, seriously propose that Lesbian Nation must be established through armed struggle. In retrospect, it is evident that lesbians in that era were influenced by the wars of national liberation in Vietnam and Algeria and by the Black liberation struggle, all of which shaped the consciousness of the generation that came of age in the sixties. Although we claim outsider status for ourselves, we adopt some of our ideas and language from other political and literary movements. The figure of the warrior woman flourished in the novels of the 1970s because war and revolutionary struggle were in the air (and on the airwaves). The context of that era accounts for the occasional glimpses we see of warrior women, such as the Shirley Temples Emeritae in *Sister Gin* (1975), a bridge club of old women who expose and humiliate abusive men, or the hidden collective in *Angel Dance* (1977) who castrate and murder a rapist.

But even in novels of the 1970s, other factors began to undercut the militancy inherited from the social movements of the sixties. For example, Joanna Russ, in *The Female Man* (1975), implies that Whileaway, a female utopia, resulted from the overthrow of men by women—but the lesbian figure in the novel is a pacifist while the warrior is aggressively heterosexual. Although Ellen Galford bases *Moll Cutpurse* (1985) on the adventures of an Elizabethan "amazon," no other lesbian writer has written a novel about such historical warriors as the amazons of Greek myth, Joan of Arc, or the palace guard of Dahomey (although some of Audre Lorde's poems in *The Black Unicorn* evoke these last figures).[54]

By the 1980s, the warrior archetype faded from view. As lesbian culture incorporated the notion that violence is essentially "male" and nurturance essentially "female," the warrior woman was redefined as a symbol of female courage and survival. In *Contract with the World* (1980), for example, Alma feels like "a woman warrior who had finally reconquered her own kingdom" when she moves into her own house (158). Today, writers use "warrior" or "amazon" primarily as a code, or synonym, for lesbian, as does Georgia Cotrell in *Shoulders* (1987) or Vicki McConnell in *Double Daughter* (1988).[55] Although these authors retain the symbolic identification of lesbian and warrior, on a practical level they have put their weapons away.

Outlaws may be heroes, but they may also be victims and prisoners. Since the lesbian mythos precludes dwelling upon our powerlessness, only a few novels, such as *The Winged Dancer, Ambitious Women,* and *This Place* incorporate prison scenes. Nor do we find many examples of lesbians incarcerated in mental institutions, although this is a not uncommon obstacle along the lesbian path, especially prior to the gay liberation movement. The criticism generated by Carol Anne Douglas's portrayal of a Black woman as victim of the psychiatric establishment in

To the Cleveland Station indicates how thoroughly we dislike seeing lesbians, especially lesbians of color, as victims.[56] We prefer to see the incarcerated lesbian turn warrior, as in Lee Lynch's *The Swashbuckler* or Madelyn Arnold's *Bird-Eyes,* and successfully fight the system. In contrast to heterosexual feminist literature, very few contemporary lesbian novels depict the hero as a madwoman.[57] Moreover, although many books include incidents with therapists—indeed, the encounter with therapy may well be one stage of the lesbian journey—the lesbian protagonist is as likely to be the therapist as the client.

The only victimized figure to have captured the lesbian imagination is the witch. Rehabilitated as a feminist hero as early as 1969 when one of the first women's liberation groups named itself WITCH (Women's International Terrorist Conspiracy from Hell), the witch is a female archetype that incorporates aspects of both victimization and power.[58] Within patriarchy the woman outlaw is traditionally perceived as either a whore or a witch. Since the former is a heterosexual symbol (despite the actual sexual preferences of many prostitutes), the latter is the outlaw figure adopted by lesbian writers. Historical evidence suggests that the women accused of witchcraft were those existing on the fringes of society, women who had no men to protect them or who lived at the edges of villages.[59] So it isn't unreasonable, despite the absence of concrete proof, for writers to imagine some of these women as lesbians, or to suggest that modern lesbians—women living on the borders—are the witches of our time.

One of these outcast women, Aurélie in Jeannine Allard's *Légende,* lives outside a village, on a cliff by the edge of the sea. Although in touch with supernatural power, Aurélie is never persecuted by the townspeople because of it. Only long after her death, when the villagers discover that she was living as a married woman with another woman who passed as a man—in other words, that she was a lesbian—do they desecrate her memory. Lesbianism taints the witch, rather than the other way around. In Jane Chambers' novel, *Burning,* Martha lives as an outlaw outside a town in colonial times, becomes lovers with Abigail, and, since the townsfolk conclude that a woman who loves another woman must be in service to the devil, is burned as a witch. In an interesting twist, the author parallels this lesbian revision of a witchcraft tale with the modern story of two women who lay the spirits of their dead foremothers to rest by reenacting their love affair. In the course of their possession, Cynthia and Angela discover for themselves and reveal to the reader that lesbians have taken the place of the witches of yore. Martha was burned as a witch for defying male control of women; Cynthia is almost raped by a gang of men who wonder "if lesbians *were* witches" (135, 138).[60]

The image of the witch as powerful victim appeals to lesbians in part because it confirms our collective anxiety; persecutions and witchhunts prove that things really are as bad as we say they are. The sheer number of women who were killed as witches (although not the inflated nine million popularized by some feminist writers) provides grisly proof that misogyny is deadly.[61] But the image of power associated with the witch is even more appealing than that of persecution. Because the witch is in touch with the forces of nature, because she is an independent and dangerous woman, because she courts punishment and persecution, she is a heroic figure in contemporary lesbian feminist culture.

Traditionally, the witch has a male counterpart in the wizard, or magician, who—like Merlin in the Arthurian tales, Gandalf in *The Lord of the Rings,* or the figure in the tarot—is a paragon of wisdom and power. Children of my generation also grew up with Mr. Wizard, the television character who taught us about science. Since science and magic are ways of manipulating the patterns in nature, the magician (like the modern-day scientist) is a *patterner,* one who sees the patterns in nature and in human acts and then transforms them from one medium into another.[62]

The magician, or patterner, has become a lesbian archetype because the lesbian transforms what are conventionally identified as the laws of nature. She takes one set of rules and changes them into another. The lesbian magician is also in tune with the power of women, a deeper rather than higher power. In this way, she resembles the High Priestess, the card of the lesbian according to *The Feminist Tarot.*[63] Myrtle, in *Say Jesus and Come to Me,* feels herself to be "a proud transplanted African queen" who is "savioress and high priestess of her people" (1). Similarly, Patience claims that Sarah "made me feel like the Lord's High Priestess" (*Patience and Sarah,* 187). Because the lesbian is not distracted by men, her connection to ancient female power is not as disrupted or defused as that of a straight woman. She can focus her attention on being a "seer"

(Marilyn Frye defines lesbians as those who "see" the female background behind the central male action), or a wise-woman.[64]

There is a touch of the magician in many lesbian characters of the 1970s, such as the Carpenter in *The Cook and the Carpenter,* Mamie Carter in *Sister Gin,* Celeste in *Six of One,* and the utterly magical Veronica in *Lover.* In the 1980s, even a traditional realist like Lee Lynch adopts the magician figure in her short stories. In "The Lopresto Traveling Magic Show" (in *Old Dyke Tales*), for example, the narrator's aunt, a magician at a local carnival, represents the path of lesbianism that the young girl will take. Lynch's most striking exemplar, the title character in "Augusta Brennan," is a lesbian Merlin conferring upon a young Queen Arthur the sign of what she calls "the royal dykedom." For Augusta, being a lesbian makes her "special, lucky, touched by some magic and given some knowledge that brings [her] a certain majesty and power" (*Old Dyke Tales,* 31, 33).

Faultline (1982) presents the most fully-developed example of the lesbian magician and patterner. Born on the San Andreas Fault, Arden Benbow is particularly sensitive to the movements of nature. She is an artist creating patterns first by writing poems, then by building a motorcycle out of a heap of spare parts, and finally by pulling together a motley crew of eccentrics and outsiders into a united family. As Arden becomes more of a magician and more of a lesbian, she also reclaims her Indian heritage and grows into a shaman. Arden is a favorite of nature: a lesbian, a mother, an Indian, a poet, and a keeper of fantastically fecund rabbits.

Lesbians often claim for ourselves a special magic, fantasy, and joy; as one of Lee Lynch's characters says, "to be gay is to be specially blessed" (*Home in Your Hands,* 197). *Faultline* substantiates this claim by making an extended comparison between being a lesbian and being the leader or patterner of an unconventional human family. The novel's cast of characters includes unconventional people with little fear of taking risks. They are chosen people who feel the earth trembling beneath their feet, people who move against the tide of ordinary existence. Not all these characters are lesbians, or even women; in fact, only Arden and Alice are lesbians, and only Arden could be said to have a lesbian consciousness. But it is Arden's family, her party.

The author intimates that to be a lesbian, especially a lesbian mother, is the most unconventional, risky, and even absurd thing one can do. As we saw, it's an oxymoron, a pulling together or patterning of two apparently antagonistic terms. Like the poet that she is, Arden sees many patterns in nature, some of which emerge only when a convulsion, an earthquake, rearranges the old elements. Arden is able to help these rearrangements along because she can see and grasp the hidden meanings within the natural world. And although Arden, the seer, understands the alignments of nature and is able and permitted to restructure them, she is also surprised by those realignments, specifically by the earthquake. Since nature after all is unknowable and uncontrollable, the novel reminds us, we must be constantly open to shock and change rather than deluding ourselves into imagining that we can define what is natural and right.

Two novels published in 1984 connect the figure of the lesbian magician with the theme of women's power in a more ambivalent fashion. *Paz,* by Camarin Grae, presents the most extreme version of the lesbian patterner. As a result of a freak accident, Drew gains the power to make people believe whatever she tells them. She can literally change the patterns of their minds. Throughout the novel, various characters debate whether this power is malevolent or benign, until Drew puts it to use in lesbian interests by creating a separatist utopia. The title character of *Iris,* by Janine Veto, is an outlaw, witch, magician, and high priestess. With her long golden hair, Iris evokes the image of the lorelei, the femme fatale, the classic heterosexual form for the magical woman. Although women's magic may be dangerous to men, the novel shows how well it serves women. Communing on the ancient island of Santorini with the "line of women who pass along magic and knowledge of healing and curing as well as of vengeance and death," Iris learns that women have a source of primeval power rooted in nature that helps them battle the political authority and sexual violence of men (208).

ANDROGYNES AND ARTISTS

The figures of the outlaw, warrior, witch, and magician are archetypal; that is, they are larger-than-life forms handed down through myth and literature. They are modified by the particular history of the lesbian community into other heroic representations. Lee Lynch, for example, sometimes portrays the archetypal patterner as a bartender. Numerous stories in *Old Dyke Tales* and *Home in Your Hands* take place in Cafe Femmes, a bar run by Sally, the best bartender in the world, who is priest, shrink, mother, and mayor of her own small community. Rivaling Sally as a patterner is Lane (*Spring Forward, Fall Back*), the owner of another magical bar, who serves as a shuttle weaving connections between various gay communities.

The way writers transform an archetype into a specifically lesbian figure is also demonstrated by the transformation of the androgyne into the butch. In her inventive mythic history, *Another Mother Tongue,* Judy Grahn argues that gay people change the shape of gender: "in the long patriarchal history that has gradually enveloped the world's people, the Gay function has been to make crossover journeys between gender-worlds, translating, identifying, and bringing back the information that each sex has developed independently of the other."[65] Gay men and lesbians, in her view, are the first true androgynes.

The heroes of lesbian feminist fictions occasionally "make crossover journeys" from a land marked by strict gender-role division to one where the distinctions are deliberately blurred. Inez Riverfingers says, "I love to walk arm in arm with them [women] and tumble through all the disguises we can think of for one another, the end of gender identification" (*Riverfinger Women,* 169). When Sarah, in *Patience and Sarah,* passes in the world as male, she discovers that, not being a woman, she is still not recognized as a man. The best she can be is a boy. Similarly, the lesbian characters in Grahn's story, "Boys at a Rodeo" (*True to Life Adventure Stories II*), discover that they are not feminine enough to be women, nor masculine enough to be men; in society's eyes, they are just boys. These examples demonstrate that gender is more complicated than the simple dualism of masculinity and femininity. Lesbians are neither "women" nor "men." In that way, the lesbian merges with the figure of the androgyne.

In the 1970s, a few writers enthusiastically pursued this manipulation of gender categories. June Arnold, for one, states in the foreword to *The Cook and the Carpenter* (1973) that if gender matters so much, the reader surely can figure out which characters are male and which female without any help from pronouns. She then proceeds to use the invented pronouns "na" and "nan," and either sex-neutral names or titles for her characters. In Monique Wittig's *Lesbian Peoples* (1976), the amazons' preferred style of dress is androgynous dyke-dandy and the words "woman" and "wife" are labeled obsolete, leaving as the only gender category "lesbian."

Gender ambiguity is rampant in the fiction of Bertha Harris. A source for some of her ideas is opera, with its theatricality and its women singing the roles of boys. In *Confessions of Cherubino* (1972), Ellen and Margaret dress up as the characters in *The Marriage of Figaro,* while *Lover* (1976) opens with a plot summary of *Der Rosenkavalier,* in which the main character is a boy sung by a woman who masquerades during part of the opera as a girl. The novel presents an historical counterpart to this plot in the Chevalier D'Eon, "a woman disguised as a man forced by circumstances to dress as a woman" (70). Lest these references prove insufficiently ambiguous, Harris dresses the characters in *Lover* in ways that deliberately mock gender roles—lesbian feminist camp. Gender roles are no more real than the clothes we wear, she seems to be saying. Ultimately, as we shall see in the next chapter, Harris subsumes all gender and sex roles under two generic and interchangeable categories: lover and beloved.

We might expect lesbians to be particularly free and creative with gender categories. By deliberately adapting the figure of the androgyne (as did Renée Vivien in *A Woman Appeared to Me* and Virginia Woolf in *Orlando*), lesbians could highlight the way in which homosexuals have defied, or "deconstructed," conventional gender roles. But novelists abandoned self-conscious "gender-bending" after the experimental period between 1973 and 1978 (a date that marks the demise of the publishing house, Daughters). An unusual example of the androgyne in more recent fiction is the title character in Ellen Galford's *Moll Cutpurse,* a "monster that was halfway between man and woman" (11).

Both literary and political factors inhibit the lesbian writer from exploiting the possibilities of the androgyne. First, as I pointed out above, after 1978 lesbian writers grew increasingly reluctant to use experimental, nonrealistic techniques. As much lesbian fiction became formulaic, one-dimensional, and overly-literal, writers lost, or never adopted, such tools as irony and ambiguity. Moreover, many feminists reject androgyny as a political position because, historically, it has only provided a means for men to incorporate into their own gender role those "feminine" traits, such as artistic sensibility, they deem desirable. Women, on the other hand, are never allowed to claim such masculine traits as leadership or ambition—or high-paying jobs. To many feminists, androgyny is a political cop-out, indeed, a retreat from feminism.[66]

Lesbians, in addition, may suspect that "androgynous" is yet another code for "lesbian" and thus a capitulation to homophobia. It is more palatable, perhaps, to think of one's self as androgynous than as lesbian, as Val does, in Katherine Forrest's *An Emergence of Green,* before she claims a lesbian identity: "What Alix perceived in her and was attracted to was the androgyny all good artists must possess, nothing more. . . . It was the reason for her own attraction to Alix. . . . a lesbian lifestyle was a complication anyone should avoid who had any choice in the matter" (61–62). Finally, at least throughout the seventies, lesbian feminists vigorously combated the popular stereotype that lesbians want to be men by insisting that we were "real women," or, in Jill Johnston's words, "woman prime."[67] Many lesbian writers dissociate their lesbian heroes from any taint of masculinity. They refuse the flexibility and multiplicity of selves implied by the androgyne in favor of a unified self who is unambiguously female.[68]

In the 1980s, however, some writers have begun to reshape the androgyne in accordance with that classic lesbian hero of the 1950s and 1960s, the butch. Rarely does the contemporary butch hero identify with men, however. She is no Stephen Gordon, no male spirit trapped in a female body. The butch, as author and historian Joan Nestle nostalgically recreates her, is instead a symbol of lesbian courage:

> None of the butch women I was with, and this included a passing woman, ever presented themselves to me as men; they did announce themselves as tabooed women who were willing to identify their passion for other women by wearing clothes that symbolized the taking of responsibility. Part of this responsibility was sexual expertise. In the 1950s this courage to feel comfortable with arousing another woman became a political act.[69]

Since butch-femme women, until the more blatant seventies, were the only women willing to declare themselves lesbians to the outside world, the butch merges the figures of the androgyne and the outlaw. Inez

Riverfingers anticipates Nestle when she venerates the "butch bartenders" she meets once she joins the lesbian community: "These women, I think, are my true foremothers. They became strong and independent in isolation. . . . they committed that act [of defiance], and gave me the courage to commit mine" (*Riverfinger Women,* 174).

Lee Lynch, among recent writers, pays particular homage to the butches of the past and celebrates the butch in women today. Frenchy, the hero of *The Swashbuckler,* defines butchiness as style, bravado, and open lesbianism: all aspects of that sexual courage Joan Nestle extols. Frenchy "diddy-bops" through the Village, angering straight people, defying convention, and swashbuckling after other women. She simply loves being a lesbian. As admirable as Frenchy is, however, *The Swashbuckler* concludes with a "taming" of the butch. But, as I discuss in chapter 6, the fiction of the late 1980s once again celebrates the butch as a heroic figure.

The last role we find for the lesbian hero is perhaps the most pervasive in western literature, that of the artist. One of the basic forms for the developmental novel is the *Künstlerroman,* or portrait of the artist, which connects the creation of the self to the creation of works of art.[70] The classic lesbian novel of this sort is *The Well of Loneliness,* in which Stephen Gordon's journey toward self-understanding and self-acceptance leads her to write the story of the invert's pain and passion, the story that is Radclyffe Hall's novel.[71] Feminist critics have demonstrated that the artist/heroine often must reconcile her quest for selfhood with society's assumption that artistic creation is a masculine pursuit.[72] Stephen Gordon, however, experiences a different struggle, since she already has a "male soul" trapped in her female body. She is inhibited by the conflict between her private lesbian self and her public attempt to pass as normal. Like Lee Lynch's character, Johnny, a passing woman who disguises her sex by pretending to be mute, Stephen distorts and silences her true voice.[73] Her best novel is written when she is happy and integrated in her love for Mary Llewellyn. Not until Stephen accepts her destiny as a lesbian does she come to fruition as an artist.

Since the contemporary lesbian novel also concerns the creation of a lesbian self in a territory marked by silence or falsehood, it is not surprising that the lesbian hero is often a writer or visual artist. We find heroes who are writers and poets in *Riverfinger Women, Sister Gin, Lover, Contract with the World, Blood Sisters, Prism, Loving Her, Faultline, Lovers in the Present Afternoon, Légende, Toothpick House,* and *Spring Forward, Fall Back.* There are visual artists in *Patience and Sarah, Rubyfruit Jungle, The Threshing Floor,* and *An Emergence of Green.* Autobiographical works, such as *Zami* and *The Woman Who Owned the Shadows,* often show the writer coming of age. Some narratives, like *The Notebooks That Emma Gave Me, The Notebooks of Leni Clare,* and *Between Friends,* are structured as pieces of text: letters or journals. The heroes of Barbara Wilson's novels are often printers, who give concrete shape to empowering language. Others, finally, are teachers, perhaps of literature or art, as in *Desert of the Heart, In Her Day,* and *Valley of the Amazons.*

Lesbian feminists define lesbian oppression primarily as a mutilation of self characterized by speechlessness, invisibility, and inauthenticity. Lesbian resistance to this oppression necessarily lies in telling our stories and naming ourselves. Our power, as individuals and as a community, flows from language, imagination, and culture. By controlling and defining images and ideas, lesbians "reconstitute the world."[74] For all these reasons, the lesbian feminist novel often presents the writing of a text or painting of a picture as both means and metaphor for the creation of the lesbian self. *Riverfinger Women,* for example, is the story of Inez Riverfingers' life as Inez is currently writing it:

> In a moment I will conjure Abby Riverfingers and Peggy Warren and the burden of inventing myself again will wear off, the story will begin. . . . The hammering of myself into the background will seem to be over. This hammering, this background—the language of our getting older, the time of our being no longer children but young women, that is to say, forming into identifiable shapes, it is not simple. From time to time you will hear that faint tackety-tackety-tackety, like kids at summercamp, making bronze name plates in relief dot by dot:
> these are our lives, these are our lives, these are our lives (6).

Or, like its early twentieth-century predecessor, *The Well of Loneliness,* the contemporary lesbian feminist novel may conclude with the artist/ hero coming out through the production of her art. In *Sister Gin,* for example, Su ties the emergence of her lesbian self and a lesbian community to the creation of a literary text: "She wanted to climb to the top of the tree and hang from its five-hundred-year-old branches and shout so that all the women could hear, even those who didn't listen any more: *All out come in free!* That would be her play. Or book. Or . . ." (205). Through the exercise of her art, the lesbian artist/hero, like Inez or Su, shapes the story of her life, and the life of the lesbian community, into a new tale of lesbian heroism.

The lesbian hero, in all her various shapes, journeys through patriarchy to its point of exit, the border of an unknown territory, a "wild zone" of the imagination.[75] Along her path may wait a woman with whom the hero establishes a relationship, so that the individual lesbian journey leads at first to the lesbian couple. And a step beyond lies that place where male culture, male law, and male power can no longer touch them. At this point, their individual lives and individual coming out stories connect, reflect, and interact: "There are all the places where these stories touch each other and make the start of a common life, the beginning of an idea about community" (*Riverfinger Women*, 14). Lesbian Nation is the cumulative product of each lesbian journey toward self-hood. It begins in the telling of individual coming out stories, in the formation of alternative images of lesbians, in the search for lesbian "herstory" and "heras," in the assertion of "I am my true self, as I really am." The creation of the lesbian self, then, is the first myth of origins for the lesbian peoples.

3 〜〜〜〜

"Lovers in the Present Afternoon":
The Lesbian Couple

The house has simple graceful lines. The woods are right for Lori to grow up in, Lynn thinks. For us to be together every day in a place of beauty, to wake up to the trees around us every morning, is to come home, she thinks. "Remember your poem?" she asks.

"Which one?"

"The one that ended 'with you I am come home'?"

Ruth nods.

"This is the right place."

—*Kathleen Fleming,* LOVERS IN THE PRESENT AFTERNOON

I imagine, starved to death, that I am making love to her in my first memory. I am in some summer house, in some country with a season of heat no other place in the world can match. It could be Alabama; it could be the Isle of Capri and I a wealthy, pre-war lesbian. . . . There is nothing inside the summerhouse but the two of us and that broken shard of teacup where a sleeping garter snake lies curled. The summerhouse eventually collapsed, broken by the weight of the green.

—*Bertha Harris,* LOVER

"I don't see what women see in other women," I'd told Doctor Nolan in my interview that noon. "What does a woman see in a woman that she can't see in a man?

Doctor Nolan paused. Then she said, "Tenderness."

—*Sylvia Plath,* THE BELL JAR

*L*ove, we know, makes the world go 'round. Love is certainly the axis around which most definitions of lesbianism and most plots of lesbian novels turn. Throughout the twentieth century, lesbian literature explored the mysterious ramifications of falling in love, discovering a language for sex, and establishing a relationship. Contemporary feminist fiction continues this tradition. Most heroes of lesbian coming out novels end their quests by falling in love and setting up housekeeping with another woman. Romantic love stories, differing only slightly from the pulp fiction of the 1950s and 60s, are the staple offerings of certain lesbian publishers, in particular The Naiad Press. The dynamics of love, sex, and "marriage" are as integral to contemporary lesbian fiction as they are to all other current fiction. As the first myth of origins in contemporary lesbian feminist literature tells of the creation of the lesbian self, the second myth recounts the formation and definition of the lesbian couple.

The contemporary lesbian romance, like the coming out novel, has been created in part to replace the old false stories of the past with a new and ostensibly truer love story. Prefeminist literature, while it claimed to be about love, did not, in fact, portray anything recognizable as love; it depicted instead obsession, vampirism, or a narcissism in which a woman possesses herself by possessing another woman. Love was defined as seduction and control: an older woman seducing a young girl; a butch controlling a femme. Relationships were characterized by violence, alcohol, and faithlessness. Lesbian lovers sometimes appeared as two immature children escaping from real life and responsibility into each other's arms. In other works, they presented a sexy challenge to men (both characters and readers), or appeared as they are portrayed in David Hamilton's photographs, veiled and soft and barely sexual.[1] This chapter illustrates how contemporary lesbian fictions dismiss many of these stereotypes, alter and subvert others, and create new ones that are challenged and revised in their turn.

Love and Marriage in the Western World

Contemporary lesbian love stories draw their primary metaphors and themes from the western literary tradition of romantic love. Love in the western world is a transfiguring experience that carries one outside the quotidian world of marital entanglements and domestic responsibilities. Love is transcendent, mystical, even religious. The condition of being in love isolates the lovers in a world of their own making. This romantic state, paradoxically, flourishes best when it is thwarted, when it is hopeless and illicit and thereby outside the ordinary conditions represented by marriage. As the great historian of western love, Denis de Rougemont, contends, "romance only comes into existence where love is fatal, frowned upon and doomed by life itself."[2] Our paradigm for romantic love, therefore, has always been the adulterous relationship, a type of love that, in literature, inevitably leads to death. The central love myth of our tradition is that of Tristan and Isolde, who love without consent or control, flee to the woods away from civilization, continually separate from each other, and finally die in each other's arms. As a companion to this paradigmatic tragedy of romantic love, western culture offers us the domestic comedy, in which marriage functions as a symbol of harmony, balance, and unification between the sexes.[3]

Neither the romantic tragedy nor the domestic comedy would seem to be the stuff lesbian dreams are made of. Adrienne Rich, in her "Twenty-One Love Poems" (a cycle of poems loosely modeled after sonnets, the traditional form for western love poetry), proposes that lesbians ought not to succumb to western romantic myths:

> *Tristan und Isolde* is scarcely the story,
> women at least should know the difference
> between love and death. . . .[4]

Nor is marriage possible for lesbians, since marriage is by definition public and regulated by laws, and lesbian love exists outside the boundaries of code and custom.

If we can claim neither romantic love nor marriage, upon what can the lesbian relationship rest? In theory, lesbians are creating new models and codes for interpersonal relationships. But few entirely new models and codes exist in literature, and lesbian romantic literature utilizes the conventions of western love. Lesbian (or homosexual) love is a twentieth-century revision of the illicit adulterous love that is the staple of romance from *Tristan* to *Anna Karenina*. It is the love that "dares not speak its name." Although, as Rich insists, we may think we know the difference between love and death, many of our fictional codes are otherwise congruent with those of the western romantic tradition.

Nature, the Garden, and the Green World

Lesbian romances most often take place in the green world, a literary convention that critic Annis Pratt defines as "a sense of oneness with the cosmos as well as of a place to one side of civilization."[5] The green world, first, evokes nature, particularly the freshness of spring that we associate with young love. It also represents a locale existing outside time and space, uncontaminated by social convention or the daily responsibilities of marriage and reproduction. It is the closed magic circle that lovers create around themselves, a protective cocoon that isolates and insulates them. Finally, the green world symbolizes the "infinite transcendence" of love, the place in which we realize what Plato called "the age-old desire—the coming together and merging with the one [we] love so the two become one."[6] *Nature, isolation,* and *transcendence:* these three characteristics of the green world are pervasive motifs in the lesbian novel of romantic love.

Nature, the blooming nature of springtime, is the preferred landscape for young love. Springtime reminds us that we human beings are part of the natural world, that like all other animals we lust and mate and carry on the endless procession of generations. Although in spring a young dyke's fancy may turn to love, lesbian love, in other ways, does not fit this paradigm. Since homosexual love does not reproduce the race, we would not necessarily expect to find it depicted through the vernal imagery that is a cliché in heterosexual romance. And in fact, a significant body of lesbian and gay male literature situates sexuality not in a green world, but in the dark and smoky world of city streets and underground bars. This is a model rooted in deviance, perhaps best captured by Sartre's image of Hell as a claustrophobic room in which sinners (among them a lesbian) are locked up forever.[7] In the pulp romances of the fifties and sixties, with Ann Bannon's *Beebo Brinker* series as a representative example, lovers come together and drift apart in the dismal mob-run bars and small closet-like apartments of New York City.

In contrast to novels that place the lovers in the city, those that celebrate the naturalness of lesbian love adopt the imagery of nature and the countryside. Perhaps no novel better illustrates this dichotomy between city and country than *The Well of Loneliness*. Stephen Gordon feels at one with Nature for the first time in her life when she falls in love with Angela Crossby; although she is forced out of her edenic home, Morton, and exiled to the city, she rediscovers her place in the green world on her honeymoon with Mary Llewellyn in the opulent gardens of Tenerife. On their return to Paris, however, their love is asphyxiated in the hellish dives of the gay underworld that serve as a prototype for all those life-denying bars of the pulp romances.

The gardens of Morton and Tenerife are deliberately intended to recall the ancient western symbol of the Garden of Eden. Both the origin and the epitome of the green world motif, the garden is where we abide in perfect solitude and innocence when we first fall in love, when we experience once again the transcendence and unification associated with innocence and infancy. Only later, when we discover how much pain accompanies love, are we exiled from the lover's paradise.

The garden shelters lesbian lovers in numerous contemporary novels. Often it is generalized to represent any natural landscape, but certain novels make the connection to the biblical Garden explicit. In Lisa Alther's version of the myth, which appears in a tapestry one woman weaves for her lover, Eden is populated by two Eves, "both smiling and eating apples" (*Other Women*, 17). This fantasy of a lesbian Eden, a place outside conventional society, is also expressed by one of the characters in Paula Christian's *The Cruise:*

> There was something special about Mazatlan . . . something even magical. A feeling of timelessness or a tropical Garden of Eden. . . . Donna knew she would be very happy to retire to this beautiful place. . . . [They could] one day live out the rest of their lives, growing old together, watching the perfect sunsets knowing that all's right with the world. (171)

Not all lovers are allowed to dally in Paradise, however. *Desert of the Heart,* as we saw, evokes the Garden not as a place of retreat and retirement but as the place we must leave, like our ancestors, to begin our difficult journey toward human love and companionship. Jane Rule reminds us that Eve, in Milton's version of the myth, is already a housewife who retreats to her rustic kitchen while Adam and Raphael speak of lofty things. The protagonist of M. F. Beal's *Angel Dance* comments wryly that Eve may very well have found the expulsion from the Garden a relief. Because the biblical myth is so oppressive to women, some novelists, as we shall see in the next chapter, shift the lesbian garden from the Judeo-Christian Eden to Sappho's pagan island.

Although Rule's characters leave the garden, many other lesbian novels situate the lovers in an edenic landscape. In one bold brushstroke, the artist-hero of Katherine Forrest's *An Emergence of Green* transforms her entire landscape into a green world: "She smiled into Carolyn's green eyes. 'I think I've definitely entered a green period. I'd like to be in a place where it's all green'" (268–69). In the prototypical lesbian green world romance, Patience and Sarah set up housekeeping on an isolated farm in Greene County, New York, where, Patience says, "the world was out of sight, and right there in the wide-open of our yard Sarah held me close and kissed me" (181). These bold kisses in the open contrast with their furtive lovemaking back in Yankee civilization, and convey the message that lesbian love ought to be fully and openly a part of nature, rather than covert and illicit.

Many other writers use the green world motif to evoke the freshness and innocence associated with new love, thereby revising the patriarchal notion that lesbian love is deviant and sterile. In a short story by Maureen Brady, an artist's studio, surrounded by "gentle California green" becomes a "paradise" for two lovers (*The Question She Put to Herself*, 105, 108). Valerie Taylor sets the love scenes in *Prism* in an apple orchard, although the apple evoked is not the fruit of the tree of knowledge but Sappho's "topmost apple the gatherers could not reach, reddening on the bough" (51).[8] *Anna's Country* is particularly saturated with references to gardening and nature; Hope and Anna even fall in love on a camping trip. When lovemaking is done indoors, as in *Iris, Zami, Curious Wine*, or *Toothpick House*, it may be in a house or apartment surrounded by nature, thus recreating the Temple of Friendship in Natalie Barney's Parisian garden.[9] Writers may draw upon nature imagery for romantic descriptions such as Ramelle's dying dream of eternity with

Celeste who "kissed her amid the tulips and butterflies" (*Six of One*, 323); or Jenny's reverie, in the first flush of romance, about kissing Sandy in "a field of tall grass," a kiss that is "the most natural thing in the world" (*Choices*, 28).

The green world in lesbian romances may be imagined as the wet world, as well. Even in *Desert of the Heart*, which resolutely rejects the notion of love as an idyllic sojourn in the Garden, Evelyn and Ann travel from Reno to the desert to make love on the shores of Pyramid Lake. Swimming in another desert lake, this one in Israel, foreshadows the future love affair between Elisheva and Deborah in *The Law of Return*. Sandy and Jenny, reunited in *Choices*, kiss on the beach in Honolulu, while Clare, in *Abeng*, realizes her love for Zoe as they sunbathe by a stream.

Why, we might ask, do we find all this water imagery in lesbian literature? One answer is that no other metaphor so accurately evokes the liquidity of oral sex, often argued to be the quintessential lesbian sexual technique. Hence, associations with water and the sea have become clichés in lesbian sexual writing. But references to water in less sexually explicit and more romantic contexts also reinforce the symbol of the self-contained island that is ubiquitous in lesbian literature. Lesbian writers draw upon the age-old association of water with sensuality, which re-creates the oceanic feelings of limitlessness and fusion supposedly experienced in the womb, and upon the connection between water and re-birth. Lovemaking by or in water, therefore, represents a baptism into the joys of lesbianism.

The freshness and fertility of nature is only the first association evoked by the green world. The protagonist of Joanna Russ's coming out novel, *On Strike against God*, describes her lover as "snowfields and mountains," bringing to mind the isolation and transcendence characteristic of romantic love (54). The green world is both a place of refuge for the lovers and a limitless zone outside time and space where they soar and merge.

The connection between love and refuge has its source in more than literary convention although, to be sure, writers have always associated romantic love with the rejection of the mundane world. Lesbians are also attracted to the idea of a refuge from a hostile and dangerous world because, as both fiction and real life demonstrate, the world is not particularly safe for women who prefer to be with women: "Under siege by the dominant culture, we feel we cannot afford anything but security, mutual validation, and predictability within the private world of our relationships." [10] Furthermore, society revolves so tightly around heterosexual couples and families that it affords no legitimacy to lesbians and acknowledges no place for us. The contrast made between a lesbian sister and her heterosexual brothers in Dodici Azpadu's *Saturday Night in the Prime of Life* makes this point poignantly clear, not the least because the illegitimacy of the lesbian choice has been internalized by the protagonist. Her lover's warning sounds a familiar note to many lesbians: "You'd never *say* your life with me is of less account than your brothers' marriages. But that's what the actions you are proposing come to. Your fantasy of belated respectability frightens me" (70).

The combination of covert rejection and overt violence leads many lesbians in real life to retreat into the safety of a relationship, a home, a closet. One sociologist names this replication of the green world fantasy in actual relationships the "insulation" period, during which "time and space are deliberately put between 'them' as a couple and the outside world." [11] Doris Grumbach, in a novel based upon the lives of a historical lesbian couple, the Ladies of Llangollen, imagines their celebrated Bed as "a lost continent on which they could live, in harmony, quite alone and together" (*The Ladies,* 182). This insulation period is certainly an actualization of "a universal fantasy about secluding oneself with one's lover forever." But the fantasy resonates particularly strongly for gay people, who "must get away from where they are because the community is hostile to their choice." [12]

However, we don't just choose seclusion because our excursion into the public world is threatening or, at the very least, uncomfortable. A pleasant and sufficient life can be created by two nesting women together—Eve and Eve at one in the Garden. The longing for home moves from the metaphoric to the realistic through carefully crafted descriptions of living spaces that depict women together creating a beautiful home. In *Prism, Say Jesus and Come to Me, Folly, Toothpick House,* and *Lovers in the Present Afternoon,* the couples dream together of a house with rugs and curtains and a warm kitchen. Even the archetypal butch, Stephen Gordon, desires to make a nest for Mary Llewellyn. The novel implies that had she also been able to make her a baby—as today's lesbians can—their relationship might have survived the onslaughts of a hostile society.

The lesbian couple is "home" for the participants in the metaphoric sense as well. The couple is the resting place that awaits the quest hero at the end of her journey. Coming home to one's lesbian self has as a corollary coming home to one's green world lover. This is the meaning of the words, "with you I am come home," that head this chapter (*Lovers in the Present Afternoon*, 248). Virtually identical words are spoken by the lovers in Ellen Frye's *Look under the Hawthorne* ("'You're home for me, Edie. . . . Let me come home to you,' whispered Anabelle" [192–93]), and appear in several stories in the appropriately titled *Home in Your Hands* by Lee Lynch. The original (and superior) title of *Patience and Sarah*—*A Place for Us*—captures this longing for a home that provides the self-sufficient lovers refuge from patriarchal society. In their new world of Greene County, Patience and Sarah, true pioneers, do everything for themselves. Sarah would even build their roof except that Patience, the practical one (the one more connected to society), recommends a professional. At the end, Patience bakes a cake to feed their love (symbolizing nurturance and fertility) and Sarah, in a gesture that would have appealed to the Ladies of Llangollen, builds their bed. [13]

Beds and houses are but two of the locations in which lesbians consummate their love. *The Wanderground, This Place, Prism,* and *The Cook and the Carpenter* all use images of nests and cocoons to inscribe the isolated and protective circle of the lesbian couple. In *The Cook and the Carpenter,* for example, one character describes her relationship as "so safe, like being wrapped inside a pillow with a mirror" (118). A magical shed in Jane Chambers' *Burning* serves as a portal to that space outside time in which the lesbian spirit waits to be absorbed by any women who chance to enter. In that space, the lovers are literally oblivious to anything or anyone outside the lesbian love tragedy they reenact. The cover artwork for *Iris* presents an archetypal image of two women locked in an embrace, oblivious to the world around them, rising together from a shrouded, mystical island.

Lovers in lesbian literature usually find fulfillment in their safe havens. Occasionally, however, the lovers' space may be invaded by the outside world. Unlike many other writers, Jane Chambers, in *Burning,* is not sanguine about nature's protective powers. Her violently sundered colonial lovers, by merging with two modern women, finally "marry" each other in "the darkening forest that surrounded them" (112). They choose the dark woods instead of the broad daylight because, unlike Patience and Sarah, but like Tristan and Isolde, they cannot openly declare their love. They find no refuge in nature, however, for men from town pursue and interrupt them in their refuge.

Traditionally, the green world is also a magical dimension in which lovers transcend time and space to be one with each other and with the universe. Of course, the longing for transcendence may be denied, particularly in prefeminist times. Emily Dickinson's suggestively lesbian poem, "I showed her Heights she never saw," is imbued with the feelings of pain and loss caused by an ambivalent lover who, when invited to share the poet's life, cannot "find her Yes." [14] In Paula Gunn Allen's *The Woman Who Owned the Shadows,* Ephanie and her girlhood friend climb a peak they have never climbed before, and, at the top, tremble on the brink of lesbianism. Ephanie reaches out to touch Elena's face, but she, like Dickinson's timid lover, turns away toward the conventional world. Instead of soaring, Ephanie contemplates falling and smashing on the rocks below. She does not recover until she is well into adulthood.

On the other hand, Annie and Victoria, in Lee Lynch's *Toothpick House,* successfully climb the heights together:

> From Vicky, Annie felt no ending, but an opening, a doorway to a path. . . . She pictured Vicky and herself hand in hand on a path in the mountains, barefoot, the grasses and clover tickling their ankles. They climbed higher and higher. At each new elevation they became giddier from the purity of the air and their feelings. They never let go of each other's hands, and they lay down in meadows along the way. For a love like this what would Annie not do! (90)

It is hardly original to imagine romantic love as a transcendent state akin to religious or spiritual experience—the transfiguration of ordinary life into the extraordinary, or what Patience calls "this mighty mystery and astonishment" (*Patience and Sarah,* 32). Annie and Victoria, in *Toothpick House,* journey together "through all the space in the universe," while the lovers in *Iris* feel themselves to be "removed from time . . . [and] the rational order of things" (116; 55). Love (or sometimes sex—the difference is not always clear) releases one from the cramped prison of the self or from the confines of time and space.

To Merge or Not to Merge: Myths of Mutuality

For many lesbian writers and readers, this romantic convention takes on a political shape. The ability of two women to permeate each other's skin, to blur the boundaries between self and other, to escape the linear dimensions of patriarchal time and space, becomes a symbol of the superiority of the lesbian choice, or lifestyle. But, like other myths of lesbian culture, our myths of mutuality take on complex and contradictory meanings.

In June Arnold's *The Cook and the Carpenter,* the Carpenter seeks to blur the boundaries between self and other by changing the shape of wood through carpentry, by altering the patterns of her brain through alcohol, and finally by merging with another woman through love-making. This image of total fusion between lovers is commonplace in lesbian literature. Lovers do not possess or own each other in a patriarchal fashion; each becomes the other, fully and mutually exchanging souls until they grow into one stronger and richer being. As the seventeenth-century British poet, Katherine Philips, wrote to her "excellent" friend, Lucasia, the ideal of lesbian lovers is to be able to say "I am not thine, but thee." [15]

In *Burning,* Martha, outcast and witch, dreams first of merging with Abigail for protection: "Martha fancied somehow that they could blend and merge into one richer, fuller being. As the two rough-hewn planks hard-nailed together in the center of the cabin formed a stronger ridgepole, so she and Abigail, their arms entwined, their bodies pressed thigh to thigh, formed a woman strong enough to fend off any danger" (82). But two women, no matter how merged, are still not strong enough to stand up to the patriarchal order. Martha and Abigail must merge with contemporary women who then reenact, in a magical space outside time, their tragically interrupted love story: "To merge, to find one's self and double it, twice gentle, twice needing, twice whole" (97).

Loss of boundaries, and merging with the other, may characterize all deeply-felt love and sex. But some feminist theorists argue that women's boundaries of self are especially permeable and, therefore, lesbian lovers are uniquely prone to merging and fusing.[16] This fusion is certainly valued, indeed idealized, by lesbians, but it is also subtly feared and questioned. Hence, *Burning* is a somewhat sinister ghost story, and merging becomes but another name for possession. A second ghost story casts an even more jaundiced eye upon the transcendental fusion of two lovers. When Karen Lathem, the protagonist of *The House at Pelham Falls,* by Brenda Weathers, rents a country house, she is possessed by the spirit of a long-dead woman whose lesbian love affair had been tragically and prematurely interrupted. The ghost pulls Karen away from this world into "uncharted atmospheres" and "a starless space empty of all but them" (56, 59). Night after night they make love, succubus possessing mortal woman, until Karen is almost drained of life. Their lovemaking evokes and yet, by denying ultimate completion, subverts conventional lesbian descriptions of romantic love: "They flew to an airless, lofty place where they made love without touching, where their bodies clung and writhed but never merged, never quite met" (146). *The House at Pelham Falls* and *Burning,* through the device of the ghost story, both reveal an ominous subtext beneath the familiar fantasy of two women soaring and merging in a green world beyond time and space. This is not the only fashion in which lesbian writers criticize the green world motif. Lesbian literature is so consistently self-critical and self-reflexive that we must consider further what values in addition to isolation, insulation, and fusion between lovers are encoded in lesbian romances.

If we turn from literary conventions and myths to community discourse about relationships between women, we find considerable ambivalence over, or oscillation between, the poles of fusion and separation, or, as psychologist Letitia Ann Peplau terms it, attachment and autonomy.[17] The lesbian myth claims that our relationships are uniquely close because of the similarity and identity of the lovers. Two women, sharing the same socialization and the same bodies, can achieve a union far deeper than that of a man and woman:

> Being a woman loving women . . . the lines blur. With great beauty
> though, like undulating lines of sun on the waves, in the middle of
> the ocean, half-way between one continent and the next, the lines of
> definition barely existing, at least always moving, never holding

still, between being a woman loving yourself and being a woman loving women. Same breasts. Same warm skin. Same softness, and particularly female sense of life and joy, such laughter and nurturing possible.[18]

This description is rooted in the mythic sameness of all women, and thus resembles the psychodynamic theory of homosexuality as narcissism.

According to this theory, a woman who loves another woman actually uses her as a mirror reflecting the self that is her real love. But Tretona, in *Who Was That Masked Woman?*, uses her powers of observation to reject this position. She refutes her therapist's Freudian "mirror theory" by describing the sexual preferences of two actual lesbians: "what each did for the other was significantly different from what she wanted for herself" (148). We find a more extensive examination and rejection of the mirror theory in *Desert of the Heart*. When Ann and Evelyn first meet, they immediately notice how similar they look. Perhaps, they muse, they are doubles, or relatives, or mirrors of the other. Perhaps their relationship is an example of what Ann labels (in a different context) a "Freudian embarrassment" (28). But we learn that, in Evelyn's words, there is "no family resemblance" but rather "an impression" that evokes "a memory, not a likeness" (10). They are not the same; instead, they are two individuals who develop a mature relationship in which each sees the other as a separate being. In its concluding words, the novel returns to the image of the mirror, not as a symbol of narcissism but of relationship: "And they turned and walked back up the steps toward their own image, reflected in the great, glass doors" (222).

Psychoanalysis is not the only theory to associate lesbianism with sameness. Lesbians also appropriate the feminist concept of sisterhood—a model of sameness and equality—to characterize our relationships. Monique Wittig, for example, gives a lesbian twist to a famous line from Baudelaire's "L'Invitation au Voyage": "You say, mon enfant, ma soeur, songe a la douceur" (*The Opoponax*, 231). The lesbian couple, as sisters together, may "dream of the sweetness" of perfect equality and mutuality.

Consequently, lovers may be symbolic or even actual sisters. Before fear of lesbianism separates them, Ephanie and Elena, in *The Woman Who Owned the Shadows*, "understood the exact measure of their relationship, the twining, the twinning. . . . With each other they were each one doubled. They were thus complete" (22). The author further adopts the Indian legend of Double Woman—women "who were sisters, born of the same mind, the same spirit"—to represent lesbians (211). Since Ephanie and Elena are described as dusky and fair, Rose Red and Snow White, their sisterhood also bridges the separation of race. Similarly, Ellen, in *Confessions of Cherubino,* makes love with Venusberg, her Black half-sister. Love between sisters, for Bertha Harris, suggests the achievement of perfect mutuality. Gina Covina, author of *The City of Hermits,* uses the sister relationship in a manner that is humorous and metaphoric at the same time. Silvia and Lucile Handy are two orphans who, in making love, "mixed essential juices in a ritual that made them sisters. The orphans were reunited with all that had been lost" (69). As the novel moves through its Dickensian plot, the women discover that they are in fact twin sisters separated at birth.

The symbol of the *doppelgänger,* one's perfect twin, reaches its sinister apotheosis in Camarin Grae's *Soul Snatcher.* Another set of identical twins separated at birth stumble upon each other, but for them the result is possession and death, not mutual love. Sharla becomes convinced that her twin snatched all positive traits in the womb, leaving her weak and sickly. In a ritual that parodies the sadomasochistic lovemaking characteristic of Grae's fiction, Sharla tries to switch their souls. As *Burning* and *The House at Pelham Falls* undercut the lesbian myth of merging, so *Soul Snatcher* unravels the myth of sisterhood and sameness.

Sisterhood is deadly in *Soul Snatcher,* however, only because it is not premised upon equality. In contrast, lesbian characters often idealize the mutuality found in their relationships. These declarations may be rhetorical, reflecting the heady intoxication of coming out rather than the hard work of building an ongoing relationship. Characters in *Between Friends* and *Blood Sisters*—both born-again lesbians—describe their relationships in politically correct terminology: relationships are "honest and, above all, equal"; or they have "a balance of power and space" not possible with men (*Between Friends,* 34; *Blood Sisters,* 104). Lesbians outside literary texts also argue that our relationships are superior to heterosexual ones because they allow or encourage independence and autonomy within the couple. Psychologist Peplau found that, while all lesbians claimed to value attachment and autonomy equally, not seeing these as mutually exclusive values, feminist lesbians placed a particularly high value on autonomy. In *Iris,* the title character voices the argument that patriarchy is not threatened by lesbian sexuality itself, but by "what grew out of that pleasure and satisfaction . . . the notion of self-worth and autonomy that a woman's love could give to another woman" (162). According to the lesbian myth, women encourage each other to be the best they can be, in contrast to men who thwart a woman's growth into adult selfhood. This ideal is expressed in one of the lesbian relationships chronicled in *Légende:* "It is a slow process, that of two people adapting the rhythms of their lives to each other: not becoming each other or even part of each other—Aurélie and I could never do that, we were too much ourselves—but adapting to being with each other" (97).

A slow process, and a difficult one. So strong is the inclination to merge and lose the self in the other, that lovers must sometimes wrench apart to maintain their individuality and autonomy. Like other lesbian myths, our myths of relationship rest upon an idealistic assumption of sameness. But lovers may discover that the differences between them are as significant as the similarities, and that love may grow best in the space created by these differences. Elisheva, in *The Law of Return,* thus wonders if she and Deborah "had finally to listen and know we were not the same person, not even identical twins, but different in ways that jarred and chafed. Nothing had prepared us for the attention our love required" (230).

Even in romances, such as *Loving Her, Curious Wine,* and *Anna's Country,* lovers must separate before they can unite. In *Anna's Country,* for example, the protagonist tells her new lover, "I need time before I'm up to you. Where most novels end—girl gets girl—is the beginning. And I'm not up to telling that story yet" (175). Because these are romances, of course, the separations are merely perfunctory. A month or two apart and the lovers move back to an ecstatic reunion. Just as the reader of romance always knows, from page one, who is going to fall in love, she also knows that, regardless of obstacles, the lovers will be together on the last page. In fiction that aims at a realistic representation of life, on the other hand, separation may be permanent or, if not, reuniting entails considerable work to construct a sense of autonomy and "wholeness." Barbara Wilson, for one, breaks with romantic and lesbian tradition by sending her hero's lover away at the end of *Murder in the Collective.*[19] Whether romantic or realistic, however, these texts reveal that the values of wholeness and autonomy have become as important to the lesbian feminist myth of relationship as are fusion and interdependence.

The interplay between intimacy and autonomy, finally, may be integrated into a theory about the basis of sexual identity. In *Burning, Choices,* and *Between Friends,* characters link sexual preference to the need for separation or closeness in relationships. Women represent safety, security, and strength through bonding, while men represent separation and otherness—or, quite often, alienation and invasiveness. Hence, one of the characters in *Burning* describes making love with a man as two hands applauding, with a woman as two hands clasped. In *Between Friends,* Amy fears the closeness that can exist between two women, the mirroring and identification that can lead to loss of self. She is incapable of maintaining a separate space with a woman, and so chooses to be heterosexual. Meg, on the other hand, fears the loss of autonomy in a relationship with a man and feels suffocated by male demands and possessiveness. She best maintains her selfhood with women and feels most comfortable as a lesbian. These novels suggest that the satisfaction a woman finds in a relationship depends, in part, upon which sex allows her the healthiest balance between intimacy and autonomy.

Dismantling the Myth of the Couple

Even as lesbian novels idealize the isolated and self-sufficient couple, they criticize and subvert many of the assumptions upon which this myth is built. As the quotation from *Lover* that heads this chapter suggests, our relationships sometimes threaten to collapse beneath the weight of our green world baggage. Consider, for example, how Maureen Brady, in *Folly,* transforms the metaphor of home. The lovers, who live in separate trailers, dream of buying a home together, but by the time they have accumulated the money to do so, Folly has awakened to a different reality:

> They could live in a house together with the children, take care of each other, curl up curve to curve in the night and be restored. . . . What kind of house would it be? She tried hard to see it. But what

she saw was an old factory, a line of women sewing, a sign out front:
WOMEN OF VICTORY CO-OP MILL. (194–95)

This author associates "home" with a private haven set apart from the world, an individualistic and selfish fantasy that must be replaced by the collective factory. *Folly* is but one of many lesbian novels that insist on placing the isolated couple in a larger political and social context.

Although thoroughly imbued with the green world/garden motif, Valerie Taylor's *Prism* gently criticizes the insular lesbian relationship as well. When Ann, a city lesbian who has never found true or satisfying love there, moves to the country in the winter of her life, she falls in love with a widow who raises cauliflower. Their romance unfolds in an apple orchard imbued with green world symbolism through plentiful references to mythic lesbian lovers: Emily Dickinson and Kate Anthon, the Ladies of Llangollen, Patience and Sarah, and, of course, Sappho herself. The apple orchard is a secret, hidden place, "empty of people but full of life," where "the air was sweet with growing things and the scent of apples pinkening in the sun" (73). The orchard also protects the lovers from external dangers as, Ann muses, it might have protected generations of lesbians who found refuge in their love and in this orchard.

But nature has one fatal flaw: it is green, safe, and protective during part of the year only—at least in the northeast. After spring and summer comes winter, the green world turns white, and lovers who hide themselves away in a garden or orchard grow cold. The two women must make a life for themselves indoors, in a community, in the civilized world, if their love is to survive. Not even separatists, Ann comments, can live apart completely.

Ann and her lover must transform their affair into a marriage, and rewrite their green world romance as a domestic novel. As Ann puts it, they must "reconcile the literal [marriage] and the transcendental [romantic love]" (119). The prism of the title—a simple domestic object, hanging from lamps, which breaks up ordinary light into rainbows—symbolizes this reconciliation. At the novel's end, the two women share a home and a bed when the orchard grows cold, and, more important, begin to expand their relationship into a community.

Prism does not repudiate the monogamous relationship; indeed, it bases everything, including the community that is hinted at in the novel, upon the love of one woman for another. June Arnold, in *Sister Gin,* casts a rather more skeptical eye at the monogamous relationship as the basis for a healthy self-image or a lesbian community. In the 1970s, when the novel was written, monogamy had come under attack in the lesbian community as an unhealthy vestige of patriarchy, associated with jealousy, possessiveness, ownership—all of which were deemed contrary to the ideal lesbian relationship.[20] Open, nonmonogamous relationships and plentiful sexual experimentation were expected, indeed mandated, for politically savvy lesbians. So one myth, that of Patience and Sarah or the Ladies of Llangollen faithful until death do them part, was countered by another, that of Molly Bolt sleeping her way through the rubyfruit jungle.

The lovers in *Sister Gin,* Su and Bettina, have lived together monogamously for twenty years when the novel opens. Before that Su had lived with another woman for ten years. Both relationships were comfortable, soft cushions that stunted Su's growth into a healthy lesbian adulthood. Su is adult, in the sense of being balanced, reasonable, and repressed, but the wild, crazy, witchy, angry part of her has never been allowed to develop. Su is so frightened of that self, which includes her lesbianism, that it only emerges when she is drunk, as she often is. Bettina is an equally disturbing example of what happens when a woman retreats from life into an insulated, protective relationship. When we first see her, she is literally unable to get out of bed. She neither works nor communicates with anyone outside of her family; she is as wrapped up in the relationship with Su as she is in her "soft pillow of what others call fat" (4–5).

Sister Gin portrays the lesbian couple as a debilitating unit in which the strengths of one woman feed off the weaknesses of the other, so that neither is whole on her own. Nor does it matter which is which: first Su is strong and Bettina weak, later Bettina is strong and Su is weak. Only when the couple breaks apart does each woman begin her developmental journey to healthy selfhood. For Arnold, the couple is a private structure that must open out into the world of politics and communal activity. Monogamy shelters lovers against life and change. In both of Su's relationships the lovers mistake protection for love, or turn their love into protection, rather than using their love as the basis for new growth. The protective circle of the couple causes them to shrink, like Su's handwriting. When Su falls in love with Mamie Carter, however, she cannot create a protective couple relationship. What, asks Mamie Carter, does monogamy, till death do us part, mean to a seventy-seven-year-old woman? Instead of a closed circle, Mamie Carter offers Su an open-ended relationship leading toward a community of women.

Arnold presents relationship as a complex of oppositions: dependence and independence, weakness and strength, intimacy and autonomy, monogamy and nonmonogamy. She stands at one end of the lesbian spectrum by elevating autonomy, and all it represents, over intimacy. Representing one part of the lesbian feminist gospel, she extols the amazon qualities and discourages the rest. Nevertheless, life can wound so deeply that we may need to return to a source of absolute, unconditional nurturance. We still dream nostalgically that we *can* go home again. Hence, intimacy and attachment may take the form of mothering and sometimes—the pun is unavoidable—smothering. As Bertha Harris puts it, "There is no intimacy between woman and woman which is not preceded by a long narrative of the mother" (*Lover*, 173).

The need to give and get nurturance is a fundamental human need. It is certainly patterned after the mother/child relationship, one that begins with the act of feeding and is then generalized and extended throughout life. Typically, women remain the givers and men the receivers of nurturing, an inequality that has been extensively explored in literature and popular psychology. It was one of the factors that precipitated the early women's liberation movement, since women resented constantly catering to men's emotional needs. We asked, who nurtures the nurturers? Who mothers the mothers? Conversely, in much lesbian feminist literature, one of the joys a woman discovers when she comes out is that another woman is sensitive to her emotional needs and nurturant in ways that men have not been. This is one reason women turn to or stay with women.

At the same time, of course, psychoanalysis has interpreted this emotional and nurturant configuration as yet another sign of pathology. Writing in a decade when psychoanalytic definitions of homosexuality were virtually unchallenged, Jane Rule was the first lesbian novelist to reject the claim that lesbians are women who never resolve the oedipal crisis or who have regressed to an infantile stage of sexuality. In *Desert of the Heart,* the lovers initially act out the paradigmatic relationship between mother and daughter (to such an extent that Ann's last name is Childs and Eve-lyn describes herself as "mother of all the world" [121]). They are confined within Freudian conventions and evade a mutual adult lesbian relationship. At the end, however, each grows out of her need to play a role, and they walk together toward an open, undefined future.

The feminist ideal is for lovers to give and take nurturance freely and equally—thus rephrasing the old Freudian cliches. In many lesbian novels, however, the couples fail to achieve such mutuality. Two women may freeze into roles, one always being the mother and the other always the daughter, as we see in Donna and Sandy's relationship in Paula Christian's *The Cruise*. Both may be so well-trained as nurturers—as Lisa Alther's *Other Women* amusingly demonstrates—that they compete to see who can take better care of the other. Or it may be that their needs are different: one may need to mother much more than to be mothered and vice versa, causing an imbalance or dependency within the relationship. Mothering then becomes a source of weakness rather than of strength.

This is the pattern found in *The Cook and the Carpenter*. The Carpenter needs mothering from the Cook to break down her rigid barriers, to help her return to the polymorphous perversity of infancy. She reaches out beyond the walls of self—the model of the relationship without walls is mother and child—and asks, in Arnold's phrase, for someone to carry her tune. The Cook, quintessential mother and nurturer, gives that help, that love. But the novel never satisfactorily resolves the question of what the Cook gets out of it. What needs of hers are met, especially since her personal journey is toward separation as the Carpenter's is toward involvement? Like a mother, the Cook seems to sacrifice her own needs for the Carpenter's. *The Cook and the Carpenter* (1973) was written at the very beginning of the lesbian feminist movement, but the question it raises—can a lesbian relationship successfully balance the needs of individual autonomy, unconditional nurturance, and social involvement—has yet to be answered.

Writing the Lesbian Body

Having discussed the fictional representation of love and bonding in lesbian relationships, I now want to turn to sex and desire. Sexuality follows romance by design in this chapter, because, contrary to what some might expect, sexuality has been less central to the novel of relationship than romantic love. Lesbian writers more often associate love with refreshing spring breezes than with the summer heat of desire. Sexual language, readers have been quick to point out, is surprisingly absent or muted in lesbian fiction and, when present, is not always satisfying or convincing.[21] For this reason, a pleasant and unassuming love story like Katherine Forrest's *Curious Wine* became (and continues to be) a smash hit almost entirely because of its numerous detailed scenes of lovemaking. At the same time that lesbian writers created an intensely romantic literature, they struggled to find a language for sexuality. As Virginia Woolf observed about women writers of the past, contemporary lesbian writers have been fettered by their own version of chastity.[22]

Monique Wittig postulates that this struggle results from the patriarchal control—the "phallogocentrism"—of language, which eliminates the possibility of meaningful words for a female sexuality independent of men. The warriors of *Les Guérillères* reject the language of the past entirely: "They say that all these forms denote an outworn language. They say everything must begin over again. They say that a great wind is sweeping the earth. They say that the sun is about to rise" (66). Although Wittig alerts us to how masculine language has defined female sexuality, she does not demonstrate how to create a new language for female and lesbian sexuality. That language remains implicit in the gaps, the absences, the empty space inside and between words.

This absence defeats Alma, in *Contract with the World,* as she tries to become a lesbian writer:

> I have no language at all for my body or Roxanne's body that isn't either derisive or embarrassing. . . . We make love without nouns as much as possible, speak directions instead. . . . a love letter filled with nothing but adverbs is ridiculous. Gertrude Stein tried to invent a new language for lovemaking, but it was more a code to be cracked than a communication. (131)

Not all writers are stymied by the absence of words. The protagonist of *Lovers in the Present Afternoon,* Lynn, easily shares words with women. Words are safe, words carry "both intense meaning and muted mystery"

(98). Touch is threatening, because touch belongs to men. Lynn keeps the realms of language and sexuality separate, or experiences the latter only through the former: "I wrote poetry about the Word becoming Flesh and Love being the Word as though I bypassed the way our bodies acted" (99). Similarly, Elisheva, in *The Law of Return*, describes the relationship she ultimately achieves with her lover in much the same way that Jane Eyre writes about her marriage with Rochester: "in talking with each other we will build a home of language, a nest of words" (248).[23]

Are lesbians at home with words, or are we alienated from our sexuality by language? Do lesbian writers "bypass" the way our bodies act? This confusion over the power of words results in part from the damage inflicted upon lesbians by conventional language and mythology. Lesbians have been reticent and uncomfortable about sexual writing in part because we wish to reject the patriarchal stereotype of the lesbian as a voracious sexual vampire who spends all her time in bed. It is safer to be a lesbian if sex is kept in the closet or under the covers. We don't wish to give the world another stick with which to beat us. Private lesbian gossip and humor can be very salacious, but our public writing is more likely to be circumspect. We can further trace this reticence about sexuality to a lesbian myth promulgated in the early days of the lesbian feminist movement. According to this myth, lesbians (or women in general) are more sensual than sexual; lovemaking between women is characterized by "touching and rubbing and cuddling and fondness." Goal-oriented behavior, on the other hand, is either gauche, politically incorrect, or—that most condemnatory of words—male. Lesbians are above "the Big Orgasm."[24]

Just as the intimacy found in lesbian relationships is argued to be proof of their superiority, so too this sensuality can be offered as evidence of the superiority of lesbian sex to heterosexual sex. One could gather from lesbian writing—and not just fiction—that all men are hopeless sexual neanderthals: insensitive, violent, and, in Rita Mae Brown's words, "boring" and "dull" (*Rubyfruit Jungle*, 159). What men lack, and women possess in abundance, is gentleness, tenderness, and an integrated sensuality. We see the impact of this perception, or myth, as recently as 1987 in a parody news item by "a. prilfool" in *off our backs*. A survey supposedly revealed that, as a result of the AIDS hysteria, college women were turning to each other for sex. Once having tried it, most said they wouldn't go back to men. *Lesbian Connection,* a national newsletter, then reprinted the item without noticing the "a. prilfool" joke, and, although they later acknowledged their gaffe, I suspect some lesbians will continue to offer this story as proof of the superiority of lesbian sex.[25] Evidence certainly exists for men's bad behavior in bed and out; nevertheless, the consistent stereotype of the brutal rapist in lesbian fiction often compromises its integrity.

In *Curious Wine,* Katherine Forrest contrasts lesbian and hetero- sexuality in a description that constructs and then deconstructs the formulas of lesbian sexual writing. She describes men and women oppositionally: men are "firm, hungry, exciting"; women are "sweet, soft, melting" (119). Men control sex, directing it for their own excitement and orgasm, while women give sexual pleasure to each other rather than taking it for themselves: "His arms, his body—insistent, carrying her, sweeping her with him. Her arms, her body—tender, giving, dissolving her."

But then, Forrest abruptly reverses the meaning of her signifiers. For the protagonist, sexual fulfillment with a man is "diffuse" and "enveloping"; with another woman it is "strong and pure." This would seem to contradict the contrast the author has previously made. Lesbian sex should lead to a diffuse and enveloping orgasm, if any at all, and heterosexual sex to a strong and pure one. But it is possible to interpret Forrest's sexual message as a subversion of heterosexuality. Because female sexuality is totally embodied—in Freudian terminology, polymorphously perverse—sex that is timed to male rhythms leads only to a diffusion of a woman's sexual potential. With another woman, who attends to her lover's total sexuality by following her particular rhythm, orgasm is pure, ecstatic, and transcendent. These are the heights never seen of which Emily Dickinson writes.

Katherine Forrest is one of a number of writers who are attempting to find, or create, a language for lesbian sexuality. Many of these writers adopt words that represent specific physiological characteristics of female sexuality and female bodies. Women's bodies are, in general, softer and smoother than men's. Female sexual response is liquid, especially when oral sex is the chosen technique. Orgasm, for women and men, causes a momentary loss of self-consciousness or ego-boundaries. Lesbian sexual language employs these signs of softness, liquidity, and merging copiously and consistently. By and large, then, descriptions of sex rely on the same green and wet world imagery that we have already noted in descriptions of romantic love. This similarity confirms what virtually everyone, expert and layperson alike, agrees is characteristic of female sexuality: for women, sex and love are intermingled. A lesbian love affair, then, is uniquely intense and satisfying because both parties share the same desire for intimacy and fusion in sexual contact.[26]

While lesbian sexuality may be satisfying in real life, the fictional representation of it very often is not. But the dissatisfaction many readers express about lesbian sexual description arises not, as it is often phrased, because too *little* of it exists. Rereading the past two decades of lesbian fiction, I discovered (somewhat to my surprise) that, from the very beginning, lesbian novelists describe sex in greater detail than do most heterosexual female novelists. Instead, our dissatisfaction with lesbian sexual language is due to the undeniable fact that most of this language is repetitive, predictable, unimaginative, and dull.

Scenes of lovemaking have developed an iconography unique to lesbian literature. The following passage from Rita Mae Brown's *In Her Day* illustrates several modes and styles characteristic of lesbian sexual language:

> Slowly she would turn Carole into an ocean of hot tides. The power of her own sexuality made her heady. She used to think of her clitoris as a red acorn but now she thought of herself as a sea anemone. She could no longer localize her centers of pleasure: Carole synthesized her body. She had her first multiple orgasm with Carole and she loved her for that.
>
> That time they were leaning up against the pillows, Carole drinking a coke as usual. She stored ice cubes in her mouth and kissed Ilse's whole body. When Carole buried her lips between Ilse's open legs, she lost the boundaries of her conventional self. Maybe it was the shock of ice on steam heat but Ilse didn't know where she left off and Carole began. Once you know how, it's easy, she flashed. She was learning to slip in and out of physical peaks at will. She felt a tremendous bond to Carole. Lying on top of her, she feared their rib cages would lock. Their thigh bones would merge. They'd have to learn to walk all over again. (76–77)

Like the language that describes romantic feelings, this passage over-determines the fusion that occurs between lovers during sex. Phrases like "no longer localize," "lost the boundaries," "Ilse didn't know where she left off and Carole began," as well as the words, "bond," "lock" and "merge," are piled upon each other to the point of redundancy. As a result of this merging into one being, like the double-creature Plato has Aristophanes describe in *The Symposium,* Ilse and Carole discover a new way of existing in the world. Furthermore, this sexuality is extraordinary, instinctive, and magical, resulting in transcendent multiple orgasms.

Brown intermingles several different modes of writing in this passage, all of which can be traced through lesbian literature. The first paragraph consists of the maritime tropes that even by 1976 had become clichés: the "ocean of hot tides" and "sea anemone" are complemented later in the section by "she had ridden out a tidal wave" and "Carole engulfed her with affection, kissed her, licking the salt." The metaphors found in the second paragraph are basically dead ones that no longer signify anything concrete; this language describes lovemaking in terms of other activities, such as locking, merging, and bonding. However, one dead metaphor does engender a reasonably fresh one: if the lovers' thigh bones "merge," then they truly will have "to learn to walk all over again."

Finally, Brown occasionally writes nonmetaphoric descriptions in answer to the inevitable question, but what do lesbians *do?:* "She pulled her fingernails along the older woman's sides, then slid her arms under Carole's shoulders and cradled the back of her head. With mounting force Carole moved further and further into Ilse's own body" (77). Even here, however, we note an ambiguity about how Carole actually moved into Ilse's body. Similarly, in an earlier sentence—"She used to think of *her clitoris* as a red acorn but now she thought of *herself* as a sea anemone" (italics mine)—Brown ambiguously and perhaps unconsciously slides from the sexual organ to the disembodied self, a substitution that is emblematic of lesbian sexual writing in general (76).

The metaphors and euphemisms found in this passage characterize existing lesbian sexual language as a whole. To depict the lesbian body, writers employ, with varying degrees of originality and success, a variety of tropes, most often drawn from the green world. Although Wittig's warriors refuse to make symbols of women's bodies, lesbian writers do not hesitate to do so. Maureen Brady, for example, creates a complex and highly metaphoric description of the vagina first as "a close cave, warm and moist and soft as velvet. A home. A mystery," and then as a "beautiful pink garden" in which to plant the seeds of love (*The Question She Put to Herself,* 110–111). To Rita Mae Brown, of course, the vulva is a "ruby fruit jungle" (203); to Audre Lorde it is a "peony" (*Zami,* 139). Even the protagonist in *Prism* comments that the apples and cauliflowers so plentiful in the text are "symbolic" of female sexuality (139). Other figurative descriptions are euphemistic, not imagistic: "the delicate crevice between her hips," "the dark mass where love is made," or "life's origin" (*Curious Wine,* 97; *Loving Her,* 6, 48). Fewer metaphors exist for the clitoris, even though this is argued to be the truly lesbian sexual organ. Brown, as we saw, refers to the clitoris as a red acorn or (perhaps) a sea anemone; to Red Arobateau it is a "pearl," and to Kate Millet, a "blossom once blasted, damaged" ("Susie Q" in *True to Life Adventure Stories I,* 108; *Sita,* 79). Other metaphors depict the rest of the body: Forrest describes flesh as "warm sculpture" (*Curious Wine,* 95); to Lorde, in a particularly evocative metaphor, flesh is "sweet and moist and firm as a winter pear" (*Zami,* 139).

Some of these metaphors work well; most, however, are clichés. Occasionally an author invents original and unforgettable figurative language, as in this description from *Sister Gin:* "Memory moved her hand to Mamie Carter's belly—skin white as milk, finely pucked like sugar-sprinkled clabber; memory dropped her hand to Mamie Carter's sparse hair curling like steel—there was strength between her legs and no dough there where the flesh was fluid enough to slip away from the bone and leave that tensed grain hard as granite and her upright violent part like an animal nose against Su's palm" (129–130). Skin has often been described as "white as milk," but never, I suspect, as "sugar-sprinkled clabber," nor has anyone invented a more startling and delightful simile for the clitoris.

Descriptions of lovemaking draw with predictable regularity upon dead metaphors or the overdone clichés that readers find particularly unsatisfying. Typically, the act of sex evokes metaphors of water, as we have seen in *In Her Day,* or as we find in the following description from *Look Under the Hawthorne:* "Fingers have explored spiral depths, tongues have tasted fresh salt brine. Sea anemones have opened and closed, their juices drawn from full and succulent petals" (193). After reading much lesbian fiction and poetry, one might be inclined to demand a moratorium on all metaphors drawn from the sea. Occasionally we do find an original use of water imagery, as in *Riverfinger Women* (whose title evokes lesbian sexuality with a subtlety worthy of Gertrude Stein):

> The river is over us and under us and I am on top of her, pushing down, pushing down with my pelvis, my breasts sweeping across her chest, and her hands locked into the skin on my back, and she is pushing up, with the same rhythm, the same breath, the same motion of fins gliding upstream. One wave, one rush, one which is us, the river everywhere, clear and fast, licking the pebbles of it, cold and fresh. (93)

This is poetic language that does not bypass the way bodies act. Nor is the reference to water rote and conventional; the metaphor is precise and extended throughout a relatively long passage.

More often, however, figurative language lacks any concrete references. The metaphors and descriptive phrases are vague, generalized, detached, and repetitive. The language acts like quicksand into which meaning slowly but inexorably sinks. Lesbian erotic language, in the space of not much more than a decade, has become as formulaic as homeric or medieval epic language. Instead of the rosy-fingered Dawn, we have bodies that are always soft and warm, lovemaking that is always slow and liquid, orgasm that is always enflaming or electric. The lover's body arches or vibrates, she melts and opens, waves sweep through her, she murmurs or moans softly her pleasure and/or desire.

To give one striking example, in three descriptive passages that chart the courtship of the lovers in Katherine Forrest's *Curious Wine* (pp. 55, 75–77, and 93–97), the word "soft" is used twenty-five times, "warm" seventeen times, "gentle" eleven, "tender" eight, "caress" and "pleasure" thirteen times each. One could reasonably conclude that, in lesbian lovemaking, soft, warm, gentle caresses bring pleasure—leading to "excitement" (seven appearances), "ecstasy," and "desire" (five each). Interestingly, this is very much how the iconoclastic manifesto, "Smash Phallic Imperialism," described lesbian lovemaking in 1971 (although Forrest does permit her lovers ecstatic, melting orgasms).

Occasionally, of course, the absence of textual models to describe lesbian love may be the very point of the description. Having no words for their sexual feelings, Patience and Sarah invent their own: they call it "melting" (95). Melting does indeed convey the sensation of loss of boundaries and liquidity that results from sexual arousal. At the time that Isabel Miller wrote the novel, "melting" was a fairly fresh word. But the language that writers typically choose for their love scenes has become so routine that, when Sophie Horowitz tries to write lesbian pornography, she finds that "none of the words were right," and turns to creating gay male porn instead (*The Sophie Horowitz Story*, 108). It is understandable that the lesbians who inserted sadomasochism into lesbian sexual discourse in the late 1970s invented the term "vanilla sex." The overwhelming impression of lesbian sexuality drawn from these novels, and from lesbian theoretical writing as well, is of a deep communion of spirit more than of body, of merging and tenderness contrasted with the beastly invasiveness and physicality of men. It is hard to imagine what kinds of orgasms the women of the Wanderground could possibly have.

Writers who attempt to make lesbian sexuality fully present by writing explicit, nonmetaphoric descriptions of lovemaking—Nancy Toder in *Choices* or Red Arobateau in "Susie Q," for example—are not successful either. Satisfying sexual writing places the act of sex in a context, evoking eroticism through representations of the fantasies, images, sensations, and forms of communication that give the act meaning. Most descriptive sexual scenes in lesbian fiction, however, are divorced from any such context. They also lack particularity, an incident or image that distinguishes this sexual encounter from generic sexual experience. *In Her Day*, despite its formulas and clichés, contains one such image, that of Carole placing an ice cube on Ilse's clitoris. Although the "shock of ice on steam heat" results in a familiar loss of boundaries for the character, for the reader it functions like Wittig's "great wind" sweeping away the outmoded and dead language in which female and lesbian sexuality has been inscribed.[27] It creates an empty space in which the reader can interject her own erotic experiences and fantasies, thus proving as stimulating to the reader as it is to the character in the story.

Joanna Russ, in *On Strike against God*, puts it another way: "There is this implacable barrier between everyday life and sex . . . some sort of gap you have to jump with your eyes shut, holding your nose (so to speak) as if you were jumping into water" (53). If, in reality, there is a barrier between everyday life and sex, in literature there is an equivalent gap between sex (experience) and text (language). Lesbian eroticism may well lie as much in what language does not say as in what it does.

So far, however, lesbian novelists have barely begun to develop a lesbian language through which to encode the erotic. Some writers have succeeded in creating, or recreating, a symbolic system for sex through writing about food. Food can represent all the intimacy, nurturance, warmth, and sensuality that women claim to find in lesbian sexuality. Nurturance begins with feeding, and women, whether lesbian or straight, are the feeders of the world. Some of the most sensual language in lesbian literature, therefore, is not about sex but about food and cooking. Or to be more accurate, the descriptions of both are deliciously intertwined.

The Sophie Horowitz Story, a culinary picaresque, follows the hero from Lower East Side dairy restaurants to Chinese feasts shared with a lover in the bathtub. Even Sophie's sexuality is teasingly oral: "we kissed just like two women. Cheek to cheek, bites and licks, lips melting into each other. It was wonderful" (128). The most erotic scenes in *Zami,* perhaps the most convincingly erotic lesbian narrative, involve food. At Audre's menarche, the ritual of mashing and pounding spices with her mother's pestle, "until its velvety surface seemed almost to caress the liquefying mash at the bottom of the mortar," suggests the erotic nature of her love for her mother (79). In a later description of lovemaking, closely related language turns Audre and her lover into human versions of that mortar and pestle: "the deep undulations and tidal motions of [her] body slowly mashed ripe banana into a beige cream that mixed with the juices of [her] electric flesh" (249). Alice Bloch also draws upon the food of her culture for a sexual vocabulary. In addition to expected green world imagery, she suggests the taste and scent of sex through references to "the juice of a pomegranate of an oyster. . . . Marmalade and curry, a plum for each one in the class, oh these kisses are sweeter than any" (*The Law of Return,* 227). Although all three authors use familiar words (melting, caress, sweeter), the juxtaposition of food and sexuality in these examples produces a tantalizing eroticism.

Often the preparation of food symbolizes the dynamics of the relationship itself, rather than providing metaphors for sexuality. Dorothy Allison, whose elaborate descriptions of food in "A Lesbian Appetite" complement those of Sarah Schulman in *The Sophie Horowitz Story,* writes that "food is more than sustenance; it is history. I remember women by what we ate together, what they dug out of the freezer after we'd made love for hours" (*Trash,* 151). Samaria, in *Lover,* worries that Veronica does not eat enough: "I am going to make a garden for you to eat—that is what they meant when they thought of Eden—and then the seeds from that food and then the seeds from those foods. I will plant all there is to eat, and you will eat it" (120). If there was any sin in Eden, it wasn't that Adam and Eve ate the apple, but that they didn't eat enough. Lovers are eaters; women fill out as they become lovers. Karen, in *The House at Pelham Falls,* in her healthy, mortal love affair, "was struck as never before by the intimacy of preparing and eating food together. . . . They were preparing this for one another. Each would eat, taking the offering into her body" (55). Eating, as a prelude to lovemaking, is like a religious rite. Not surprisingly, then, the kitchen can be a temple and refuge for lovers:

> First of all, everything is a sensual delight. This is the living room, the kitchen of our utopia and there is a continuous feeding, suckling, loving here, or often enough that it seems continuous, or there always is this red kitchen. . . . It is wonderful to cook and eat in this kitchen, alone with the jars and smells or laughing playing with each other so engrossed so much to be in each other that we laugh at the long mornings and evenings just around the kitchen—never getting too far from the source.[28]

Appropriately, this author attempts to capture the free rhythms of Gertrude Stein, the writer who more than anyone before the contemporary feminist era celebrated the lesbian body and the eroticism of food.

Passion and Desire

As I have shown, lesbian writers have created a repetitive and often formulaic language for writing about sex. They also fall short in their depictions of intense passion and desire. Lesbian fiction abounds with falling in love, romance, the thrill of anticipation, but not much passion, obsession, loss, or intensely painful desire: the stuff that most heterosexual literature is made of. No lesbian who has ever been in and then out of love can argue that this absence is due to some quality unique to lesbian love. Instead, we have come up against another lesbian myth. Lesbian writers often want to give their readers the happy endings denied us in real life, and so write upbeat romances and domestic comedies (comic in the sense that they lead to happy, harmonious endings). Passion and desire are the stuff of tragedy, and our community has had enough of that.

Some writers of the 1970s, however, such as Bertha Harris, Monique Wittig and Kate Millett, dissected these myths. What, they asked, *is* sexual desire? What is love? The majority of authors assume that we know the answers to these questions, and then write what we all recognize as charming love stories. Harris, Wittig, and Millett do not. They make few assumptions, and what they write cannot always be described as charming.

Confessions of Cherubino, written by Bertha Harris and published at the onset of the feminist movement, is shaped around the conflict between desire and fulfillment. Harris describes desire as the condition of longing, of being unfulfilled, of living in a state of absence and gaps. The theme of *Confessions* recalls that of Keat's "Ode on a Grecian Urn": the pursuit of love is more stimulating than its achievement. Similarly, the anticipation of sex is more intense at times than the sex itself. Moreover, a forbidden love is the most exciting love of all. Harris's themes are separation, longing, and the violence of unsatisfied desire—all of which keep passion painfully alive. The characters Margaret and Ellen, separated from each other, are both driven into states of madness—Margaret permanently, Ellen only temporarily—by desire.

Since homosexuality is a forbidden love, it represents the most absolute separation; at the same time, because the lovers are of the same sex, it can also symbolize absolute identification. For this reason, in counterpoint to the reality of separation, Harris posits an equally strong longing for fulfillment, unification, and stasis: the perfect identification between lovers that is the dream of lesbian fiction. After their separate journeys into the hell of lust and desire, Ellen and Margaret are reborn together, in the closing words of the novel, into pure timelessness and stasis: "all the sounds ran together, reached silence, stopped, dissolved. . . . it seems to Ellen that they are approaching the conditions of perfect love"

(211). Love equals fulfillment and closure, as desire equals absence and openness. More than any other lesbian novel, *Confessions of Cherubino* explores the ramifications of Plato's allegory of love, that we begin as one double-creature, are split by lust and desire (the inevitable conditions of life), and move back toward union with our other half through love.

If the central theme of *Confessions of Cherubino* is desire (the two women only reach that condition of perfect love in the last paragraph of the novel), then the central theme of Harris's more overtly feminist novel *Lover* is, not surprisingly, love. But where *Confessions* is a dark and decadent tragedy, *Lover* is a bright and buoyant comedy. Indeed, it is a domestic comedy about a matriarchal family of lovers. Harris replaces outworn categories like woman and man, lesbian and heterosexual, with a new dualism of lover and beloved. Lover and beloved, however, are not biological or even sociopolitical categories, but states of achievement, or ways of being. Moreover, this is a fluid dualism, since love is never static. In *Lover,* unlike in *Confessions of Cherubino,* Harris proposes reconciliation rather than conflict between desire and love. The lover loves the beloved and becomes a beloved herself, oscillating effortlessly between the two poles. Subjective and objective are wiped out; Flynn and Veronica, two of the characters, and even "Bertha," are sometimes the "I" and sometimes characters in another "I"'s narrative. There is no stasis, fulfillment, perfection, or, death. All is movement and change. Daughters love mothers and sisters love sisters; love banishes all taboos.

Lover replaces categories based on gender and sexual preference in order to transcend nature. Transcending nature does not mean denying the body, however. Paralyzed by the dualism of mind and body, and fearing the power of love (desire, lust, the physical), Flynn dreams of being pure brain and of stopping her daughter Nelly's growth into a woman. Flynn and Nelly are alike in wanting only the mind—the realm of pure rationality, of "true facts." But love and sex imply illusion, falsehood, and transformation. Veronica—who holds that truth resides in the body and who celebrates sex and food—defeats Flynn's plan to build a "brain machine" by sending her a fantasy lover to rouse her lust and desire (9). Although the novel ends traditionally, with lovers living happily ever after, it also concludes with an image of Flynn as a rope-dancer—an image of magic, illusion, and constant motion.

Monique Wittig also shapes her texts around these themes of passion and desire. Her first novel, *The Opoponax,* written in 1966 and published in English translation in 1976, is imbued with the symbols of and references to traditional literary romances, particularly *The Romance of the Rose.* The gardens that create the landscape of the novel, the schoolgirl dance of a knight and lady, the rose petals Catherine Legrand drops on Valerie Borge's face, the vision of the latter as a lady with flowing hair riding a wild horse—all contribute to the novel's atmosphere of courtly love. Catherine Legrand is the young knight yearning after the unreachable, untouchable lady on the pedestal. Such is the condition of desire: the gap between feeling and fulfillment, the separation between the lover and beloved. This absence is painful and, as in *Confessions of Cherubino,* separation is associated with violence. Throughout *The Opoponax* the motif of war evokes the violence of unrequited love. The lady on the pedestal, Valerie Borge, puts not a flower or a pennant in Catherine Legrand's hand, but bullets. They have been born into a state of knowledge and desire, not a peaceful Eden. Their world is already touched by longing, violence, and even sadism. These young girls will have to fight to fulfill their passions.

In this way, the gardens of *The Opoponax* open directly onto the fantasy landscape of *Les Guérillères.* In their struggle against phallogocentrism, the female warriors reclaim their sexuality for themselves. But the treatment of sexuality in *Les Guérillères* is primarily philosophical. Despite an occasional erotic image of women dancing drunkenly, the narrative emphasizes the absence of female sexuality, and in particular lesbian sexuality, from patriarchal culture, not its presence. Furthermore, the young men are eventually welcomed back into the female circle, which mutes the impact of *Les Guérillères* as a lesbian text.

Les Guérillères depicted a political, desexualized version of lesbian feminism; *The Lesbian Body* brings sex back into the center of the screen. It is as if one group of victorious warriors refused reconciliation with men and moved to their own island, where they enact a drama of violent passion and desire. *The Lesbian Body* is inspired by Sappho's celebrated prayer that the goddess Aphrodite visit upon the poet's beloved the same pangs of unwilling desire that she feels.[29] The unnamed narrator of *The Lesbian Body* tells a story of possession and loss—a story of intensely romantic love—in a loose series of prose poems. As in *The Opoponax,* the "I" occupies the position of a courtier yearning after an impossible dream; even when fulfilled—for this *belle dame sans merci* does yield at times—the "I" is not satisfied since she desires total possession of and fusion with the beloved. Only in words—in literature—is such possession and merging possible.

In *The Lesbian Body,* Wittig encodes desire through shocking and unusual metaphors of eating, dismembering, dying, penetrating, thrusting, and impaling. Used with intense and clinical precision, her words seem to lose the aura of metaphor. In her next work, *Lesbian Peoples,* Wittig claims that a true women's language would be purely literal; it would have no space between sign and referent, and thus no metaphors. In a subtle self-contradiction, this serves as a metaphor for the lover's own attempt to overcome the distance between desire and fulfillment. Such deliberate blurring of the metaphor also accounts for the discomfort some readers articulate about *The Lesbian Body.* How can Wittig write so objectively of cannibalism? Of viscera and excrement? She does so to render lesbianism corporeal, to recreate the lesbian body that feels the pangs of desire. Love, lust, passion, desire are all physical, residing in the physical body, and not just in the mind (or on the page). Lovers (particularly lesbian lovers) claim to want to possess the other, consume them, be them; our culture refers to cunnilingus as "eating"; lesbian writers adopt the metaphors and language of fusion and food for their descriptions of sex and love. Through her vivid and disquieting language, Wittig makes explicit what is already implicit in lesbian feminist sexual myths.

Wittig also gives to lesbian literature an eroticism that is violent, physical, consuming, and marked by hatred as well as love. Her writing contrasts sharply with more "orthodox" lesbian feminist romances that create a version of love always tender, gentle, warm, and comfortable. For Wittig, love is not comfortable. In *Lesbian Peoples,* she writes that the companion lovers pay for the word "love" with their skin (100). In the evolution of the lesbian romance, then, *The Lesbian Body* stands out as an anomaly. It is traditionally romantic and intensely mythic. But it also depicts with brutal honesty those facets of passion, lust, and the desire to merge and possess that most lesbian love stories evade.

The only American writer to equal Wittig in her evocation of the pain and violence that can be attached to love is Kate Millett. *Sita* is a "confessional"—a memoir structured like a novel—that recounts the end of a love affair. Love affairs end in other lesbian texts, but not often and not with the searing pain we experience in real life. (June Arnold, in *Sister Gin,* uses an elaborate and brilliant gustatory conceit to represent the pain of separation and loss: "At the table Su saw only division. The chicken on its platter seemed separated into two opposing armies, breasts against thighs—white meat for Bettina, dark for herself. The rolls pushed at their saucer's edges, one against one. The onions fell too neatly into two servings, the salad hunched equally on either side of the wooden servers; only the rice fluffed together as a unit and Su reached hungrily for it" [151].)

Millett, however, does not distance herself from the pain of separation through either metaphor or fictionalization. As in her other memoir, *Flying,* she proves uniquely capable of giving textual form to raw emotions. Her emotions are not pleasant and they are definitely not politically correct. One critic has even labeled *Sita* "sexist" because Millett seems so submerged in patriarchal romantic myths of loss and agony.[30] Millett is more self-revealing than most feminist writers, lesbian or heterosexual, have allowed themselves to be. The narrator, "Kate," may seem so thoroughly at the mercy of her worst emotions that the reader wants to reach into the text and kick her, but I would praise rather than condemn Millett for so successfully provoking us to recall our own experiences of love and loss.

In *Sita,* Millett illustrates how destructive romantic myths can be. Like Wittig's characters, Kate is in the position of a lowly courtier worshiping her "Lady" (the term of endearment she and Sita use for each other). When Sita returns her love, Kate walks in the green world: "We are entire and made whole, one in the unique separateness of us, each for a moment beyond self into a further place beyond reason and finally even beyond consciousness into a distant and momentary peace" (79). When Sita refuses her love, Kate ruefully contemplates the cost of this romantic fantasy: "What is it about this love that destroys the self? When it was reciprocal, mutual, joyous and fresh, I lived in a shocking state of self-esteem. Hubris even. And now, loving and unloved, I fold like a broken tent" (299).

The serpent in her garden, the flaw in the myth of romantic love, is inequality. Although no *institutionalized* inequality may exist between lesbian lovers, as it always does between men and women, a different inequality, unique to love itself, is possible: the inequality of desire. Because she loves more, Kate lacks power or control. Like Bertha Harris's categories of lover and beloved, Millett's desirer and desired transcend gender; they are intrinsic to the course of love itself. Denied the fulfillment of love, Kate, like a traditional woman in love, submerges herself in madness: "I insist upon my sickness, even arguing its value, turning it into a perversity, something clung to. Because it is mine, because it is my whole life now, my obsession. Sita" (235). Although the storyline brings Kate close to self-destruction, she retains the constructive power to turn her obsession into literature.

The interplay of power in *Sita* and of violent longing in *The Lesbian Body* both prefigure the development of a new erotic discourse in the 1980s. The literature produced by the sadomasochistic, or S/M, movement within lesbian culture—primarily personal narratives, short stories, and a few erotic novels—fictionalizes its theoretical position that power is erotic in our society.[31] Lesbian feminists claim that since relationships between women are based upon equality, power is removed as an erotic element. For this reason, lesbian sexuality is purported to be superior to heterosexuality. Lesbian sexuality is defined as free from power, coercion, and violence, while heterosexual relationships are rooted in these very dynamics. But advocates of S/M claim this argument to be a myth, and deride "vanilla" sex as boring and cloying. In contrast, they model sexuality upon the interplay of power between lovers.

Camarin Grae's well-plotted novels incorporate both models of sexuality. She first creates a sexual relationship based on dominance and submission that overwhelms the character and educates her about the nature of power. The author describes this S/M relationship in the conventional terminology of the lesbian romance: lovers long for "orgasmic submission," to "lose" themselves and "merge" into the other, to "consume or be consumed" (*The Winged Dancer*, 141, 161, 171). Like Wittig and Millett, Grae pushes the lesbian myth of sex and romance to its extreme limit, and then over the edge into its exact opposite. Following this intense but unequal passion is a gentler, feminist partnership based upon equality and mutual respect, as if the protagonist, having been educated and exorcised, can now get on with egalitarian sex.[32] These latter relationships are established in feminist utopias, perhaps the author's subtle suggestion that equality and mutuality are idealistic dreams that can only exist "after the revolution." In the real world, we still dominate and submit.

The Bridging Novel

The pattern we see in Grae's novels—an unequal relationship giving way to an equal one—introduces a specific form of lesbian romance I call the "bridging novel." In these novels, lovers overcome, or "bridge," structural differences between them. The lovers may be of different ages, classes, or races; they may have different political views; or they may simply have contrasting personalities. Opposites initially attract, but through the development of a relationship between two women, the writer minimizes, eliminates, blends, or integrates differences. In some cases, this relationship serves as a bridge to a diverse community built upon love, sisterhood, and mutual respect. Two contrasting individuals or groups, either through a love affair or some other cataclysmic event, draw each other and the reader to a "correct" political position. In this way, the bridging novel is a political version of the romantic love story.

This type of novel requires a formal contrast between lovers. Contrast plays an important role in sexual relationships—more, perhaps, in literature than in real life. We are all familiar with the *vive-la-différence* contrast between male and female. Upon the obvious biological difference is built a mystique of sexual otherness and attraction, which is formalized in heterosexual relationships. Our dualistic culture also associates "male" and "female" with a spectrum of attributes—such as light and dark, rational and emotional, human and animal, good and evil— far removed from sexuality. Often in literature, in the nineteenth-century domestic novels of George Eliot for example, marriage represents the ideal state of unification between maleness and femaleness. Difference leads to sexual desire, and marriage resolves both difference and desire. The couple is now one unit, grown alike (recall the folk wisdom that long-married individuals begin to resemble each other), and perhaps bereft of sexual tension. Whether these assumptions can be substantiated or not, literature clearly bases romantic attraction upon otherness and difference.

Heterosexuality contains a built-in otherness of gender. Some lesbians before the feminist era built alterity into their "erotic statements" by creating the roles of butch and femme.[33] These roles to some extent mimicked heterosexual ones, but more profoundly, they created order in lesbian society. One knew whom to approach, how to structure a relationship, even how to have sex. Furthermore, and I am theorizing here, the introduction of "gender" difference into the uniformly female lesbian community created that gap in which lies erotic desire. Butch and femme desire each other because they differ from one another.

With the rise of feminism (and even before that, as novels like *Desert of the Heart* or *The Price of Salt* indicate) butch-femme roleplaying was redefined as an anachronism, even an embarrassment. Accordingly, contemporary novels often bridge the gap between butch and femme, offering a new model based upon sameness and equality: "the taming of the butch." Femmes, unlike butches, usually do not change, since their role is less rigidly defined. (The femme counterpart to the "taming of the butch" novel is the "sleeping beauty" novel in which a heterosexual woman awakens into lesbianism.) The butch characteristics that are tamed are not typically the public persona; ironically, lesbian feminist chic in the 1970s and early 80s—jeans and flannel shirts, short hair, taboos on cosmetics, a tough and purposeful stance and stride—hardly differed from butch styles of previous decades. Nor do these butches feel they have the soul of a man, like Stephen Gordon, although they may be uncomfortable with certain aspects of their femaleness. Frenchy, the hero of Lee Lynch's *The Swashbuckler,* considers a butch to be better, "lighter and more graceful" than a man (2). Still, she feels defeated by menstruation, "weary and drained by her womanhood" (38).

What the butch must change in these novels is her behavior within a relationship. If butch-femme behavior sets up inequality, if the butch mimics men in trying to dominate and control sexuality, or in refusing tenderness and vulnerability, then the characters must overcome and eliminate the differences. The stone butch protagonist of *Look under the Hawthorne* is taught that "you've got to let other people love you, too. Loving's got to go both ways, it won't last long if it's always one way" (108). Inflexibility, not roleplaying, is the obstacle along the path to equal relationship.

The Swashbuckler presents a particularly clear example of "the taming of the butch." The hero, Frenchy, and her friends, for all their denials that butches are like men, adopt unappealing masculine characteristics. Frenchy seduces and quickly discards women. She will not allow herself to be touched. She acts tough and cocky, and disdains tenderness. But then, by the beach in Provincetown, she undergoes a dramatic change. To her horror, she falls in love with Mercedes, another butch. Although it takes years for these two women to free themselves of their rigid taboos against "homosexuality"—butch with butch—and establish a relationship, eventually both are "tamed":

> I see all of a sudden that every butch is a femme; every femme is a butch. I know the lips of my friend could get me hotter than the lips of any femme in the room. I remember how it looks like femmes and butches went out of style in this bar. I think, as I slip into Frenchy's arms, maybe I'm going out of style too. (66)

After a time, Frenchy also acknowledges the "common experience" of women, and the two women reunite as equals, sharing a house together "in a way Mercedes never imagined two butches could" (128, 274). In a coda that characterizes some bridging novels, the entire community converges at an anniversary party for the two lovers.

The differences built into the central relationships in lesbian feminist novels are less likely to be based on sexual roles than on sociological, political, or psychological categories. Patience and Sarah, for example, are often read as a butch-femme couple, but a closer look at the text reveals that the more significant difference between them is class. Age and personal history is the significant difference between the characters in *Desert of the Heart*. Evelyn is a previously-married, well-educated, conventional older woman, while Ann is single, experienced with women, self-made and iconoclastic, and several years younger than Evelyn. Each is attracted to the other because of their differences. Class, age, and especially ethnicity separate Lindy and Neddie in Dodici Azpadu's *Saturday Night in the Prime of Life;* the strong ties that bind Neddie to her Sicilian family are hard for the Nordic Lindy to comprehend. *Loving Her,* by Ann Allen Shockley, is one of the few lesbian novels to be structured around an interracial relationship.[34] Rather than creating tension within the couple, racial difference is an external force they must overcome to survive. Lesbian identity makes it possible for a

Black and a white woman to live together.[35] The author's message is summed up in the Black character's statement that "you can't confine love to color or object. Love is what you see, like and admire in a person, how you feel and respond to that person" (84).

While in *Patience and Sarah, Desert of the Heart, Saturday Night in the Prime of Life,* and *Loving Her* the lovers all overcome their differences (through love, the great mediator), the central relationship in these works remains isolated from any larger community. Other novels present the couple as a symbol of the community. Sandy Boucher's novella, *The Notebooks of Leni Clare,* explores an idiosyncratic opposition within the lesbian community: the city and the country. To city women, the city is the place of politics, diversity, life and energy, engagement, technology, and people. The country, on the other hand, is empty, isolated, a retreat from life. For country dykes, the city is the location of patriarchy, men and machines, old values, sterility, and constriction. The country is Lesbian Nation, Mother Nature, the new age, the green world—the site of culture and community. All define the opposition as politics versus culture, involvement versus separation. Although Boucher's lovers break up over this dichotomy—the city woman mistrustful of the country, the country woman contemptuous of the city—each eventually comes to terms with the opposite terrain. In the tradition of the bridging novel, each character recognizes that lovers and friends need not split apart over false dichotomies: "Grass, she said to herself, grass and trees. And she thought how weird and symmetrical their lives were, winding up now one place, now another, where they would never have expected. And somehow still together" (150). Ultimately, urban and rural terrains can both exist in Lesbian Nation.

In Her Day also concerns a love affair that, despite its failure, symbolizes the creation of community out of difference. The characters of Ilse and of Carole are, for this reason, drawn quite differently. Ilse is young, political, upper class, an out and active lesbian. She embodies the future—the brash, forward-looking mover and shaker. Carole is in early middle-age, an academic, working class in origin, and closeted. She represents the past, in that she lives a traditional lesbian life and is a historian who appreciates roots and origins. As an art historian, she also represents culture in the relationship: Ilse represents politics. Carole lacks Ilse's energy and direction, Ilse needs Carole's perspective and wisdom. The novel is virtually an allegory of the early lesbian feminist movement (although the Ilses far outnumbered the Caroles). Through their love affair they attempt to bridge the differences between them and between the different characteristics necessary to a successful movement.

To an extent, the two women succeed. Carole comes out to her co-workers and discovers the necessity of political change. She plans, at the conclusion of the novel, to write a book on medieval women, her way of putting culture and history at the service of present-day politics. Influenced by Ilse, Carole also becomes more self-conscious and aware of her identity (foreshadowing the direction taken by the lesbian feminist community). At the end of the novel, Carole (like Su in *Sister Gin,* and like Rita Mae Brown, the author of the book) thinks of returning to her southern roots. Ilse has changed Carole considerably, making her a fuller, more complex person.

Ilse in her turn is changed by Carole, although her change is more ideological, in keeping with her character. Whereas Ilse saw herself and the movement as cut off from the past—"reborn" into a new world free from original sin—she now begins to appreciate the longer view of history, the inherited experience of the past (95). She also understands that if we are to be born again, we need new language, new images, and new concepts—in short, we need artists. In this way, both women (and perhaps the author) reconcile politics and culture. They also reconcile history and vision, past and future, through their present-day love affair. Although Carole and Ilse don't survive as a couple, they have their moment, and each "in her day" moves herself and, symbolically, the women's movement, closer to the reconciliation of opposition and difference.

In two other novels the bridging of difference creates lesbian community on a narrative as well as a symbolic level. *The Cruise,* by Paula Christian (who began writing lesbian novels in the fifties), seems on the surface to be little more than a potboiler. But even the most frivolous of lesbian novels may carry a serious and educational message. *The Cruise* takes place on the S.S. Sisterhood, a lesbian love boat, and the women aboard this floating wanderground are presented as a cross-section of the population (overrepresenting, to be sure, white and middle class lesbians) superficially separated by lifestyle and individual attributes. We find, for example, a white collar/blue collar difference between the "gold-earring" and "camper" sets, and a contrast between old dykes and new militants, as well as differences between generations and races. At the beginning of the cruise, the women are separated from and mistrustful of each other: they act in old ways and cling to old ties; they are rigid in their beliefs; and they fail to understand themselves as individuals or as community members. But a series of crises—involving the testing of personal relationships and a communal catharsis that exposes the absurdity of heterosexuality—deepens their self-awareness, relationships, and communal ties.

Step by step, the characters in the novel overcome opposition and antagonism. Erica, a tough old butch, spirals down through an alcoholic crisis and is helped by her opposites—the radical feminists—to leave her lover for the women's community she never knew existed. Felice and Margaret both change through their cross-generational relationship: Felice abandons her little girl poses and attitudes; Margaret becomes convinced that age does not erase sexual desirability. Donna and Sandy, representing the camper set, become friends with Felice of the gold earring set. And so it goes: Carmen and Amanda, white woman and Black, fall in love; the two rejected lovers of a bisexual femme fatale get together. What was Sisterhood in name becomes sisterhood in spirit as well: "There was an electricity in the atmosphere, a charge of solidarity. Seven days before, they were mostly strangers to one another; now they shared a bond" (215). The cruise, and the novel, concludes with a utopian vision of lesbian community.

Finally, in *Toothpick House,* an exemplary bridging novel, the happy ending to its love story unites the two communities to which the lovers belong. Annie is a working class bar dyke, a part of the old gay world. Victoria is an upper class Yalie, still nominally heterosexual and not even a feminist. Both are firmly placed within their separate worlds: Annie's of butches and femmes and hard drinking in the bars; Victoria's of budding lesbian feminists and poetry readings at the university. They seem to abide in "the house of difference," as Audre Lorde puts it, and this difference often threatens to destroy their relationship.[36] Eventually, however, Victoria and Annie discover that they are not so different after all. Annie is a cab driver with middle class aspirations and tastes; Victoria is genteel but impoverished, lacking the privileges class provides. Annie is not a bar dyke at heart, nor is Victoria a college snob. Both are really declassé. Annie says to Victoria, "let's learn who we are together. Maybe it'll have something to do with feminism" (169).

Together Annie and Victoria dwell in their own special country—Toothpick House—and gradually the world their bond creates expands to include the other worlds to which they belong. The two separate communities of university feminists and bar dykes merge into one lesbian feminist community. In a nice intertextual touch, the community is cemented through a poetry reading by Judy Grahn, one of the actual writers who bridges the gap between the historical gay community and lesbian feminist culture. Victoria and Annie's relationship is a microcosm of the novel's social movement: alone and separate at first, they struggle to create a relationship despite differences, and finally unite through love and through their feminist commitment to women and the emerging lesbian community.

Annie and Victoria are just two of the lesbian characters who meet, fall in love, carry on a courtship, and, in both pain and joy, evolve into a lesbian couple. Although all love relationships share many characteristics, few concrete models exist for women living in a society that denies both legitimacy and visibility to the lesbian couple. Fiction, then, provides one format through which we create, adjust, revise, and reshape models for our relationships. But as we have seen, many women learn in the course of their mutual journey that an isolated couple—no matter how satisfied—cannot live forever in the green world and still sustain the full weight of individual and mutual needs. Like a butterfly, the lesbian hero must break through the chrysalis of the couple, and continue her flight toward community. The formation of this community, Lesbian Nation, out of disparate individuals and couples, is the third and, arguably, most pervasive myth of origins created by lesbian feminist culture.

4 〰〰〰

"An Island of Women": The Lesbian Community

"I don't want anything from you, Erika. You're not even my type. I'm just one of thousands of women who want to help other women. We're here for you, expecting nothing in return. You don't have to stay with me, if you're worried about 'complications.' There are plenty of other women willing to give a sister a helping hand. For the first time in history, we've got a network of our own. Come with us . . . start over again."
—*Paula Christian,* THE CRUISE

The floor of the huge ballroom was filled with women of every size and shape, with skin from deep rich black to tawny brown and lighter and lighter to almost white, wearing costumes of every color, pattern and design. They made a vibrant grouping as they came together on the dance floor, interspersing, joining, creating a rich varied harmonious blend, each one adding her uniqueness and helping form the whole.
—*Camarin Grae,* PAZ

The very last nation to exist before the beginning of the Glorious Age was the Lesbian Nation.
—*Monique Wittig,* LESBIAN PEOPLES

*T*he third formative myth in lesbian literature, and the keystone of lesbian feminist culture, is that of the community. The individual's quest ends in the location of a supportive community of women, and the couple finds its resting place there. The lesbian community is an environment in which women-loving women find freedom and wholeness, as well as sanctuary from a threatening world. The lesbian community functions as an alternative reality to heterosexual society, providing the individual quest hero with validation, pride, joy, and self-affirmation. From the earliest days of contemporary lesbian feminism, the notion of a unique lesbian space—sometimes actual, sometimes mythic or spiritual—has guided our visions and politics.

Jill Johnston assigned a name to this lesbian community when she first referred in a 1971 *Village Voice* article to "lesbian nation," a phrase which later became the title of her groundbreaking book.[1] The concept captured the radical separatist and tribal inclinations of lesbian feminism:

> In 1968 in London for the first time I observed women tribally excluding the man and I didn't know what to make of it, it seemed bizarre if not just unchristian. By that winter of 69 I could appreciate it better out of that personal urgency of my last trip to save myself and the world by living happily ever after with my one true beloved who had the means to buy up all the space we needed to establish the new lesbos on the mainland. (93)

Lesbian Nation is a separate lesbian space inhabited by a community of women who share a lifestyle, a set of beliefs, an ethic, and a culture, or who at least are struggling toward that end. Sociologist Susan Krieger further defines the lesbian community, as

> the range of social groups in which the lesbian individual may feel a sense of camaraderie with other lesbians, a sense of support, shared understanding, shared vision, shared sense of self "as a lesbian," vis-a-vis the outside world. Some lesbian communities are geographically specific . . . some exist within institutions . . . some exist only in spirit; some are ideological . . . some, primarily social. All

are groups in which an individual may share her distinctively lesbian way of being with other lesbians.[2]

The lesbian community is a space, or a group of people, or even a concept, within which the individual lesbian feels herself welcome and at home.

Symbolically that lesbian space may be envisioned as a garden, an island, or a territory. Mythically, as Johnston noted, Lesbian Nation existed on Sappho's island of Lesbos. In actual life it may be realized in a bar, a political group, a music festival, or a family. Several novels locate Lesbian Nation imaginatively in another time or on another planet. Wherever it is placed, however, Lesbian Nation gives concrete shape to our dreams of what a society of women-loving women, focused totally on ourselves and our relationships, might look and act like.

Novels about lesbian community (whether they belong to the genre of speculative fiction or not) tend to be intensely idealistic and utopian. They may establish myths of origin explaining or justifying all-female collectivity, and attempt to develop a feminist code of ethics. Some fictions explore the relationship of men to the female community, most asserting an absolute difference between the sexes and identifying men as a snake in the garden. A few, however, expand the lesbian community to include men, thereby transforming it into a gay or human community. Finally, as I will discuss in the next chapter, many communities discover and confront the differences and tensions that lie within their boundaries.

The Origins of Lesbian Nation

The notion of lesbian community, or Lesbian Nation, did not materialize out of thin air, of course, but arose from a variety of historical, political, and literary sources. The first of these is the legacy of gay life that preceded the emergence of the gay liberation movement in 1969, an underground existence mandated by strong cultural taboos against homosexuality. Lesbians banded together in bars and private homes—at times with gay men, at other times separately—because only in their own communities could they openly and safely be themselves. Everywhere else they had to adopt pretense and fear exposure. Although memoirs of those days recall the psychic pain and anxiety caused by living in the closet, at the same time they look back with some nostalgia at the close-knit communities that once existed in the shadows. A respondent in Sasha Gregory Lewis's 1979 study, *Sunday's Women,* expresses this ambivalence about moving from inside to out: "In all the words about coming out, about lesbian revolution, about a brave new world, it seems like we're losing touch with the best of what we had: our tribes, our lesbian nation, our partisan underground if you want to call it that."[3] The old gay world was a closed world—a closet—but it also served as a wellspring of strength and nurturance. Lesbian Nation, then, is a concept aimed at preserving the unique qualities of the deviant subculture while still demanding the recognition due an emerging nation.

A second source for Lesbian Nation can be found in the communal ideals of the 1960s counterculture. Since many of the women who fashioned the early visions of lesbian feminism came out during that era, they were shaped by its values. One source of Johnston's "Lesbian Nation" is "Woodstock Nation," which in turn pays homage to the historical and spiritual legacy of Indian Nation. From this and other historical sources—such as American utopian experiments and twentieth-century socialist revolutions—the sixties generation adopted the principles of collective decision-making, utopian socialism, and experimental sexual norms, and further fantasized about a perfect society that some individuals, both straight and gay, tried to actualize in country communes. Among the best fictional inscriptions of this vision is Marge Piercy's feminist utopia, *Woman on the Edge of Time,* which incorporates the values of sexual and racial equality, decentralized government, economic anarcho-syndicalism, and complete respect for the individual and for nature. These principles, lived out in a pastoral setting, are characteristic of virtually all lesbian utopias. Even in those lesbian fictions that are neither utopian nor pastoral, communalism is often a central ideal.

A third source for Lesbian Nation is feminism, of course, particularly radical feminism, which emphasized the virtues of universal sisterhood and women working together to create new institutions, new ways of being, or, in the words of Adrienne Rich, "a whole new poetry beginning here."[4] Radical feminism also developed a particularly pointed critique of men and patriarchy, and thus led more logically to female separatism than did socialist or liberal feminism. Once infused with cultural feminism—which extolled the special nature and creativity of women—and invigorated by the many heterosexual feminists who discovered lesbianism and lesbians who embraced feminism, it was hardly surprising that the ideology of radical feminism became an integral part of the lesbian movement.

Finally, the fourth source for the myth of Lesbian Nation can be found in the historical transmission of symbols from text to text.[5] Lesbians have often looked back to an imaginary golden age when we lived free and proud in our own separate territory. At the beginning of the twentieth century, Renée Vivien and Natalie Barney first grasped how significant Lesbos could be to women-loving women. They traveled from Paris to Sappho's island in order to recreate, in the words of literary historian Elyse Blankley, "a visionary female city." Lesbos (or, as it was called at the time, Mytilene) was to be an authentic community of women poets: "Unlike the small lesbian 'islands' perched precariously above water in Paris, Mytilene is a firm island that can be as large as a continent or a universe."[6]

But Vivien and Barney discovered what generations of lesbians have discovered since, that lesbian community and female space exist more happily in literature and myth than they do in real life. Once in the Aegean, they found that the passage of time had wiped out all vestiges of Sappho's spirit. Even so, Vivien remained "an indefatigable traveler," shuttling between Paris and other urban centers and Lesbos, while Barney, for her part, realized their dream of a circle of lesbian artists with her Academy of Women in Paris rather than on Mytilene.[7]

As Karla Jay points out in her biography of Barney and Vivien, they, like contemporary lesbians, were engaged less in "an act of resurrection than one of invention of new modes to suit the requirements of their own situation."[8] The Lesbian Sappho they invented has been transmitted further through the texts of Monique Wittig, particularly in *The Lesbian Body* and *Lesbian Peoples*. As Barney was called "*l'Amazone*" by her contemporaries, so Wittig envisions Sappho as an amazon queen, and her island, equated both actually and symbolically with Lesbos, as a "domain of women" upon which to establish a contemporary lesbian community:

> We already have our islets, our islands, we are already in process of living in a culture that befits us. The Amazons are women who live among themselves, by themselves and for themselves at all the generally accepted levels: fictional, symbolic, actual . . . we possess an entire fiction into which we project ourselves and which is already a possible reality. It is our fiction that validates us. (*The Lesbian Body,* ix)

Wittig here refers to the process by which contemporary lesbians establish a separate female and lesbian space that can exist in a geographic locale, but more importantly, takes shape through our symbols of Lesbian Nation and through the literature, particularly the fiction, that recreates that place imaginatively.

The community to which the lesbian hero journeys, as Wittig indicates, is repeatedly imagined as existing on an island. Although there is no actual lesbian territory or island of women, Sappho's island resonates in our dreams and fantasies, and is recreated imaginatively in lesbian feminist literature. The companion lovers of *Lesbian Peoples* create their new world on islands ringed around the equator. Flynn, in *Lover,* and Tretona, in *Who Was That Masked Woman?,* both dream egocentric dreams of reigning over an island of women. In *Anna's Country,* Hope's lifelong dream is to stand on an island within a lake within an island. Actual islands also figure extensively in lesbian novels: Catalina in *Spring Forward, Fall Back;* England in *Who Was That Masked Woman?;* Jamaica in *Abeng;* Carriacou in *Zami;* Hawaii, Santorini, Lesbos, and Key West in *Iris;* and, of course, Manhattan, location of the lesbian mecca, Greenwich Village. Moreover, novelist Lee Lynch wonders about the prevalence of islands in the real lives of lesbian writers: "Jane Rule, like Sappho, lives on an island. Is this coincidence, or a signpost to success for all of us singers of lesbian tales? Is the island the perfect lesbian literary zone? A realm of seclusion, inspiration and safety?"[9]

Why, we might ask along with Lynch, do islands resonate so strongly in the lesbian imagination? Writers and readers alike have been inspired by what Lesbos represents: an island in the safe sea of women, a symbol of female separation, community, and author/ity that can be recreated in contemporary lesbian lives. Had Sappho not been historically associated with an island, Barney and Vivien and all their followers might have placed her there just the same. The nature of women's bodies suggests a metaphoric connection between islands and the female, and water is conventionally connected to the feminine and the maternal. The floating island thus evokes a growing fetus cradled inside the womb of Mother Nature.

Judy Grahn, in her unique mythopoetic fashion, expands the associations we can make with this inspirational symbol of Sappho's isle of Lesbos:

> Sappho wrote to us from an island, a lavender-flowered island as travelers describe it. . . . everything she represents lives on an island. That island is separate from, even though it is central to, all of that ancient, ritualized and mundane life of thriving, gorgeous Greece. Sappho wrote from an island, an island of obvious natural beauty, grace and apparent safety for women. . . . In her world, women were central to themselves; they had to have been for her to write as she did. She lived on an island of women, in a company of women, from which she addressed all creation. [10]

Grahn here identifies three main concepts—separation, safety, and centrality—that account for the prevalence of the symbol of the island in lesbian feminist fiction.

In the first place, an island is a territory surrounded by the natural protective medium of water. Since it is isolated from the mainland, in fantasy, at least, an island need not be taken and defended with arms. There need be no contact between island and mainland at all (although contact and communication may be a theme of island-hopping novels like *Spring Forward, Fall Back*). An island nation appeals to a community that claims to abhor violence and embrace pacifism, and whose preferred political mode is separation and withdrawal rather than confrontation. It may also appeal to that part of us that is indifferent or hostile to the rest of the world. Islands are remote, existing outside the stream of patriarchal time and space. Island civilizations (at least before the advent of modern technology) were left alone to develop in their own fashions. One aspect of the lesbian fantasy, then, is to become precisely what John Donne preached against: an island, entire of itself.

Because it is isolated and separate, an island can be a place of safety for a group accustomed to ideological and physical attack. The island nation protects lesbians from the storms swirling around the patriarchal mainland. The protagonist of *Iris,* for example, claims that islands create natural boundaries that reinforce her isolation. In the same way that islands center the individual, they provide an image of cohesiveness for a group that has been physically scattered. Alone and self-contained, Iris turns inward to encounter and tap the female power that resides in islands. So too does the island community of women.

Author Lee Lynch is therefore very canny in proposing the island as a lesbian "literary zone," or as a correlative to the "wild zone" that critic Elaine Showalter identifies as lying outside the domination of patriarchal language and authority. Although neither writer articulates what kind of culture might exist beyond the pale, the wild zone suggests Inez Riverfingers' magic forest, Wittig's mythic island, Johnston's Lesbian Nation. It is the place separate from and undefined by men, a space in which we can "dwell," as Emily Dickinson wrote, in the house of "possibility." [11] According to critic Namascar Shaktini, lesbian writers evoke "the metaphor of embarkation as an image of displacement from the 'dark continent of femininity which Freud never really penetrated.'" [12] If patriarchal thinkers define Woman as a dark continent, it is hardly surprising that lesbian writers sail away to islands in order to create and define a separate discourse about women and sexuality. Turning our backs on the mainland, like the lovers in H. H. Richardson's "Two Hanged Women," we gaze into the "safe sea of women"—our individual and collective consciousness—to "reconstitute the world." [13]

Lesbian Separatism and Women-Identification

Wittig argues that the lesbian community includes actual, symbolic, and fictional islands, and I would add that we have as well a *political* manifestation of the island in the theory of lesbian separatism. In articulations of lesbian- or women-focused community, we can observe two main tendencies. One focuses on the unification of all women, on the basis of shared female experience, into a "women-identified" collectivity that includes but does not require lesbian identity. Many novels, particularly those that center on feminist political activity—are "women-identified" in this way. The second tendency emphasizes the uniqueness of lesbian experience, separate from female experience in general and most emphatically from the world of men. These novels are more likely to be idealistic and utopian than overtly political. The two positions of lesbian separatism and women-identification are important intellectual developments within contemporary feminism that provide a theoretical grounding for the concept of community in lesbian fiction.

Lesbian separatism has had exceedingly bad press since its main tenets were first expressed in 1972. Some responsibility for this must be accepted by those who participated in its articulation: our language was extreme and our minds were often closed. But much of the reaction of nonseparatists was equally extreme, based as it was upon fear or prejudice. Looking back from the distance of fifteen years, we can see how lesbian separatism carried through to its logical conclusion one fundamental principle of the women's liberation movement: that of *autonomy* (which, in turn, derived from Black separatism of the 1960s). Women's liberationists argued that the movement must be autonomous from men and male political groups in order to allow women the "free space" to develop self-confidence, personal authority, and an independent theory and politics. [14] The notion of separate space originated not in the lesbian community but in the women's liberation movement. Separatism made profound sense to many lesbian feminists, however, because it is considerably more congruent with the lesbian lifestyle than with the heterosexual female lifestyle.

Separatism was never one monolithic theory. Shaped initially in 1972 and 1973 by the Furies collective in Washington, D.C. (whose members included Rita Mae Brown and Charlotte Bunch) and a few other small groups, separatism at first asserted that lesbianism was a political choice challenging male supremacy at its root: institutionalized heterosexuality. [15] Men as a group and as individuals maintain power by controlling women as a group and as individuals. Accordingly, one strategy for attacking male dominance is refusing the individual control of a man; in other words, by opting out of heterosexuality and choosing lesbianism. Women who remain heterosexual—indeed, women who give support to men in any fashion—uphold the system of male supremacy. Although the arguments put forth by the Furies are certainly dogmatic, they are also logical. Nevertheless, the most glaring flaw in their reasoning—the narrow focus on heterosexuality as the single cornerstone of male supremacy—led to the implication that lesbians were the vanguard of the women's movement, that lesbianism (and specifically lesbian separatism) was the only legitimate strategy for transforming male supremacy. This conclusion, not surprisingly, angered heterosexual and nonseparatist lesbian feminists, who were excluded from the ranks of the elect.

The politics of separatism grew increasingly murky through the 1970s, as various groups debated whether or not separatism required separation only from men, or also from heterosexual and bisexual women, or even from nonseparatist lesbians. A kind of separatist physics developed, positing that every woman has a quantifiable and limited amount of "energy" constantly in danger of being ripped off and given to men. If a women loses some of her energy, her power is diminished; should a man receive some of it, his is enhanced. Straight women, or even another lesbian who "gave energy" to men, were the medium by which energy was exchanged and hence were to be avoided. Partly as a result of this thinking, instead of empowering women, as the Furies collecive or, later, philosopher Marilyn Frye envisioned it, separatism tended to degenerate into a defensive effort to conserve precious lesbian resources.[16]

Despite this degeneration, lesbian separatism was an impressive theoretical position and an invigorating political and cultural development. Lesbian separatists provided the energy that fueled cultural institutions of the 1970s—such as Diana Press and Olivia Records—that are prototypes for current independent women's businesses and collective endeavors. Moreover, the principles of separatism—women withdrawing from daily struggle with men and male-defined institutions in order to develop their own autonomous values and visions—are evident in the writings of feminists, both lesbian and heterosexual, who would not consider themselves to be separatists.

The second way in which lesbian fiction imagines community is through the concept of women-identification. Ironically, when the Radicalesbians collective coined the term in 1970, they used it as a synonym or euphemism for lesbian; a "woman-identified woman" was a lesbian, in contrast to the male-identified heterosexual woman who defined her interests in terms of men. In 1974, songwriter Alix Dobkin expressed her separatist politics through a rather convoluted use of this concept: "To me, 'Lesbian' is a much bigger framework than 'woman.' When I write for Lesbians I'm writing for all women. If I just wrote for women, as opposed to women-identified, women-committed women, I would be much more limited." [17]

Like "lesbian separatist," however, "women-identified" has gone through many interpretive twists. Sometimes it serves as a code for lesbian: for instance, my university course on lesbianism is titled "Women-Identified Women" to protect students from potential recriminations by a homophobic society. It may even be used to refer to a feminine woman in contrast to the "male-identified" butch lesbian. Most typically, however, the term defines a category encompassing lesbians and all other women who value and bond with women. "Women-identified" and "lesbian" are concentric circles of definition, the first containing the second. The category of "women-identification" includes all loving and primary relationships among women—those of friends, sisters, mothers and daughters, and colleagues, as well as lovers—on what Adrienne Rich has named "the lesbian continuum." [18] Women-identified feminism overlaps with lesbian feminism—and many of the writers whose works are "women-identified" are themselves lesbians—but it attempts to include, not exclude, women who have not chosen or affirmed a lesbian identity. Some lesbian novels focus on communities of women who have built solid edifices inside Lesbian Nation; others attend to the way in which many women visit or set up camp right at its boundaries. All, however, place lesbian existence at the heart of the community of women.

Historically, however, no idea of community can be found in the earliest examples of contemporary lesbian fiction (between roughly 1964 and 1973). These novels were written in the period between the decline of the gay underground and the emergence of a lesbian feminist community. They differ from the pulp paperbacks of the 1950s and 60s, such as Ann Bannon's *Beebo Brinker* series, in that the protagonists lack even the protective community of the bar. Couples in *Desert of the Heart* (1964), *Patience and Sarah* (1969), and *Confessions of Cherubino* (1972) are utterly isolated. Molly Bolt's journey in *Rubyfruit Jungle* (1973) is one of splendid isolation and her unbounded egoism places her above and beyond everyone in the novel, including all other lesbians. The bars and parties in *Rubyfruit Jungle* are populated by pathetic manipulators or losers. Molly lives in a world with just one inhabitant, rather like a god. She develops no social or communal self, partly, to be sure, because no community exists to which she can belong. But Molly remains separate and alone primarily because her sense of superiority sustains the drive and ambition that allows her to triumph over adversity. She remains a radical individualist, the token woman, the grand exception—which reminds us how conventionally American a novel *Rubyfruit Jungle* is.[19] Molly Bolt is a role model to an extent, but she is also a solitary figure standing on a side path just off the main road taken by most other lesbian novelists.

That main road was staked out in the early 1970s particularly by other writers associated with the publishing house, Daughters, which was founded as a model for how separatism could "change the world." For the Daughters writers and publishers, separatism provided a strategy of withdrawal "to gather their strength and find their individual and collective voices," rather than secession into an alternative society. Their press was one step in actualizing Charlotte Bunch's vision of a feminist future: "women building new institutions that control increasingly larger portions of their lives—and, ultimately, of the nation's life."[20] This active and political vision of separatism involves a "commute" between islands of women and the mainland centers of political life. The Daughters philosophy was recreated in novels published between 1973 and 1978 that began to establish the boundaries of a new culture.

Women-Identification and the Lesbian Novel

The separatist philosophy of Daughters was more akin to the autonomous politics of the women's liberation movement than it was to pure lesbian separatism. Even their most explicitly lesbian novels— such as *Riverfinger Women, Sister Gin,* and *Lover*—articulate a women-identified vision rather than a lesbian separatist one. Writers like June Arnold and Elana Nachmann were particularly instrumental in using the political agenda of the women's liberation movement as a lesbian literary theme. (Certainly these writers were not alone in this; political novels about the women's liberation movement, sometimes incorporating lesbianism, were written by Marge Piercy, Alix Shulman, and Ruth Geller, among others.)[21] *Riverfinger Women,* for example, presents a radical, 1960s-inspired revision of Sappho's island in the shape of "the first promise of an armed women's nation" (6). This Lesbian Nation begins in women's individual lives touching to "make the start of a common life, the beginning of an idea about community" (14).

The Cook and the Carpenter, chronologically the first lesbian novel about political community, was based on the author's involvement in an actual attempt to take over a public building and turn it into women's space. In the novel, a group of lesbians live and work together collectively to create alternatives to the nuclear family and other social institutions. Their living collective is, at first, an island of safety within a hostile, indeed violent, world. But, at the same time, they try through their political work to reach beyond that island, to stretch and grow and create change.

This theme—that women together can create safety for themselves and then effect change in society—is repeated with particular success in June Arnold's next novel, *Sister Gin.* This novel is replete with examples of women bonding together in communities, the most celebrated of which are the Shirley Temples Emeritae. We also find a community of old women—Luz, Miss May, and Mamie Carter—who support Su through her menopause; the actual sisterhood of Bettina and Adele; the friendship between Su and Daisy; the political group that forms around Mamie Carter's campaign; and, eventually, Su's forecast of a politicized southern women's community. Women create these forms of nurturance and support around the lesbian couple. Arnold proposes what many lesbian feminists subsequently argued, that love and support between and among women leads them logically and naturally to Lesbian Nation. Appropriately enough, Su and Mamie Carter, the lesbians, are at the center of all these networks.

But lesbianism also threatens to dissolve the women's community. Su's mother, Shirley, exemplifies how homophobia destroys ties between women. Inspired by her daughter's "confession" of lesbianism, Shirley reclaims the lesbian moment in her own life when she visits a girlhood friend under the pretense of a dental appointment. Drugged by gas at the dentist's office, Shirley then forges a bond of womanhood with the dental assistant as a defense against the unwelcome advances of the unctuous dentist:

> They had won, she and the other woman; the victory was orange and the afterworld green. Against his drugs and jokes, her old battered mind had stood up and now she and the assistant and all women

swam in a field of brilliant green, buoyed up by unbelievable green—gathered in a giant sweep all yellow and blue and scooped it into one untouchable safe sea of women. (92)

Shirley luxuriates in that "safe sea" until, in her drugged state, she feels the moment become frighteningly sexual. Lesbian sexuality disrupts the prenatal safety she had momentarily found in the assistant's eyes. Rather than returning to her friend, a return that would confirm Shirley's place in the lesbian community, she calls her husband for rescue exactly as Su calls a male friend every time she is confronted by Sister Gin, her lesbian alter ego.

Sister Gin portrays with painful sympathy how some women drop away from the community of women and search out a different kind of safety with men, simply because that community includes—is even powered by—lesbian sexual energy. Shirley is never again mentioned in the novel, but the community of southern women continues without her. Toward the end of *Sister Gin,* Su calls on all women to come *in,* not *out,* and be home free.

Later novels continue to propose a "women-identified" strategy for feminism by concentrating on the ways lesbian and straight women bond together. In "On the Way to the ERA," a short story by Maureen Brady, for example, a sense of community arises among women trapped in an elevator on their way to a political benefit. Political activism in Verena Stefan's *Shedding* leads the protagonist to a community of women in which she discovers her selfhood; in Gillian Hanscombe's *Between Friends,* several women with varying politics and lifestyles resolve their differences by planning a campaign against the marriage license. These texts resemble each other in their emphasis on organized confrontation rather than separation as a political strategy, and by including all women within the community rather than just lesbians. Their utopianism, therefore, lies in their optimistic view that lesbians and straight women together can build women's community.

Like June Arnold's novels, a number of these narratives that depict a community of women emerging from political action are set in the South, a legacy perhaps of the civil rights movement. *Say Jesus and Come to Me,* written by a Black woman about Black women, presents so clear and consistent a message of unity among women that it even makes a place for insufferably racist white women.[22] Black street prostitutes, representing the intersection of sex, race, and class oppression, form a veritable chain of protection around the central character, Myrtle, as she organizes a unifying Take Back the Night March:

> They *were* history, this moving blanket of women. The March showed strength and unity. Sisterhood in more than words, a political statement of determination in planting the seeds for a new southern woman. . . . No doubt, there was a silent legion of lesbians striding along with her, dreaming of a different southern march someday for another purpose. (267)

Since, as the novel puts it, women helping women is a "cover" for lesbianism, lesbianism is the heart of women's community, as Myrtle, the closeted lesbian, is the soul of the march. For the author, Ann Allen Shockley, like many others, lesbian love is both motivation for and microcosm of women's community.

In another southern novel, *Folly,* Maureen Brady draws women together around a factory strike, precipitated by the woman's issue of responsibility to family as well as by economic need. As the two main characters, Folly and Martha, walk the picket lines together, they fall in love and Folly comes out. Other women explore friendships and potential relationships across racial lines. The weaving of connections between women is symbolized by the movement of a copy of *Sappho Was a Right-On Woman* from one woman to the next. The strike succeeds, the factory workers take a few tentative steps toward overcoming racism, the lesbians come a bit closer to establishing a community, and Folly dreams of a cooperative factory run by and for women—a working class variation on the utopian theme of Lesbian Nation.

The plots of *Folly* and *Say Jesus and Come to Me* revolve around the creation of feminist political networks. "Networking"—one of the most popular words to arise out of the professionalization of the women's movement—derives from the traditional association of women with needlecraft. In the seventeenth century, Anne Bradstreet protested the idea that her hand "better fit" a needle than a pen. But contemporary feminist critics and writers exploit the metaphors of weaving, knitting, spinning, sewing, and piecing to represent the way women connect disparate elements into a varied and colorful whole.[23] It is not incidental, then, that the political struggle in *Folly* is set in a garment mill, and that the language of *Say Jesus and Come to Me* includes such metaphors as "cover" and "blanket" to refer to feminist and lesbian activity.

Two British novels demonstrate the similarities of form and content among Anglophone writers by drawing even more pointedly upon needlework imagery. At the climax of Anna Livia's *Relatively Norma,* the women converge at a marketplace where, ignored by men, they begin to connect and take care of each other, a simple but eloquent definition of "the beginnings of a women's community" (198). When the police enter the scene, the women fight them with female weapons like balls of wool and knitting needles: "A roomful of invisible women sat knitting their way into an invisible we(b) which wove around the hall in glorious twists of colour growing centimetres per second in long woolly tentacles" (187–188). Trapped in this female we/web, the police are forced to retreat and all the women escape.

A second British novel, Caeia March's *Three-Ply Yarn,* uses language drawn from needlecraft to symbolize both the weaving of women's community and the construction of a text (which, of course, derives from the same Latin root as textile). The story is told alternately by three first-person narrators whose individual lives weave in and out of one another's. One of these narrators, herself adept at needlecraft, develops a unified system of textile/textual metaphors through which she weaves her story: she "grafts" together memories, "sorts" the colors and patterns of her life, "spins" threads into a new "weft" and "warp," "unpicks" and "unravels" certain stitches, and collects women's words like "staples of sheep's wool" (59, 63, 126, 153, 179, 191). By the end of the novel, she defines both her literary craft and her new sexual identity as cognates to the weaving and knitting she has done all her life: "I shall become a spinner of words. Independent woman, without a man. Spinster, proud to be, cherishing the gathered staples, spinning them so carefully, not wasting them. Spinning yarn as did my foremothers, and theirs before them, miles and miles of yarn reaching back into the past. Life lines. Ready to be woven into the future" (191).

Three-Ply Yarn is one of many lesbian feminist novels that parallel the metaphor of weaving with the device of multiple narrators creating a communal voice. Although a few authors—Bertha Harris in *Lover* and Gina Covina in *The City of Hermits,* for example—adopt this decentered point of view in a postmodernist fashion to disrupt our complacency as readers, more commonly lesbian writers use it to make a political statement that no story is ever one woman's story. Valerie Miner explains this position in the introduction to *Movement*, a novel that frames the main character's story with vignettes from other women's lives: "I write these stories to break through the isolation and the individualism of the *Bildungsroman*, the conventional novel of development. Susan [the protagonist] does not know, and may never meet, any of these women. Their stories are told as shadows and illuminations of our mutual momentum" (xiii).

To be sure, the majority of lesbian novelists adopt a transparent first-person voice or create a conventional third-person omniscient narrator. But some—Jane Rule in *Contract with the World*, Sheila Ortiz Taylor in *Faultline*, Gillian Hanscombe in *Between Friends*, Sally Gearhart in *The Wanderground*, Barbara Wilson in *Ambitious Women*, Jeannine Allard in *Légende*, and Rochelle Singer in *The Demeter Flower*, among others—move in and out of interconnected subjectivities. Lee Lynch and Lesléa Newman interweave characters between stories or novels, creating an enclosed and unified fictional universe—a narrative community. Through multiple points of view or narrative voices and interwoven characters, the lesbian writer attempts to create an egalitarian, democratic novel.

A World of Lesbians Only

Relatively Norma, with its fantasy ending and its inclination toward female separatism, provides a transition between novels that imagine a *women's* community and those that recreate a specifically *lesbian* community. Unlike the earlier novels, these narratives rarely suggest that lesbian community can be created or expressed through public confrontation and activism. They propose that lesbian tactics involve the creation of a separate world, whether it be a secure enclave within what Janice Raymond labels "hetero-reality," or a complete revisioning of "a world of women only." [24]

Lee Lynch's *Toothpick House,* for example, opens with a weak and fearful Annie telling a friend that she'd like to "build a little shack on an island and not let anybody but dykes live there" (17). Annie's idea of Lesbian Nation derives from the closet, a tight little island that imprisons rather than frees the spirit. Her friend, who has already attended some women's liberation meetings, counters Annie's limited vision with an expansive one of her own: "I think that's what the libbers are talking about. Only they're saying we're already on an island and when a lot more women join us we can have the rest of the world too" (17). The characters subsequently share their various dreams of starting a women's center and resort, a printing press, a magazine, a bar, a band, a cab service, a restaurant, and even a fishing business. Unlike the confrontational and political activities illustrated in "women-identified" novels, their projects are separatist and primarily cultural (although a few are gratifyingly economic). As the most theoretically inclined member of their group observes, they have begun to envision the macrostructure of Lesbian Nation. She suggests that they create an educational slide show, "like the slides parents show when they get back from another country. Because we're *in* another country now. And our country has a history and a literature and even a language all its own" (253). Like the women who founded Daughters, this group envisions a "gay world" that expands beyond the bars until it encompasses a whole, separate society (254). By the novel's close, Annie's vulnerable little shack, Toothpick House, is solidly connected to the terra firma of Lesbian Nation.

Valley of the Amazons, by Noretta Koertge, also revolves around explicitly lesbian, not just women-identified, groups. Tretona, the reader's guide through the valley, takes up residence in neighborhood after neighborhood of Lesbian Nation as she drifts from lover to lover, in this way finding her community through sexuality. Each lover introduces her to a different cultural or political group: in one she discusses definitions of lesbian identity and the politics of monogamy; in another she performs witchcraft rituals; and in the "Feminist Theory Ovular" she discovers "the strange new world of Amazonia" (31). But Tretona eventually tires of their separatist and utopian revisioning: "All this group ever does is trash what there is and dream about perfect little doll houses in the big separatist sky. I think it's time we started with the here and now and started talking about alliances and working to really change things instead of trying to define perfection" (58). As we shall see, a frustrated Tretona moves on to explore instead the possibility of creating a politically united gay community.

If purely lesbian community is only occasionally found in political groups, it is often located in country collectives. The country serves as a green world not only for the couple, but also for the community. Lesbianism, particularly the separatist variety, and country living are closely connected, accounting in part for the ongoing success of women's music festivals. For a time, moving to the country was a lesbian fad. In fact, we might consider it part of a typical lesbian history. The lesbian interlude in Lisa Alther's *Kinflicks,* for example, is set in the country. The autobiographical narrative, *The Notebooks That Emma Gave Me,* includes such a rural sojourn, and famous lesbians, such as Jill Johnston and Kate Millett, write of their rural retreats.[25] The country collective may be for some contemporary lesbians what the military is for others: an assured place to find women like one's self.[26]

Historically, gay literature has been more likely to endorse the move from the country to the city than the reverse. The country, or small town, represents the narrow world of convention and prejudice, the closet, oppression. It represents the inability to be one's self, or to find other gay people, including someone to love. The gay landscape, on the other hand, is the city, typically at night. Stephen Gordon leaves the British countryside for Paris; Beebo Brinker leaves the boondocks for New York. Others leave for San Francisco or Chicago. This kind of "gay movement" is as characteristic of real life as it is of literature. In contrast to the pattern that critic Tony Tanner notes in western literature, in gay literature (and life), the country is the zone of restrictions and rules, and the city, because of its size and anonymity, the realm of freedom.[27]

With the ecological and feminist movements of the 1960s and 70s, however, a counter-movement developed. The country was glorified, and lesbian novels became imbued with a profound pastoralism. We find no better example of this than *Patience and Sarah,* whose green world lovers move to a farm in Greene County to evade the prying eyes of family and neighbors. At least partly because of the antiurban bias of the "Woodstock generation" and the revision of traditional gay urbanism by contemporary lesbian feminists, lesbian fiction displays an ironic similarity to the dominant American literature of the nineteenth century with its pairs of men escaping civilization for the frontier.[28]

This is the lesbian new age idealism that Sandy Boucher explores with subtle irony in "The Notebooks of Leni Clare," just one among numerous lesbian narratives—including *The Cook and the Carpenter, Riverfinger Women, Lesbian Peoples, Burning,* and *The City of Hermits*—in which women leave the city for the country. In *Prism,* for example, Ann moves from Chicago to a small town in the country and falls in love with a farmer. Together with other lesbian couples in the area, they establish "a little gay community right in Abigail" (146). Moreover, in a number of novels, such as *Sister Gin* and *In Her Day,* a character makes a rapprochement with the South, which functions like the country to the North's city. Finally, all the utopian novels, of necessity, take place in pastoral settings.

Some novels, more often those written in the 1980s than the 1970s, locate lesbian community in an urban landscape. Barbara Wilson, for example, chooses Seattle for her terrain; Sarah Schulman, New York City. *Goat Song, Zami, Blood Sisters,* and *Contract with the World* all have a strong urban flavor. Jane Rule, in her novels, identifies the city as the place where human community coalesces, even though she herself lives on an island. Nevertheless, in several novels set in urban environments, the narrative incorporates a movement away from the city toward the country, symbolized by the quarry in *Triangles,* the beach in *The Swashbuckler,* and the West in *Sinking/Stealing.* Moreover, in novels where the protagonist is forced into exile, like Ephanie in *The Woman Who Owned the Shadows* or Clare in *Abeng,* the city is a mecca but the country remains paradise lost.

One site that seldom functions as a location of lesbian community is the workplace. To be sure, there are examples of workplace community in *Folly* and in Barbara Wilson's novels, in which the print shop may symbolize community (in *Ambitious Women*) or be an actual collective (in *Murder in the Collective*). But these are fairly isolated examples. Because most lesbians are forced to be closeted at work—as we see in Becky Birtha's story "Marisa" (in *For Nights Like This One*)—the job provides no entree to a community but, rather, exaggerates isolation and alienation. In Sandy Boucher's story, "The Cutting Room" (in *The Notebooks of Leni Clare*), the homophobic gossip of her co-workers leaves the protagonist, who has only recently come out, feeling like one of the specimens she handles. Moreover, lesbians and heterosexuals alike assign lesbian existence to the private, individual sphere of love and sexuality. Public activities, such as political activism and work, are tangential to the primary myths of lesbian fiction. The protagonist of *To the Cleveland Station* astutely notes the contrast between the feminist goal of career and the lesbian goal of relationship: "How strange—her first thought when she became a budding feminist was that she must study for the PhD she wanted—but becoming a lesbian had made that seem somehow trivial, as if all those articles about women wanting and needing to work were wrong and love was the most important thing after all" (109).

Although the public sphere (work) is muted in lesbian fiction, the private sphere, in the shape of the matrilineal family, is very much a location of, or metaphor for, Lesbian Nation. The first explicitly lesbian band, formed in Chicago in the early 1970s, named itself Family of Women after the celebrated book of photographs by Edward Steichen, *The Family of Man.*[29] Since lesbians often lose the support and validation of our birth families, we choose or are forced to replace them with the lesbian community. But we do not lose our desire for a loving biological family, as we can see in the number of novels that imagine families consisting exclusively of mothers, daughters, sisters, and female cousins. These novels differ from the gargantuan family sagas so popular today (although it would be wonderful to luxuriate in six-hundred-page epics of lesbian life) in that they move narratively through space, not through time and generations. What matters is the web of connections existing at the moment, or during a short span of time, not the extension of the family lineage through the years. The lesbian family novel presents women's love—the bonds of blood—as a vital symbol of women's community.

Valerie Miner's *Blood Sisters* presents a striking example of a matrilineal family (although it is a women-identified rather than separatist novel). Liz and Beth are the daughters of twin sisters; they are first cousins who share the same bloodline. They are also women connected by the blood of birth and of menstruation, the female equivalent of blood brothers, linked together by something deeper than social bonds. But they are also separated by the blood of history and politics. Although they share the same first name—that of their maternal grandmother Elizabeth—they have different last names. This difference represents the different fates of their mothers and, consequently, the different political perspectives of each daughter. The family of women in

Blood Sisters has a difficult time sustaining itself in the atmosphere generated by male political power. It is eventually disrupted and drowned in blood, emphasizing realities of political difference and failed sisterhood.

Bertha Harris's *Lover* creates a much more successful and joyous family in which five generations of women seem to have intercourse only in order to bear daughters. These women stand at the center of the novel's various communities, including those related through stories and legends. Although a family novel, in *Lover,* birth is not the climactic event. One character comes from nowhere and another is born from her mother's mouth. Men are irrelevant; the family of women is the natural, paradigmatic entity.

The lesbian family novel extends the ties of sisterhood through space; other lesbian novels extend women- or lesbian-identification from the present back through the past and even into the future. The characters come to feel themselves connected to a community of women located in historical or even mythic time. In *Burning,* as we have seen, Cynthia and Angela relive the three hundred year old story of Martha and Abigail creating among the four of them a tenuous community. The author of *Légende* states that, in writing the novel, she intends to create a community with women lovers of the past. Elisheva, in *The Law of Return,* and Ephanie, in *The Woman Who Owned the Shadows,* both feel connected to the legendary women of their cultural traditions; Elisheva, for example, returns to Israel to study the traditional songs of Yemeni women that are one expression of Jewish female identity.

In some of these novels, like *The Law of Return,* the characters seem to enter a mythical time zone in either an imagined prepatriarchal past or a shadowy matriarchal future. The protagonist of *Iris,* for example, uncovers a direct spiritual line to the community of women artists that once existed on Lesbos. Moreover, the ritual of lesbian lovemaking weaves Iris and her lover into a web of women transcending time and space. *The Godmothers,* a speculative fiction, imagines history as co-existing timestreams of past, present, and future. But underlying time and history is the mysterious realm of the Godmothers who promise eternal life in the Great Mother, when all selves will be one Self.

Before there were matriarchal families and visionary utopias, before political collectives and country communes, the one island of safety for lesbian women was the bar. As Joan Nestle writes, "even when I was an old femme I knew there was an amazon world—not by reading or talking but by the strength and adventure I felt in entering the bars, walking the street late at night, stepping out of bounds even if it was to find a closeness that was defined by who did what."[30] The bar historically formed the center of lesbian life, home to lesbians who had no other home, as we see in *Zami,* Audre Lorde's autobiographical narrative about the 1950s. For this reason, in fiction, the bar may function as a sign confirming individual lesbian identity. A character's actual or potential lesbianism is revealed by how comfortable she feels in the lesbian bar. The bar is a territory with "customs and rules" of its own that lesbians comprehend but straight women transgress (*Choices,* 147). The metaphor used most extensively to express this idea is that of tourism. Whereas lesbians are residents, heterosexual or ambivalent women, like Jenny in *Choices* or Anna in *Anna's Country,* are foreign visitors suspected of "looking at the interesting natives" (*Anna's Country,* 119). Even a lesbian couple, like Kate and Sita, may feel like "tourists" if they have been too long outside the lesbian bar scene (*Sita,* 143).

Although many bars in actuality were and are nasty and exploitative, in fiction they are portrayed as an idealized location of community and home. Lee Lynch, in particular, envisions the bar as a small town formed by interconnected individuals with their loves, hates, fears, and frailties. Using the intertwining narrative technique, Lynch weaves characters from one story into another until, as in *Home in Your Hands,* all come together at the bar. Two other authors, Sheila Ortiz Taylor and Katherine Forrest, create equally utopian bars. Lane, the magical patterner of Taylor's *Spring Forward, Fall Back,* creates a bar, "The Daily Planet," as her "own little world" of safety and comfort (151). The result is a rare place of beauty and comfort, a bar unlike any bar ever seen outside of literature. What Lane calls her "heavenhaven" is, in fact, symbolically similar to a utopian landscape (145). Rather than write a utopian novel, Lane creates her own version of a utopia by creating a bar where there is room for both community and individuality.

Although the name of the bar in Katherine Forrest's *Murder in the Nightwood Bar* reminds us of Djuna Barnes's nocturnal world of suffering and self-hatred, it is, instead, a wonderful place. Its uniqueness, like that of The Daily Planet, is symbolized by its being "the only bar in the world with a bookcase" (17). Both are bars that nurture the intellect as well as the body. Kate Delafield, the police-detective hero, contrasts this unique place with the "freak show" and "ghetto" she frequented twenty years before (34). The Nightwood Bar is described as "a secluded, private place," hidden away in a dark cul-de-sac, that "felt right and natural and good in every respect" (27–28). Here, lesbians can "relax and be themselves" (18). Most importantly, the bar empowers its denizens "to make [their] own families" (212). The nurturing lesbian family created in the isolated bar stands in striking contrast to the violent and hate-filled nuclear family around which the mystery revolves.

Nonetheless, negative associations with bars persist to such an extent that in some of Lee Lynch's fictions the characters, even the bartenders, abandon them for other locations. Frenchy, in *The Swashbuckler,* is at first only at home in the bar despite its disreputable qualities: "The closer they got to the bar, the more eager Frenchy became to be with her own. There, in that smoky dark place owned by racketeers, fueled by poor liquor, so crowded she sometimes could not sit and had to wait in long lines to use the toilets, where she danced on a packed floor to music most often sung by straights, she felt at home, accepted" (144). But the more that Frenchy extends herself into the world, the less she needs the bar as a retreat or a closet. The novel ends, not at the bar, but at a party where "little by little, the world is gathering in [a] living room" (277).

The problem with the bar, as we shall see in chapter six, is its focus on the sale and consumption of alcohol. Sensitivity to alcoholism within the lesbian community has grown so strong recently that it would be difficult now to write a hard-drinking novel like *Sister Gin,* or even to center the community in the bars. Sally, the bartender in Lynch's bar stories, worries about the debilitating effect of Cafe Femmes: "the kids needed a place to be together, to be away from straights and guys, a place where they wouldn't be stared at or laughed at or thrown out for being themselves, a place to go when they'd been fired. But was Cafe Femmes the best place for them?" (*Home in Your Hands,* 105). Although Sally doesn't quit her job, as she contemplates, she does deemphasize drinking by expanding the bar into a sidewalk cafe. The logical conclusion to this antialcohol development can be found in Lynch's 1987 novel, *Dusty's Queen of Hearts Diner,* where community is situated in a restaurant that does not have a liquor license.

The Lesbian Utopia

All these locations of community—the bar, the country commune, the matrilineal family—express the lesbian separatist impulse toward withdrawal and disengagement. In 1978, with the publication of Sally Gearhart's *The Wanderground*, separatism took its most comprehensive imaginative shape in the lesbian utopian novel. Although some lesbians, then and now, attempt to break all ties with male institutions, total separation inevitably proves impossible. No lesbian community has successfully created the material base or the superstructure of an ongoing alternative society. But we can dream it into existence; to paraphrase Monique Wittig, our fiction can validate our ideals when real life cannot.

Lesbians are hardly unique in turning to fictional formulations of political theories. The utopian, or SF, form (SF stands for science or speculative fiction) has always been popular with radicals and visionaries: since Plato's *Republic,* authors have produced philosophical, religious, socialist, anarchist, feminist, and now lesbian utopias. Some feminist utopian novels—such as Charlotte Perkins Gilman's *Herland,* Monique Wittig's *Les Guérillères,* or Suzy McKee Charnas's *Motherlines*—portray all-female societies, although they are not explicitly lesbian. But several others—particularly *The Wanderground, Retreat, The Demeter Flower, Daughters of a Coral Dawn, Paz,* and, to a lesser extent, *The Female Man*—deliberately place lesbianism and a lesbian program for social organization at the center of their utopian vision.

Many familiar themes and metaphors converge in the utopian SF novel: the quest/journey, exile, islands, the country and the city, and particularly Lesbian Nation. Lesbian feminist utopian novels are an imaginative response to the alienation women feel within a patriarchal society. Feeling alien, or in Simone Beauvoir's term, Other, women choose exile.[31] In some novels, patriarchy falls apart, and women are defined not only as Other but as Enemy, and forced into exile. But in other speculative fictions, women simply pick up and leave: as Wittig put it in *Lesbian Peoples,* they "take a powder" from patriarchal society. In lesbian feminist utopian novels, the heroes embark on a journey of discovery to a new land where they create Lesbian Nation. As lesbians left for Paris in the early decades of this century, journeyed to Greenwich Village in the fifties and sixties, and moved to country communes in the seventies—so some of these novels imagine the ultimate "ex-patriation," the abandonment of a patriarchal earth.

In *The Wanderground* and *The Demeter Flower,* independent women (lesbians) flee a post-holocaust world, one in which men have reasserted their brutal domination over women, to take refuge in the abandoned countryside. Drew (in *Paz*), once she has figured out what to do with her mind-changing power, does not wait for the holocaust, but leaves to create her hidden community of Dega-J. In *Daughters of a Coral Dawn,* the descendants of one prolific alien escape a patriarchal earth that seems more boring than dangerous.

The names these expatriates give to their utopian communities indicate to what extent the authors characterize Lesbian Nation as a womb, an island of safety and nurturance in a violent universe. "The Wanderground" is a place where women can wander securely because they are under the protection of nature. Similarly, in *The Female Man,* women can safely "whileaway" the time, free from debilitating struggles with men. "Retreat" implies yet another safe nook, hidden away from danger and confrontation. "Maternas" (in *Daughters of a Coral Dawn*) signifies the maternal principle, while "Demeter" refers explicitly to the Greek goddess of benign nature whose name means "mother goddess." Finally, "Dega-J" evokes Gaia, an earlier Greek goddess of the earth.

Needless to say, the utopian societies conform in theory to the non-authoritarian, egalitarian, nonsexist, and nonracist tenets of feminism (although, as I shall discuss, curious exceptions exist). They are also firmly rooted in the gender essentialism that emerged from the cultural feminism of the late 1970s and then came to dominate the discourse of some varieties of lesbian feminism. According to this view, the natures of women and men are fundamentally and inherently different in ways that (ironically) resemble the concepts of femininity and masculinity found in the most conservative patriarchal thinking. Women are assumed to be nurturant, peaceful, and empathetic; men, to be aggressive, violent, and domineering. Lesbian utopias, therefore, often prefer the "maternal" virtues of empathy and nurturance to the "amazon" virtues of strength and militancy. Although variations exist among these texts, overall, lesbian feminist utopias incorporate a social paradigm based on sexual dualism, nonviolence, a close relation to nature, and mothering.[32] This paradigm influences the shape of the utopian society, its assumptions about "human nature," and even the direction of the novel's plot.

Each author incorporates the maternal paradigm in a different fashion and to a different degree. In Donna Young's *Retreat,* the most extreme example, the Sisterhood lives by the principles of Nurturing, Sharing, and Freedom (capitalization is the author's). They may call themselves Sisters, but they are, in fact, all Mothers. In Sally Gearhart's *The Wanderground,* this paradigm manifests itself in a profound identification between the hill women and the earth. Under the protection of Mother Nature, they build a society based on spirituality, telepathy, and harmony with all living things.

In contrast, both novels, like most other lesbian novels of community, deemphasize such "male" factors as economics, science, and technology. (An exception to this generalization is the way in which the reproductive techniques of lesbian utopias—either parthenogenesis or the merging of ova—are detailed in a deliberate imitation of scientific language.) *Retreat,* for example, presents a rather curious, poorly-integrated melange of "hard tech"—roads and spaceships—and "soft tech"—telepathic weapons and pastoral villages. The women of this world nurture, heal, raise young, and, almost incidentally, operate spaceships. But little is said in either *Retreat* or *The Wanderground* about raising crops, disposing of refuse, or manufacturing durable goods. Moreover, in their reliance on psychic energy, both societies tend to be anti-scientific and anti-technological.

Katherine Forrest's *Daughters of a Coral Dawn* and Rochelle Singer's *The Demeter Flower* are more ambivalent about the nurturant paradigm than *The Wanderground* and *Retreat.* To be sure, the pioneers on Maternas are all inspired by and obedient to Mother, an alien creature who looks like an ancient fertility goddess and breeds in litters. They also name the main settlement on their fertile and luxuriant planet after the Near Eastern mother goddess, Cybele. But, with her demonic winds and hypnotic monster, Maternas can be a dangerous mother; Forrest's view of nature is less romantic than that of Sally Gearhart. Similarly, although one of the characters in *The Demeter Flower* claims that Nature killed men's civilization "because it threatened her and her children," Singer's

Nature is no more a benign mother than is Forrest's (164). She made no provision for her daughters. Only a few managed to escape as civilization collapsed, and their continued security depends entirely "on estrangement from the outside world" (27).

Despite these dangers, the communities of Demeter and Maternas thrive by living in harmony with nature. The women on Maternas build their houses as womb-like caves safe within Mother's body. They avoid, but do not kill, the monster, and turn the winds into beautiful music. They learn to eat Maternas' nourishing plants and use her one animal species as pets, not food. Like all other lesbian utopias, Maternas is vegetarian, but, unlike the society of the hill women, humans here are undoubtedly the dominant species.

Maternas deviates from the maternal model in other respects, most emphatically by being a *lesbian* world, not a world of desexualized women as other utopias are. This observation is substantiated not only by the names given to its geographical landmarks—such as Damon Point, Toklas Lake, and Radclyffe Falls (revealing Forrest to be the only lesbian SF novelist with a sense of humor)—but also by the copious sexual descriptions that punctuate the novel. The Unity (as the pioneers on Maternas name themselves) also accords much greater respect to what might be called "male" attributes such as ambition, achievement, and leadership. Before they leave Earth, each member maximizes her skills and knowledge in every field of human endeavor, including those that men monopolize. As a result, they are the most accomplished and exceptional women on Earth. Finally, this utopia does not disdain technology and science: although Forrest never details their energy source or their economic structure, both must be highly advanced, for Maternas resembles an elegant and wealthy resort more than a rustic village.

As the maternal paradigm influences the structure of these alternative societies, so gender essentialism tinges their view of the human psyche. *The Wanderground, Retreat, Daughters of a Coral Dawn,* and *Paz* (and, more ambivalently, *The Demeter Flower*) all posit a fundamental opposition between men and women. Ironically, at one time it was anathema for a feminist to link sex differences to anything other than socialization. We believed fervently in the influence of nurture, and rejected that of nature. In *Woman On the Edge of Time,* Marge Piercy had women give up childbearing and men take up breastfeeding to create absolute sexual equality. But that bias shifted to such an extent that some lesbian utopias tilt the balance if not completely, then a good way back toward nature.

The Wanderground, the earliest among these texts, establishes this dualism in a particularly provocative fashion. On the side of maleness lies civilization (the City), technology, violence, invasion, hierarchic power, and evil. On the side of femaleness lies nature (the Country), psychic power, nurturance, empathy, cooperation, benign anarchy, and good. Presumably any woman can be a hill woman, although those who remain in the City are alienated from their true woman-self to such an extent that they don't really count. In fact, in one scene, a City woman unwittingly acts as the enemy. Furthermore, there are men, the gentles, who don't conform to the masculine stereotype and who have cast their lot with the hill women. But, as they still must struggle against the original sin of maleness, they cannot (yet?) be admitted to the women's community.

Now, as one hill woman says "'It is too simple . . . to condemn them all or to praise all of us.'" Nevertheless, the hill women must act *as if* men and women are polar opposites: "'But for the sake of the earth and all she holds, that simplicity must be our creed'" (2). Otherwise, the novel implies, they would suffer a potentially fatal loss or diminution of their feminist principles through a premature accommodation with patriarchy. As another hill woman declares, men and women "are no longer of the same species" (115). Apparently, men's bad behavior sent us off on two different lines of spiritual evolution.

Certainly the hill women and the gentles display strikingly different psychic powers, suggesting different brains organizing and using stimuli in different ways. The women's psychic power, upon which they build their community, is expressed as enfolding and encircling; adapting an I Ching image, Gearhart names it the lake on the lake.[33] But for the gentles, empathy and psychic power are "not a gift of nature, but the product of some painful growth" (170). They can only "bridge," lockstep, in a line. Not only is their power weaker, "bridging" is a benign form of invading and penetrating.[34] This *psychological* difference between the sexes is clearly analogous to *physiological* difference: the penis extends and penetrates, the vagina encircles and enfolds.[35] Gearhart thus sexualizes the spirit. She also implies a moral contrast, for encircling is presented as far superior to bridging. Sexual difference not only proves to be dualistic here, but Manichean as well.

To extend this dualism further, most of these novels answer the central utopian question—how do we get there from here?—by imagining a cataclysmic event produced by the excesses of patriarchal society. In those texts that operate within the assumptions of classic realism, the cataclysm is a nuclear holocaust or ecological disaster. In *The Demeter Flower,* for example, the world strangles itself with pollution, violence, and economic chaos, and declines into a version of a medieval theocracy run by priests and fathers.[36] *The Wanderground* also presents realistically rendered memories of events leading up to a cataclysm, the earliest of which could have been lifted from the daily newspapers. Subsequent memories that are more fictionalized—where present time begins to slide into future—foretell just what the so-called Moral Majority, given political power, might instigate: enforced heterosexuality, reeducation camps, and witch trials—a world similar to that imagined by Margaret Atwood in *The Handmaid's Tale.*

Gearhart's cataclysm, however, is not the big bang of nuclear war nor the slower death-throes of economic and ecological decline, but a piece of pure fantasy that she calls the Revolt of the Mother. Mother Earth finally rebels against rape and exploitation by "taking the toys away from the boys." Outside the City, neither men's bodies nor their machines are potent. Gearhart's Nature frees her territory—the Country, the Wanderground—from male energy and violence. Only this Revolt enables the hill women to establish their nonviolent, separatist society. Otherwise they would surely be hunted down and destroyed, since Gearhart does not follow Wittig's example by making her hill women warriors. The hill women do not, cannot, use violence, not even to protect themselves, as the scene in which one character offers her naked breast to a crazed, armed woman dramatically illustrates. The hill women would rather be destroyed than take up arms.

The lesbian utopian novel combines the themes of the use of violence in self-defense, separatism, and gender dualism in a paradigmatic plot that draws upon the biblical myth of the Garden and the Fall and the Greek myth of Kore and Demeter (which relates the disruption by rape of the primal bond between mother and daughter). The female community lives in peace and harmony until it is entered from the outside by Man, the serpent who threatens paradise. As a result of this invasion, the community gains deeper knowledge of good and evil, and its golden age passes away. Charlotte Perkins Gilman first made use of this edenic myth in her female (but not lesbian) separatist utopia, *Herland.* Joanna Russ gave it a lesbian twist in "When It Changed"—a short story later revised and incorporated into *The Female Man*—which takes place on a planet of women at the moment of its disruption: men have returned to While-away and life will never again be the same. This is also the crux of the problem in *The Wanderground, Retreat, The Demeter Flower, Daughters of a Coral Dawn,* and to a lesser extent, *Paz.* Each community must find a way to protect itself from men without succumbing to the violence they introduce.

The crisis in *The Wanderground* erupts when the gentles discover their power of bridging. Since their power is fundamentally different from and inferior to that of the hill women, we might expect that the community would remain restricted to women. But the plot revolves around the question of separatism. Through the gentles, the hill women learn that they are inextricably linked to the City, that they cannot totally separate from it even though they are materially independent of it. They still retain a responsibility, if not to the City women and the gentles, then to themselves. For, in some unexplained way, Nature exacts a price for her protection. Perhaps the hill women must liberate the rest of Mother Nature's daughters and even her sons, or, like the "dutiful daughters" mentioned in chapter two, repair the damage caused by patriarchal excess. The novel's allegorical message is clear, nonetheless: contemporary lesbians cannot be pure separatists but must live vigilantly in Man's world, doing our best to change it or at least prevent the kind of dystopia so vividly depicted in the novel.

In *The Wanderground,* although the enemy is external (men), the crisis also disrupts the community from within. No consensus exists among the hill women over the prospect of withdrawing from the City, and their town meeting, the Gatherstretch, ends without a resolution. It is possible, although hardly likely, that the community will split apart because of this. *Retreat* is similarly disrupted from within and without. The attack from outside comes in the shape of a warlike race that is neither identified nor explained. Who they are, where they come from, why they are violent, and, most important, what sex they are: all remains a mystery. This external enemy is merely a device through which the author introduces a more serious crisis, the mutation of the x-chromosome.

Retreat uses the conventions of futuristic space fiction to create a lesbian allegory of sexual evolution in a prepatriarchal past.[37] The author bases the plot upon a fanciful reversal of Aristotelian biology, postulating that men are mutated women. After a spaceship is crippled by enemy radiation, a few crewmembers give birth to strange creatures possessing damaged x-chromosomes and odd external genitalia. This ominous event, the genesis of the first males, heralds the end of the all-female community and the destruction or loss of paradise. To be fair, the author isn't committed to an absolutely biological dualism between male and female. It isn't just the y-chromosome that makes these new creatures maladjusted, belligerent, violent, malicious, untrusting, and bitter. They act as they do because they feel themselves different and alien. However, other characters who feel different (or, as the novel puts it, Self Apart) become loners or saints, not aggressive and violent sociopaths. Clearly, the novel proposes a genetic basis for masculine and feminine behavior. It also prophecies the eventual triumph of men over women since the reader knows, despite what the Sisters believe, that this aberration will not disappear after one generation. Once the new males discover that they can use their strange organs to penetrate vaginas and perpetuate themselves, the golden age will be over, and women will be forced out of paradise into exile.

The community in *The Demeter Flower* is rocked by a similar crisis over the issue of continued separation from the male world. Here too the crisis is both external and internal, since the village of Demeter is by no means harmonious. It already has split into two factions over the question of separatism: should they explore the outside world and found a second village, or maintain the status quo until they are stronger? The community's various positions (like those expressed at the Gatherstretch in *The Wanderground*) range from support for their current isolation to a desire for active engagement, even including a minority proposal to create an army to free captive women on the outside. Singer skillfully depicts the multiple strategies, from separatism to activism, voiced within the contemporary women's movement. At the same time, Demeter is split between generations: that of the founders, who lived in the old world, and that of the second generation, born in Demeter. The founders, who lived through a violent era, fear the return of the bad old days. Their daughters, who grew up in peace and security, cannot fully understand how easy it would be to lose what their mothers fought for.

Into this maelstrom comes Bennett, who embodies the external crisis. As in most of these novels, this crisis can be labeled simply "what do we do about men?" Like the men in all utopian fictions, and most other lesbian feminist novels as well, Bennett is aggressively, violently masculine. But Singer does not fall back on biological dualism to explain his behavior. Her women seem no more innately nurturant than Bennett is violent. The villagers learn that he must act as he does to survive as an independent man in the theocracy outside. Nevertheless, his presence poses a most perplexing moral dilemma for Demeter. He cannot stay, but neither can he go. Demeter has no place for a male, especially one who will not accept the dominance of women (the novel avoids the question of whether it would be possible to integrate a "gentle" into the female community). On the other hand, the safety of the community would be compromised should he leave and reveal their location to the outside world. His presence deepens all the existing splits within Demeter.

Violence has entered the village with Bennett: the women of Demeter fight each other, have disturbing dreams, doubt their strength and competence. He is clearly a serpent even if this garden is no paradise. The community is pulled apart by the most painful moral dilemma posed by nonviolence, whether it is justifiable to kill in self-defense. If they kill him, do they become like the world they abandoned? In the end, the author evades the problem by having Bennett act in a way that virtually compels the women to kill him. Perhaps the only way out of the dilemma is to wait until the intruder self-destructs. Nevertheless, one of the community strikes the actual blow; Bennett does not take his own life. As a result of this act of violence, Demeter is completely changed: "the old peaceful days were gone. Bennett was dead, but the effects of his coming were still with us. Our new knowledge of the world had changed us" (213). Like Adam and Eve, some villagers will leave the garden, and those who remain will no longer be completely isolated. Demeter has been transformed from a mythic utopia into a flawed, human community.

There is no internal conflict in *Daughters of a Coral Dawn*, the most optimistic of lesbian utopias. Bored or disaffected women can escape to another part of the settlement or homestead on another island. The serpent enters in the form of a spaceship from Earth bearing three of the most overdrawn caricatures of male chauvinist pigs in lesbian literature. Thus emerges the inevitable problem. As in *The Demeter Flower,* the problem is brought to a crisis by violence in the form of the quintessential male crime, rape. As the earthmen see it, women, under any circumstance, exist only to satisfy men. Accordingly, they can't even be imprisoned on a remote island: not only would the women be constantly threatened, the planet itself would be outraged. Nor can the men return to earth to reveal the existence of Maternas. Killing them is the only solution. As in the other utopian novels, the community is divided by this dilemma and loses its innocence. Nevertheless, although tarnished by their decision, the Unity suffers no lasting harm. The price it pays is far lower than the benefits that accrue. The reader might well wish all moral choices had such beneficent outcomes.

Utopian Visions and Contemporary Communities

Like most utopian novels, these create models for social organization and behavior that arise from and reaffirm contemporary values and beliefs. We have already seen how they address the issues of separatism and pacifism. Although lesbian feminist utopias differ in surprising and illustrative ways, together they give fictional form to what many women think of as the values and vision of Lesbian Nation. But a noticeable contrast between *The Wanderground,* on the one hand, and *Daughters of a Coral Dawn* and *Paz,* on the other, raises questions about how lesbians envision a perfect society. Moreover, the questions raised in these novels force us to consider how we confirm membership within the community. Who and what do we include or exclude?

The Wanderground is an extreme example of the idealization of the lesbian myth of community. The telepathic communication used by the hill women has its present-day counterpart in empathy, the complete experience of the other. The hill women, like many lesbians today, idealize loving freely without possessing the other. Their democratic anarchism, with its endless "processing to consensus," is the political ideal that a portion of the contemporary lesbian community strives towards. As some lesbians do, the hill women extol nonviolence and revere (some would say romanticize) nature. Overall, the community of the hill women serves as a model for communities we can build today, while the dreadful City is but an extreme version of existing capitalist patriarchy. *The Wanderground* proposes that we work in the present to prevent the hill women's past from becoming our future.

This idealism results in some artistic lapses. The reader would like to see more flaws in the community: hill women who are fundamentally bad, not just ill-tempered, or nature in its violent aspect (the crops do fail once). The pastoral blandness of *The Wanderground* can irritate the skeptical reader. The hill women are also impossibly deliberate in their political correctness. Moreover, the novel is whimsical in its depiction of talking horses, telepathic trees, and conscious water. Despite the questionable anthropomorphizing, these examples reveal how strongly Sally Gearhart and those inspired by her revere the virtues of equality, balance, harmony, and complete respect for all entities, living or not.

Maternas resembles *The Wanderground* and other feminist utopias in numerous ways: education is tailored to maximize individual health and potential, genetic differences are encouraged, and government is strictly limited. The Unity's central code—a simple assurance of peace and equality—is similar to the principles held by the hill women. However, as we saw, this novel also makes a place for "male" values of strength, leadership, and sexual assertiveness. In doing so, the author subtly revises some of the assumptions fundamental to the lesbian myth of community.

At times, *Daughters of a Coral Dawn* is so idiosyncratic that it appears to undermine the basic feminism of its utopian vision. The relationship between the central couple, for example, is a parody of heterosexual marriage. When Megan comes home from a hard day's work, she finds a warm meal prepared by Laurel, whose sweet nature soothes and comforts her. Good wife that she is, Laurel offers to style Megan's hair every morning. Not surprisingly, at their "joining," Laurel wears a white wedding dress, and Megan elegant new pants. Maternas apparently retains dualistic gender roles in both personal style and domestic life. Furthermore, only one artist exists in this settlement of ten thousand women, suggesting a creative dictatorship rather than a democracy or a community of artists. The art she produces, like socialist realism of the 1930s, is invariably monumental and representational, focusing solely on the erotic presentation of glorious female bodies. The mass athletic games that are central to the life of the community provide a disquieting parallel to historical fascism. The final and most uncharacteristic element in this so-called feminist utopia is the nature of political leadership.

The Unity is no lesbian democracy, but, rather, a dictatorship rooted in a cult of leadership. The first leader was Mother, whose rule the reader can tolerate since she is both the Unity's origin and its inspiration. But Mother insists upon Megan as her successor, an absolute leader. When Mother asks, "Who has time for democracy?" the Unity unhesitatingly accepts a benevolent dictatorship (37). Once on Maternas, Megan remains the leader: Self Apart, isolated and venerated, assigned special privileges and responsibilities. Like another Lenin or Mao, she becomes the center of a cult of adoration: "The mythology has already begun. Songs written of our departure and journey, her heroism. A giant mural is being created in Cybele's main square depicting Megan as she first stands upon Maternas" (104). Young girls copy her hairstyle (to her discomfort), and some even fall in love with her, thereby infusing her leadership with erotic energy in yet another mimicking of totalitarian style.

Daughters of a Coral Dawn is not the only one of these novels to reject a democratic approach to the political organization of lesbian feminist communities. Camarin Grae's *Paz* presents a similarly disquieting "utopia" in just a few pages at the end of the novel. Rather than try to influence those who run the patriarchal world, Drew, the novel's telepathic hero, withdraws from it and creates a utopian community of women (presumably all lesbians) on a hidden island or peninsula somewhere off the coast of South America. Women come voluntarily, but whether they stay or leave, they must submit to Drew's "zap." If they choose to leave, they are zapped to forget (neatly solving the problem of exposure and betrayal that perplexes the communities in *The Demeter Flower* and *Daughters of a Coral Dawn*); if they stay, their natural desire to create a feminist utopia is reinforced by Drew's zap. This zap, which they undergo with full consent, merely renders it impossible for them to want anything other than "compassionate, empathic resolution of conflict, and true understanding and acceptance of differences among human beings" (306).

The zap, of course, is a short-cut to utopia, taking the place of the holocaust found in most other novels. Although the author creates a very interesting utopia, she cannot solve the basic utopian problem of how to get from here to there without some kind of *dea ex machina*. Dega-J miraculously avoids the problems of difference, intolerance, self-hatred, and fear that have destroyed incipient lesbian communities. With one zap all are healed of whatever tendencies they might have that would destroy community. Hence, Dega-J, like Maternas, is based upon a cult of leadership. Drew, like Megan, is set apart from the rest of the community. Like a goddess or a mythical hero, she is reborn as Paz, the giver of peace. Without Paz, or more precisely, without her gift, Dega-J could not succeed. It is literally her world, another benevolent dictatorship. In fact, it is a particularly insidious dictatorship because its subjects consent to Drew's control. The author never confronts what appears to be a fundamental contradiction, that Paz uses the power of coercion to create a community eschewing power and coercion. I personally prefer another character within the novel: Rit Avery will visit Dega-J, but she won't live there.

It is difficult to know what to make of the fact that two lesbian utopian novels published in 1984 based their perfect society on benevolent dictatorship. Are they paying homage to George Orwell or succumbing to four years of Ronald Reagan? More seriously, these two novels indicate that some lesbians have become bored with—even cynical about—the democratic anarchism that has characterized lesbian feminist decision-making. "Processing to consensus" is time-consuming, frustrating, and at times ineffective. So, both *Daughters of a Coral Dawn* and *Paz* imply that authoritarianism, even a touch of fascism, may be preferable if the community is feminist and if the leader is capable and has the best interests of the masses at heart. One must certainly question this assumption. What if the leader mistakes her own interests for those of the masses; what if she is seduced and corrupted by power? How are Megan and Paz to maintain their objectivity, virtue? How can either society change from dictatorship to democracy?

The retreat from democracy into dictatorship that characterizes *Daughters of a Coral Dawn* and *Paz* can also be read as a response to the conformity and political rigidity that some individuals experience within actual lesbian communities. As we saw, lesbian feminists in the 1970s defined "female" or "lesbian" in a way that extolled certain characteristics while excluding others. This problem of exclusion, most particularly on the basis of race or class, eventually came to the forefront of the lesbian agenda. None of these utopian novels addresses the possibility of ethnic or cultural differences within the community beyond a formulaic description of varying skin tones. But even their one-dimensional utopian characters may feel torn between the needs of the individual and the demands of the community.

The Wanderground and *Retreat* minimize conflict between the self and the group, by uniting the community with empathy and telepathy. Individual disagreements may dilute but do not dissolve the communal cohesiveness grounded in the unique spiritual qualities of women. The principal symbol of these cultures is, appropriately enough, the circle. Both *Daughters of a Coral Dawn* and *Paz* present an explicit program, as part of the community's "bill of rights," for balancing individual and group needs. But, as in *The Wanderground* and *Retreat,* this principle—that the individual reaches her fullest potential as part of the group—is never tested by the plot, remaining instead an unproven assertion, a visionary dream.

The Demeter Flower and *The Female Man,* in somewhat different ways, stand at the other end of the spectrum. Whileaway, in *The Female Man,* is an individualistic utopia that makes plenty of room for clashes between individual and group. However, while respecting the right of the individual to self-expression, it also insists that those rights be subjected (by force if need be) to the needs of the community. Demeter, the most satisfyingly concrete among these utopias, is a tense community invigorated by individual differences. Since individuals do not always find sufficient validation within the community, separation and schism, rather than integration and identity, form the novel's theme.

The Myth of Community and the Realistic Novel

The relationship between the individual and the group envisioned in these utopian novels is replicated in novels that describe the world as we know it. In real life, the delicate balance between self and community is often a source of conflict for a woman who is forming a lesbian identity. Susan Krieger, in her study of one particular community, concludes that:

> Individuals come to lesbian communities—as they do to other groups and organizations—with the desire for being accepted as unique individuals as much as for being similar to others. Yet the desire to be accepted as a person who is different from others in a group—or from another in a relationship—is often hidden. It is not spoken of as frequently or as publicly as is the desire for confirmation of a common identity . . . we have difficulty knowing how to feel comfortable if we are not merged.[38]

The conflicts and tensions that Krieger describes in her sociological study are washed out in lesbian utopias, as well as in most realistic novels of community. These communities are painted in watercolors, not the vibrant acrylics of real life.

Although the myth of community seldom causes conflict or trauma in most fictions, occasionally we do hear dissenting voices.[39] The protagonist of *The Sophie Horowitz Story* prefers her definition of lesbian culture—"a certain cynicism developed collectively"—to the "fairy tale view of women together" (112, 126). To a limited degree, lesbian writers criticize or satirize the internal rules of the community pertaining to dress, language, sexual behavior, and political beliefs. The protagonist of a Maureen Brady story writes lovingly but critically from within a typical lesbian community: "Her community is made up of brave, rule-breaking dykes who, despite their liberationist stance, don't like to see anyone liberated at the expense of anyone else. They listen for the cues of who is most victimized" (*The Question She Put to Herself,* 13). Jan Clausen, with equal affection, parodies the excesses of new age communities in her description of "Systersea Sharespace"—a lesbian collective household—in *Sinking, Stealing* (184–198). Anna Livia, in a hilarious spoof of lesbian feminist linguistic experiments, spells "woman" and "women" eleven different ways in four pages (*Relatively Norma,* 78–81). *Valley of the Amazons,* in a more detached manner, presents itself as a satirical guide-book to the alien and sometimes bizarre neighborhoods within Lesbian Nation.

Occasionally, a protagonist feels alienated and alone within the community. Elisheva, for example, feels "homeless" for a time, while Hadel is "unhappily alienated from everything, from the straight community, the gay community, the political community. No one lived in her universe but her" (*The Law of Return,* 232; *Give Me Time,* 109). These are extreme and unusual reactions, however. Most lesbian characters find the community a limitless source of personal validation.

Nevertheless, just as some writers question the closed circle of the lesbian couple, others are skeptical about the closed circle of the lesbian community. Often, they argue, we retreat into a closet-like community, not by choice, but because the world provides no place for a despised and stigmatized minority. Community for lesbians, or gay people, may have been and may still be an inhibiting, distorting ghetto. In Dodici Azpadu's *Goat Song,* for example, racism, classism, and homophobia keep the community of dykes and street people outside the mainstream of society. Their world appears dim because it is isolated and without hope. Instead of triumphantly claiming pride, solidarity, and culture, they experience only anger and violence.

This is what disturbs Tretona, midway through *Who Was That Masked Woman?,* when she discovers in the bars and back streets a "spiritually and psychologically debilitating" gay world (179). Diana, her sociologist friend and lover, suggests that when a group is forced to live apart rather than choosing to do so, its culture deteriorates: "If all your time and energy has to go into defending yourself, into surviving oppression, there's not going to be much left over for building libraries." Diana's theory is noticeably flawed, since culture certainly flourished in the Jewish ghettoes of eastern Europe and in Harlem throughout the twentieth century. Prejudice did not inhibit Jewish or African American culture, perhaps because Jews and Blacks could draw upon centuries of tradition and history.[40] Lacking such a history and culture with which to fight against ghettoization and stigmatization, however, gays and lesbians internalize the prejudice of the dominant society to a greater degree, resulting in the impoverished gay communities that Tretona deplores.

Lesbian feminists (beginning with Natalie Barney's circle) have used two tactics to rehabilitate lesbian culture and community. One has been deliberate separation: rather than waiting to be thrust into a gay ghetto, many lesbian feminists take the initiative and withdraw both actually and symbolically from the dominant society into Lesbian Nation. We refuse to continue the debilitating struggle against oppression. Inside Lesbian Nation we pursue the second tactic, creating our own history, tradition, and culture. In a profound way this culture defines and sustains the community. A woman becomes a citizen of Lesbian Nation, a lesbian feminist, through the books she reads, the music she listens to, the heroes she identifies with, the language she speaks, the clothes she wears—even if at times she resents the required codes.

The lesbian students in Tretona's gay studies class (in *Valley of the Amazons*) argue that to construct positive gay or lesbian identities, we must reconstruct our individual pasts, rewrite our collective history, and even (although Tretona might balk at this suggestion) recreate our own myths of origins. We then validate and maintain our identities by living openly in the gay or lesbian community: "the *only* way we can get a positive identity is by finding out how healthy gay people react to us. *That's* why the gay community is so important—not just as a place to pick up lovers or get sympathy when the straight world fucks us over, it's the gay community that permits us to construct a gay identity" (136–137).

Unlike Noretta Koertge, the author of the above quote, I am not convinced that a coherent image of *gay* community exists. However, lesbian identity and community are created through history and culture.[41] Our political skirmishes also serve a useful purpose here, not only by allowing us to debate our ethical and political differences, but also by affirming group membership. One way to belong to the lesbian community is to take part in its controversies over separatism, bisexuality, or sadomasochism, to name just three issues that have preoccupied the community in recent years.

In a more uplifting manner, concerts, festivals, and conferences serve as geographical gathering places where we foster lesbian culture and community. In particular, the Michigan Women's Music Festival appears textually as a recreation of Lesbian Nation. In *Paz,* women fantasize about a year-long festival—"we could build cabins and permanent buildings and work the land and have our own town"—and Bo entertains Drew and Rit "with song after song of womanstrength and union and love and fighting back and the dawning of Lesbian nation" (85, 184). When it comes time for Drew to make use of her mind-changing power, she not unexpectedly models Dega-J—"a beautiful setting in which to develop a culture of our choosing"—after the Michigan Women's Music Festival (298). Even the skeptical Tretona is excited by this "Amazon Fair" and concedes that our community just might be rooted firmly in "our own humor and our own literature and—as the first group struck up—and, most of all, our own Music!" (*Valley of the Amazons* 61, 76).

Opening the Doors to Men

Despite her initial enthusiasm, Tretona leaves the Amazon Fair still alienated from Lesbian Nation. She journeys on to become part of a coalition that plans the First Annual Boonville Festival for Lesbians and Gay Men. *Valley of the Amazons* presents yet another way in which some writers question the closed community of lesbians: they include men, on the basis of either shared gay identity or human identity. The fragile, easily-threatened Boonville community of lesbians and gay men joins together to combat the homophobia of the outside world. Similarly, in Vicki McConnell's *The Burnton Widows,* hostility against "queers," which draws no distinction between male and female, precipitates a united gay front. Cast out of the so-called normal community, homosexuals band together to create one of their own. Unrestricted by geographical space or biological connection, they have members everywhere and in every walk of life: "even when lots of places we live in won't claim us or include us in any real sense, don't think we don't have our own network and our own way of getting the word out. People with no civil rights have a historic bonding" (181).

But this community is created by a negative factor, the absence of civil rights. The negative becomes positive in the Castle, the home of the murdered women of the title, and the focal point of the plot. The Castle of the Burnton Widows is defined not by absence (of civil rights) but by presence (of magic and love). It is "a woman's fortress" built and occupied by women, a lesbian island, a mythic location of community (18). The protagonist literally opens a closet door to discover lesbian love poems hidden within. Nevertheless, when a gay man inherits the Castle, it becomes the symbol of "Oregon's Queer Territory": because gay men give up the privileges of manhood, they are symbolically women and thus honorary citizens of the Castle. The community at the end is, therefore, a united "gay family" that even extends its welcome to straight Burnton (244). The Castle will stand as a monument to the history of gays, women, and Burnton itself. The house of lesbians has become the center of the world. Appropriately, the novel ends with everyone partying together much as, in *Valley of the Amazons,* everyone's anger and mistrust is joyously resolved when the whole community— women and men, separatists and transsexuals—takes over a local bar to dance, celebrate, and proclaim their gay identity.

The unification of women and men is evident in other novels as well. In *Six of One* a motley crew of deviants (mostly, but not entirely, women) is ruled over by a lesbian monarch, Celeste Chalfont. And *Murder in the Collective* begins with an attempt to unite a lesbian separatist print shop with a mixed socialist one, and ends with some of the members—of various sexes, races, and sexualities—understanding each other better and even working together. Two novels in particular—Jane Rule's *Contract with the World* and Sheila Ortiz Taylor's *Faultline*—exemplify this humanist (rather than separatist or even women- or gay-identified) tendency in recent lesbian fiction.

Of all the writers I have been discussing, Jane Rule is perhaps the least connected to the lesbian feminist or lesbian separatist movement. In a literary sense, she is one of the most mainstream of writers. Although a committed lesbian, she is also universalist in her views. She has written novels focused on lesbianism—*Desert of the Heart* and *This is Not for You*—and novels that include lesbians among other characters such as her recent *After the Fire.* In each case, her recurring theme is the creation of community. Hence she structures *Contract with the World* as a story told from each of six different points of view. A character who is the object in one story becomes the subject in another, Rule's model for building any human community. Since everyone is subject to her or him self, and object to all other selves, to survive we must create intersubjectivity through mutual tolerance and empathy. Most often, her community is made up of artists, as in *Contract with the World,* which suggests that art offers the best model for this empathy and intersubjectivity.

Rule's novel is rare in depicting a community composed of women and men, gays and straights (ethnically it is homogeneous). As critic Marilyn Schuster astutely explains:

> The outcasts who form these communities evolve an unwritten social contract that protects their outcast status, rejecting blind, brutal conformity to a dominant norm. They are, in a sense, communities built on a lesbian model. Lesbian identity itself is not so much subsumed into the community as kept whole within it—one aspect of identity among others, not singled out as the defining characteristic or an angle of vision any more or less valid than others. If Wittig responds to ostracism and oppression by imagining islands of Amazons, Rule responds by creating neighborhoods within the city walls, so to speak, where differences are sorted out and kept intact in spite of the leveling machines of society.[42]

Rule suggests that with some humility and much charity, we can overcome our differences and create a human community, particularly when that community is made up of the despised and rejected: the artists, outcasts, and queers. At the end of the novel, as the characters fight to defend their lives and work, we see how these separate individuals who have loved and hated and fought bitterly have become, almost imperceptibly, a community connected through art.

Faultline unites women and men, gays and straights, and people of many races, not through a symbolic language like art, but through a person. Arden the Patterner weaves a collection of oddballs and originals into an authentic family that loves, nurtures, and looks out for one another. This family then serves as a model for human community. Although Arden's own family consists of female and male, gay and straight, the mama at the center is definitely a dyke. The lesbian myth of community proclaims that only a lesbian magician can pull and hold such a disparate family together. Arden's story concludes in the best comic novel tradition, with a grand gay wedding party. *Faultline* is a joyous and communal novel, so overflowing with love and lesbian energy that it has plenty to spare for heterosexuals and men.

Whether humanist, gay-centered, women-identified, or lesbian separatist, the lesbian feminist novel of community celebrates sameness and unity. It displays an abiding faith in the ability of groups of disparate individuals to work together for common ends, subsuming individual differences and disagreements in the interest of the common good. But the experience of lesbian groups through the 1970s into the 80s raises serious questions about such optimism. The Family of Woman found it increasingly difficult to sustain a sense of unity in the face of real and enduring differences. The differences of race, class, ethnicity, age, physical ability, and political ideology shocked Lesbian Nation out of its complacency. In real life and in fiction, we continue to assess the consequences of this convulsive change. As Taylor notes in *Faultline*, earthquakes remind us that the earth is still moving; it is not yet finished changing. Neither, as we shall see in the next chapter, is Lesbian Nation.

5 ~~~~~

"Doesn't Always Mean Agreement": Community and Difference

Two women were friends; then they quarreled over politics.
—*Jan Clausen, "Thesis: Antithesis"*

How do we redefine difference for all women? It is not our differences which separate women, but our reluctance to recognize those differences and to deal effectively with the distortions which have resulted from the ignoring and misnaming of those differences.
— *Audre Lorde,* SISTER OUTSIDER

Doesn't always mean agreement
It doesn't ever mean the same

. . . .

Hang on, don't give up the ship (we're sailing)
Hang on, don't let the anchor slip
We are the sailors and we're in mutiny
The safety of this journey depends on
Unity.
— *Holly Near, "Unity"*

During the women's liberation movement of the early 1970s the slogan "sisterhood is powerful" was popular. The term "sisterhood," with its connotations of kinship and convents and its reference back to the "brotherhood" of the French Revolution and the Black-led civil rights movement, was adopted immediately and universally. We based our expectations that we could develop our power and establish a new society upon the unexamined belief that all women's oppression, and thus all women's interests, were the same.

But that myth was quickly shattered. Although the women's liberation movement from its very beginning noted that some groups of women suffered special or additional oppression, that awareness minimally permeated its philosophy and program. The oppression of Black women due to racism or lesbians due to homophobia was seen as an additional *layer* of oppression, but it was addressed in a formulaic manner. Black women were described as suffering "double jeopardy" (the title of one of the most famous and often-reprinted articles in the anthology *Sisterhood Is Powerful*); Black lesbian women, then, suffer "triple jeopardy" and so on.[1] The manifesto of the Redstockings organization specified that feminists "define our best interest as that of the poorest, most brutally exploited woman," but it is difficult to see with the hindsight of twenty years how that admirable idea translated into action.[2] We barely understood that multiple oppressions and differences among women needed to be incorporated directly into the politics of feminism. Instead, for the most part, the largely white and middle class women of the early women's liberation movement assumed, and acted upon the assumption, that our concerns would be the concerns of all women, regardless of their varying positions within United States society, let alone the rest of the world.

As early as 1970, however, the cloth of sisterhood began to unravel. The politics of identical interests began to mutate into the politics of identity. By locating political interests in the separate status of gender (as the civil rights movement had already done with race), activists rejected the western belief in a disembodied human essence. That notion of self—subjective, individualistic, and "spiritual"—assumes that what *really* matters, one's "human nature," is unencumbered by conditions of gender, race, or class. This interpretation of "self" derives from the experiences of those unmarked by such encumbering conditions: economically privileged white men. To the extent that women's liberationists substituted a universal "Woman" for human nature, we simply left our job unfinished. And so the project came undone. One of the first and most noticeable splits in the largely white and middle class women's liberation movement was over sexuality, since many women were or soon became lesbians. Between roughly 1971 and 1973, many left women's liberation groups to pursue the politics of identity on our own turf.

The radical lesbian, or lesbian feminist, movement that grew throughout the 1970s was itself pulled (and has continued to be pulled) in two interrelated directions. The first direction is toward sameness based upon a similarity of sexual and gender interests among all lesbians. We have confidently and unhesitatingly stated our conviction that we are all united as *lesbians*. But at the same time, our understanding of how, as lesbians, we differ from heterosexual women and from gay men, has made us, by fits and starts, aware that our differences—of race, class, age, physical ability—are as important as our similarities. Furthermore, the roots of the lesbian community in the radical political movements of the 1960s has required us, again by fits and starts, to pay some attention to the political dimensions of our existence. This chapter attends to these two related factors in the lesbian narrative: the politicizing of fiction and the fictionalizing of ethnic and racial particularity.

Politics and Anti-Politics

To begin, how do lesbian feminist writers interpret and use the word "political?" Derived from the Greek *polis,* the city or the collective of citizens, politics refers to issues that engage the attention of the residents of a city. *Political* implies public, confrontational, worldly, power-based; it is exemplified by elections, demonstrations, parties and caucuses, smoke-filled rooms: any activity involving struggles for power. Political subjects include war, government, law, and economics. Politics is mean, dirty, and sleazy. Furthermore, in classical Athens, the source of our contemporary notions of democratic politics, only men (and a minority of men at that) engaged in the life of the *polis*. Politics, therefore, is what men do. In a word, politics is male.

There is no single word or concept to contrast to political. In nineteenth-century Britain, middle class writers like Charles Dickens and George Eliot often contrasted the political realm, either explicitly or implicitly, to the moral or social realm. Political strategies, fueled by anger or opportunism, divided the community while moral strategies, because they were based on love and empathy, brought it back together. These strategies usually centered around class struggle, although George Eliot contrasted "political" and "moral" approaches to women's protest against gender oppression. Such a distinction continues to form part of contemporary political ideology. Political protests against oppression and exploitation are named "special pleading" by "interest groups" who disrupt the supposed harmony of the whole community.

The early women's liberation movement conceived of politics differently. Drawing upon another nineteenth century dualistic concept—the "separate spheres" of men and women—the women's liberation movement made a connection between the *political* and the *personal,* thus creating its well-known slogan, "the personal is political."[3] We argued that everything considered individual and private—the personal—was in fact influenced or even determined by forces that are collective and public—the political. The personal is roughly coexistent with women's traditional private sphere and the political with men's public realm; hence, we claimed what men had deemed of primary importance, politics, for women as well. This slogan, the personal is political, expanded women's sphere to the size of men's—even denied any significant difference between them. The personal—home, family, housework, love, sex, the psyche—was argued to be governed by the same forces as are wars, revolutions, governments, and economies. Using different phraseology, socialist feminists revised classic Marxism by relocating women's work—domestic labor and reproduction—away from the ideological superstructure into the economic base.[4] The language of "male" politics and revolutionary struggle was seized and extended to women's fight against male domination, as we see in Monique Wittig's *Les Guérillères.* Even the name we used for ourselves—the women's liberation movement or front—was appropriated from third world politics.

Many examples of women's liberation fiction of the early 1970s are, therefore, deliberately political in tone and content. The novels of Marge Piercy are perhaps the best known examples of feminist political fiction, but they are not unique. The plots of such novels are set in consciousness-raising or political action groups, the development of their characters is distinguished by movement from oppression to activism, their genre is didactic realism, and their intent is to record historical events and inspire women to join in them. These elements also characterize the earliest lesbian novels, primarily those published by Daughters between 1973 and 1976, which initiated both the "golden age" of lesbian experimentation and of lesbian political fiction. Writers of lesbian political fiction include June Arnold, Elana Nachmann, Monique Wittig (a leader of the Mouvement de libération des femmes in France), and, to a lesser extent, Rita Mae Brown.

"The personal is political" manifests itself in the first and possibly best example of a political lesbian novel, June Arnold's *The Cook and the Carpenter*. This novel preserves in fiction that optimistic time when lesbians and feminists believed self, society, culture, and language to be infinitely changeable. The personal is political, and the political personal, on three interconnected narrative levels (which parallel the three lesbian myths I have laid out): the story of the Carpenter's individual growth; the story of a love triangle involving the Carpenter, the Cook, and Three; and the story of a political collective attempting to work through differences and effect social change. As the lovers struggle with the differences between them (the personal), so too do the women of the collective struggle with their real and imagined differences (the political). As the Carpenter attempts to change the state of her mind through love, art, and alcohol, so the collective attempts to change the shape of the town through political actions. The splits the Carpenter finds within herself—between rigidity and flexibility, for example—exist within the collective as well. The differences of class and personality that bedevil the love relationships also plague the group. *The Cook and the Carpenter* is, ultimately, a morality play uneasily foreshadowing the direction of the lesbian community. As the Carpenter tells the Cook, "The two things we are trying to do—set up a counter culture and make a revolution . . . it's hard to do both things at the same time" (49).

The collective's most striking difficulty—even though they "all want the same thing"—is the lack of trust generated by their differences

(100). These seem to them so gigantic and the work required to overcome them so overwhelming that the group is paralyzed and almost
destroyed. When five members of the collective are arrested, the personal and the political are suddenly wrenched apart once again. Arnold
expresses this disjunction by suddenly replacing the invented neutral
pronoun, "na," with conventional pronouns. In their experimental
living and political collective, gender is insignificant, but in the "real
world" of police power and official violence, gender difference is maintained through language (pronouns) and force.

In jail, the only difference that seems to matter is the difference enforced by political authorities:

> As they answered official questions, they were aware of the trivial
> nature of their own differences: whereas previously they had all felt
> that their group of women, coming together from different spheres,
> lives, ages, had meant that any conclusion the group reached had the
> validity of convergence, now—the thought was a glare from the
> flatface opposite—they appeared as a collection of one minute sub-
> genre of strangeness coincidentally gathered into a tiny room. They
> were no more than a single gritty-eyed headache in the life of a giant.
> (139–40)

In this passage, Arnold articulates the tension between sameness and
difference. The group discovers that what had seemed to be monumental
distinctions among them are simply not perceived by the authorities; to
the police they are just an indistinguishable mass of "commie dykes."
But political power cannot be established and maintained on the basis of
a sameness imposed from above—whether imposed by the enemy or by
those who share class or race identity with the oppressors. Stripped of
their differences and their invigorating struggle to create unity based
upon difference, the collective feels as if "they had been rolled into one
ball in order to be stamped out by one efficient foot" (140).

At the end of the novel, then, the collective's optimism has diminished sharply. Their revolutionary political activism has narrowed in
focus to women's health and abortion needs. One by one the individuals
who established the collective leave. The author continues to use gen-
dered language to the end. But the ideals of the movement have not been
lost entirely. New women come to take the place of the old. Women's

lives are changed, if more slowly and less dramatically, and the main characters continue to hold fast to the fundamental principle of the women's liberation movement: the personal is political. As they leave the collective, the Carpenter says to the Cook: "Your telling me how strong I am is beginning to make me feel strong. Now all we have to do is change society" (179). These words remind us that in a political novel, the transformation of consciousness implies but does not assure the restructuring of reality.

The women's liberation and radical lesbian movements are the settings for other novels of that era. (Rita Mae Brown's *In Her Day,* for example, uses the movement as its backdrop.) The movements also provide figurative language such as the amazon warrior metaphors of Monique Wittig and Elana Nachmann. But few writers other than June Arnold place political activism at the center of plot, theme, and character development. With the demise of Daughters in 1978, political struggle directed outward against society was no longer noticeable in lesbian fiction. It would be surprising were this otherwise, since by the mid-seventies, the lesbian feminist movement had grown considerably less confrontational and more separatist. "Politics" had become a suspect word. If "political" signified activities performed by men in cities, then lesbians, particularly separatists, would disdain politics. Having left the city of men for the safe sea of women, we believed we had left the political realm behind.

As the seventies progressed, many lesbians felt that we had more and more reason to distrust politics. *Liberal* feminist politics narrowed its focus to the pursuit of the equal rights amendment; *radical* politics entailed condoning urban terrorism performed at times by lesbians who subsumed their interests and identities (once again) under those of men. Little wonder that some of us felt, as I wrote in response to the participation of lesbians in the 1974 Symbionese Liberation Army debacle, that we were part of a "lost generation, believing in the power of women, in collectively working for a change, for revolution, for a lesbian culture and nation" but not knowing how to do so anymore.[5] Little wonder, either, that many of us rejected the notion of politics entirely.

Harriet Desmoines, editor of *Sinister Wisdom,* summed up that position as the decade drew to a close:

> I would love to be able to declare a ten-year moratorium on the word
> *political*. The unvoiced assumptions that underlie its use are patriar-
> chal—that is, falsely universal . . . the Lesbian writing I'm seeing
> and wanting to see more of is not political and shouldn't be described
> as political. It is not engaging or taking sides in patriarchal poli-
> tics—patriarchal politics being that which can be succinctly charac-
> terized as Boys A versus Boys B and to hell with whoever gets caught
> in the cross-fire.[6]

I would call this position anti- (not a-) political. It is closely aligned with
the cultural feminism that merged with lesbian separatism to form the
distinctive position of "mature" lesbian feminism.[7] As nineteenth-
century novelists contrasted the political with the moral, and women's
liberation theorists interlinked the political and the personal, lesbian
(and other) feminists began to counterpose the political and the cultural.
In contrast to connotations of the word "political," "cultural" implies
artistic, communal, lifestyle-based, women-identified, and separatist.
Culture signifies what unites us as women, politics what pulls us apart.
Not surprisingly, the lesbian fiction published during this rather short
period (from the mid-seventies through the early eighties) consists primarily of coming out stories, green world romances, and utopian fantasies. *The Cook and the Carpenter* exemplifies the first phase of lesbian
fiction, *The Wanderground* the second.

But lesbian fiction entered a third phase in the eighties in which
writers returned to traditionally defined political issues and to the politics of difference and identity. Fiction focused both on what I would label
internal politics—such as racism and classism within the movement,
ethnic identity, and separatism—and on the external politics we had
once labeled "male," such as demonstrations, marches, and strikes. For
all the strong, often negative, reaction during the 1970s to debates over
the politics of Jane Alpert, Susan Saxe, and the women of the SLA, many
lesbian feminists and separatists were forced to come to terms with the
fantastical nature of the project to establish a Lesbian Nation within the
real world of imperialist and anti-imperialist nation-states.[8] Furthermore, within Lesbian Nation, the criticisms of women of color had
severely damaged the credibility of separatism. Finally, the landslide
election of Ronald Reagan in 1980, with its threat of a right-wing

fundamentalist political agenda in the United States, shocked many lesbians into reevaluating our antipolitical stance.

For all these reasons, around 1982—to pinpoint a watershed year—lesbian fictions began to reincorporate elements that we typically named "political" or "male": a factory strike in Maureen Brady's *Folly,* Irish nationalism and British imperialism in Valerie Miner's *Blood Sisters,* urban terrorism and grand juries in Barbara Wilson's *Ambitious Women,* street demonstrations in Ann Shockley's *Say Jesus and Come to Me,* anti-Klan activities in Chris South's *Clenched Fists, Burning Crosses.* Each novel places women's individual and collective struggles in the context of larger social and political realities. These novelists reject Virginia Woolf's claim of political neutrality in *Three Guineas;* like Adrienne Rich, they insist: "As a woman I have a country; as a woman I cannot divest myself of that country merely by condemning its government or by saying three times 'As a woman my country is the whole world.'" [9] In the late twentieth century, no woman, lesbian or otherwise, can isolate herself from history.

Equally significant, several novels written in the first half of the 1980s insist thematically upon the differences that separate women, not only the similarities that unite them. In place of the optimistic 1970s slogan, "sisterhood is powerful," they offer a demurral—"sisterhood can be divided." Miner's *Blood Sisters* and Gillian Hanscombe's *Between Friends,* for example, both explore the ways that political loyalties create barriers to sisterhood and how women can exploit and betray other women. Even Noretta Koertge's *Valley of the Amazons,* despite its utopian title, suggests that all is not perfect peace and harmony in Lesbian Nation.

Since these novels are not idealistic visions of united lesbians frolicking together, they do not focus as exclusively on lesbians as do most novels written during the late 1970s. They recall the women's liberation novels of Marge Piercy and June Arnold, and thus might be labeled "women-identified" rather than lesbian. I suggest the term "socialist-lesbian" since their political position is rooted in the material differences between women rather than in their essential similarities. Difference and dissension certainly figure in other lesbian novels, but, as we have seen, primarily as a factor to be bridged and overcome through love and sisterhood. Most of the novels I have mentioned end with a vision or hope of reconciliation and unity among women—perhaps the most notable characteristic of lesbian fiction. Increasingly, however, difference, whether of political belief or cultural identity, has become a crucial force to be reckoned with in lesbian fiction and lesbian communities.

The Politics of Identity

Novels like *Blood Sisters, Ambitious Women, Between Friends, Folly, Clenched Fists, Burning Crosses,* and *Say Jesus and Come to Me* mark a short period, between the election of Ronald Reagan and the symbolic year of 1984, during which traditionally defined political topics were popular in lesbian fictions. But politics within the lesbian community has been directed primarily inward, not outward. Because we envision ourselves as outlaws, as marginal to the dominant society, white lesbians seldom articulate internal political differences in ideological or tactical terms. In contrast, the early women's liberation movement, created by women with extensive experience in male leftist groups, typically split between socialist and radical tendencies, or between different brands of socialism. The split between lesbians and straight women was the first time that identity issues made a serious impact on white feminism. The only significant *ideological* split within lesbian feminism was over separatism, and during the first decade of the movement even this issue took a personal form such as the place of male children in the community.

The differences that lesbian feminists struggle over, and that force reconsideration of our utopian idealism, are those of identity based mostly, although not exclusively, on conditions of birth. We discover that the safe sea of women is divided into eddies of different races, classes, ethnicities, ages, physical abilities, and even sexual tastes. Or, to use another metaphor, taking note of the fact that the island model for Lesbian Nation is a white western one, created by privileged women living in Paris at the turn of the century, some writers propose a variety of islands and homelands—a cosmopolitan archipelago—to replace the old exclusivity of Lesbos. So Carriacou, Jamaica, Calafia, Aztlan, the biblical land of Moab where Ruth and Naomi pledged their devotion, all enter into the mythic structure. Lesbian Nation is becoming ethnic, particular, and diverse through the politics of identity.

The politics of identity is a phrase used in "A Black Feminist Statement," a manifesto written in 1977 by the Combahee River Collective:

"This focusing upon our own oppression is embodied in the concept of identity politics. We believe that the most profound and potentially radical politics come directly out of our own identity, as opposed to working to end somebody else's oppression." [10] Such a definition is the logical outcome of the theory and practice of feminism over the past two decades, but with a crucial difference. White feminists used the principle of fighting for one's own identity to insist that women disregard conditions of class and race, and join together on the basis of gender. The Combahee River Collective criticized what they saw as the naivete and implicit racism of white women. Several years later, Barbara Smith, one of the authors of the statement, argued that identity politics only works (positively) when individuals have "a combination of non-mainstream identities as a result of their race, class, ethnicity, sex, and sexuality" or (negatively) when "the most stringent realities of class and race are either not operative (because everybody involved is white and middle-class) or when these material realities are ignored or even forcibly denied." [11]

Smith's criticism indicates to what extent lesbian separatism—which is premised upon the belief that gender is the primary basis of identity and all other divisions are male-imposed—had lost its place as the privileged discourse of Lesbian Nation. Serious attacks and reconsiderations (sometimes resembling the "confessions" of repentant communists in the 1950s) can be found in issues of *Sinister Wisdom* and in *Top Ranking,* a collection of articles on racism in the lesbian movement. [12] By the mid 1980s, the voice of lesbian separatism had been effectively silenced (a situation that may change with the 1988 publication of *For Lesbians Only: A Separatist Anthology*). Instead, the articulation of difference had become the dominant discourse within the community. This position rejects the idea that women of color could or should separate from the men of their communities, or that "all women's interests are the *same,* thus, that all women share *identical* oppression." [13] This is a sharp deviation from earlier lesbian feminism.

As we have seen, the "true path," or central myth, of lesbian feminism is that we are all one, all sisters; our lesbian nationality or culture overrides, even obliterates, "minor" differences among us. National, racial, religious, and class differences are male defined and male enforced; accordingly, they should not matter to women-identified women. To a certain extent women's interests, female identity, and lesbian culture do transcend particular boundaries, a recognition that is the strength of the lesbian utopian vision. But our idealism has been our weakness as well. One writer in *Top Ranking* criticizes white women for failing "to examine our racism, to deal with the differences among us, differences that perpetuate *within* the sisterhood the horrors of the larger society." [14] By avoiding difference the lesbian community becomes a microcosm of the dominant culture, and our transforming myths come back to haunt us. If we predicate "sameness" and "unity" upon the culture, values, and beliefs of only one group of women, and these women (no matter how self-defined as outlaws) belong to the dominant culture, Lesbian Nation becomes an imperialist nation. We act like men, or whites, or the superpowers when they impose "unity" on women, people of color, or the Third World.

That imperialism manifests itself most strikingly in the struggle to define the community and who belongs to it. White women shaped Lesbian Nation as a room of our own with a door that appears transparent and open from the inside, but opaque and firmly closed from outside. As Bernice Reagon wryly notes, those inside may begin to say, "we better open the door and let some Black folks in the barred room," but that doesn't improve the situation. [15] Even were Black lesbians willing to enter, "the room don't feel like the room anymore. . . . And it ain't home no more. It is not a womb no more. And you can't feel comfortable no more." Reagon proposes that the very language of women's *community* would have to be replaced by that of *coalition,* as diverse women enter what had previously been a safely unified and univocal "refuge place." The repositioning of "home" and "identity," that Reagon proposes continues to be a—perhaps *the*—central theme of texts by lesbians of color.

Lesbian feminists have liked to believe that we, as lesbians or women, are exempt from imperialist original sin. "We" (white, middle class, etc.), by virtue of our essential womanness, are not racist or classist. [16] Barbara Wilson, through a Black character, exposes the white lesbian community's optimistic belief that the difference of lesbianism provides a position point from which all other differences can be understood and either appreciated or transcended: " 'Honey, you are so liberal you don't even know how liberal you are. It truly blows the mind.' She sat down on the sofa again as if exhausted. 'Though now you're a lesbian there may be some hope for you' " (*Murder in the Collective,* 176). This sentiment is not unique to the feminist era. As Audre Lorde's *Zami* shows, young white lesbians in the 1950s stated confidently that no racism existed in Greenwich Village. But Black lesbians knew about the extra IDs demanded at bars and the slurs passed off as jokes between friends.

The reader of lesbian utopias, in particular, may conclude that the community has effortlessly, magically, overcome internal difference. Unfortunately this is not so. Describing some characters as dark-skinned or nappy-haired (as Sally Gearhart once suggested) does not overcome difference.[17] A utopia imagined by a lesbian of color might look fundamentally different from one written by a white woman. (Furthermore, it is important to note that only a few writers of color have been drawn to the utopian or fantasy genres.) White lesbians thought we could transcend difference through sheer good will and enthusiasm, by asserting our sameness. We failed to understand that we could get to unity only by going through difference—and that unity would still not mean sameness. Lesbian Nation would have to be very diverse: to paraphrase Audre Lorde's oft-repeated words, the house of women is the house of difference.[18]

For many years, we (white middle class feminists) saw this difference as a failure in the model of sisterhood. One reason we feared difference was, no doubt, that we did not like to feel like bad girls. Although, as Barbara Smith puts it, "it is neither possible nor necessary to be morally exempt in order to stand in opposition to oppression," we had rather smugly assigned wickedness and impurity to men, and we didn't want to take back any responsibility for social evils.[19] For those who had adopted a virtually Manichean model (in which male equals bad, and female good), a religion was being upset. Not only might it be necessary to admit that women could be racist, and thus bad, but, if women could overcome racism (which we had to believe possible) and be good again, why couldn't men overcome sexism? We could evade this terrible dilemma entirely by denying the force of difference and oppression within the community.

Another explanation often given for why the lesbian community evades differences is that many white and middle class women are socialized to dislike and avoid confrontation. This reason underlies defensive reactions to any discussion of racism in the community, as we see in an article written by the white organizer of a racism workshop in 1979:

> While I understand their [Black women's] anger from both an his-
> toric and contemporary perspective, I question whether it is appro-
> priate or constructive to focus it on white lesbians. After all as
> women we share many, though clearly not all, of the oppressions
> perpetuated by the straight, white, male power structure. In short,
> we have more in common as women than we have differences based
> on race or ethnicity.[20]

This writer is clearly using the rhetoric of all-women-are-the-same and
men-are-the-real-enemy to evade the true source of her discomfort: the
anger of Black women.

Certainly these debates over difference raise the least pleasant of emotions: guilt, self-righteousness, exclusion, defensiveness, and betrayal,
as well as anger. And certainly the internal debate is often couched in
such a way that it is impossible to act in any manner that is not racist.
Moreover, when one's politics have been idealistic, visionary, even ecstatic, it is painful and unpleasant to be brought down to earth, down to
acrimonious fights over racism and a multitude of other oppressions. We
might ask why anyone would expect political struggle to be pleasant.
But it is equally reasonable to ask why we should expect people to
participate if it is not. No wonder many women, on both sides, retreated
from the fray. Indeed, the mere fact that I speak here of two sides is
another aspect of the problem. Few women feel that they are on a "side"
within Lesbian Nation, yet sides seem to exist.

Literature and the Dynamics of Difference

Literature is traditionally expected to bridge the gap between Self
and Other through empathy and information. So how has literature
represented differences within the lesbian community? Race, of course,
has been the most significant difference threatening to split the lesbian
community, and race involves both personal identity and political
struggle. Although the women's liberation movement and the lesbian
community have attempted (if inadequately) to address racism within
their ranks, white lesbian fiction has had only modest success in portray-
ing racism (or, for that matter, any other "ism") or in depicting with any
degree of skill and sensitivity a diverse cast of characters.[21]

Among the first authors to recreate fictionally the oppression of race was, not surprisingly, the trailblazing June Arnold. In *The Cook and the Carpenter,* the Black member of the collective describes herself as "a fucking rat's nest of oppressed parts," but it is *Sister Gin* that addresses racism in a thoughtful if oblique manner that ultimately evades the very problem it raises (100). The novel appears to end with Su's utopian call for all women to "come in" and find a home in the community of women. But a final chapter, which functions as an epilogue, presents the voice of Miss May, a Black servant who has hovered in the background of the novel. Su tries to bring her into the foreground by writing about life as Miss May experiences it. In the end, however, Su and Sister Gin break into the text with an admission that it does not work, that the "story is probably right all right but the voice is wrong" (210). Miss May will have to write her own story: "Have some gin, Su. You just can't speak for Miss May, that's all. Let her go on out the door. And she doesn't need you to hold it for her, either" (215).

This chapter, the real conclusion to the novel, attempts to come to terms with the complexities of imagining a women's community that includes both Black and white women. A novel by a white woman, if it is to be "true," must include Black women (particularly if it takes place in the South). Yet white women cannot honestly and thoroughly tell Black women's stories, interpret Black women's lives, especially when they only know them in the role of servants. Black women must tell their own tales—which, of course, is what Toni Morrison, Toni Cade Bambara, Alice Walker, Ann Allen Shockley, and many others were and are doing. How then is a white woman's novel not to be racist, either by omission or commission? Arnold's solution to—or evasion of—the dilemma is a postmodernist disruption of the text through which the author poses the problem and comments on her inability to solve it. Miss May, and all Black women, remain Other in the text as they were in the white lesbian community. This may have been the best Arnold could do at the time, but it was no solution to the racism of the predominantly white genre of lesbian fiction, especially as racism moved to the forefront of the community's political and ethical agendas.[22]

Few other white lesbian writers have focused their stories on racism, or tried to create believable characters of races other than their own. The struggle against racism in both the political and personal dimensions is central to Maureen Brady's rather didactic novel, *Folly.* On a political level, white racism almost divides and conquers the strikers: "we gotta know how easy it would be for the mill to set us up, white against Black, if we don't look out" (76). Only Folly's strenuous effort to bridge the gap created by her white co-workers keeps the Black women from abandoning the strike, which would be fatal to everyone's hopes since they are both the most politically astute and the hardest workers. The personal dimension is represented by the growing friendships between women of different races, and by Folly's halting realization that she is profoundly ignorant about Black life and about her own whiteness for that matter: "She needed to know a lot more about what it meant to be Mabel and Emily, Freena and the others, to be Black women. She needed to know herself as a white woman who didn't just take it for granted that since she was white, she needn't bother with anyone who wasn't" (76). Barbara Wilson structures *Murder in the Collective* and Chris South, *Clenched Fists, Burning Crosses,* around antiracist struggles, but these are fairly isolated examples.

One might expect writers of color to address racism; however, until the 1980s, Ann Allen Shockley was the only prominent and widely-read chronicler of Black lesbian lives (although Red Arobateau had self-published a largely forgotten novel, *The Bars across Heaven,* in 1975 and anthologies had included some short stories by lesbians of color).[23] Nor can I identify any Latina, Asian-American, or American Indian lesbian novelists before 1983. Interestingly, much of the earliest fiction published that dealt with racial or ethnic issues—for example, short stories in *Lesbian Fiction* (1981)—focused more on homophobia within ethnic communities than on racism within the lesbian movement. A notable exception to this is Shockley's story, "A Meeting of the Sapphic Daughters," in *The Black and White of It* (1980). One of the Black women who attend a lecture about "love and building a world community of lesbians" addresses the group's racism directly:

> "There doesn't seem to be anything in any of the lesbian literature on the lesbian movement addressing itself to helping the black lesbian to become free from racism—especially *inside* the lesbian community."
> Trollope looked puzzled at first, then flustered.
> "Will there be freedom from racism in your lesbian world community?" Lettie went on pointedly. (67)

Through their behavior, the Sapphic Daughters emphatically answer no. But this is rather strong stuff for Shockley. In *Loving Her* and even *Say Jesus and Come to Me* with its crudely racist white feminists, Shockley, like most white lesbian writers, envisions love and sisterhood overcoming racial difference.

In general, the reader of lesbian fiction written during the 1970s could reasonably conclude that the women who reside in Lesbian Nation are pretty much alike. The writers, whether similar in background or not, subscribed to the dominant ideology of sameness. The only identity markedly present is the regional one of southern white women.[24] Even when the writer is not herself a mainstream WASP—such as Elana Nachmann or Nancy Toder who are both Jewish—the ethnicity of her characters is neither central nor emphasized. Sheila Ortiz Taylor created a Chicana protagonist in *Faultline* (1982), but her ethnicity is not pronounced. A rare exception in the 1970s was M. F. Beal's Katarina Guerrera (*Angel Dance* [1977]), one of the most interesting characters in lesbian fiction. A detective and political radical, she is conscious of her ethnic identity and moves convincingly within a well-delineated Latino community. For the most part, however, white authors were strikingly unsuccessful in their attempts to create racially diverse characters. The character of Adele in *In Her Day* is one example; I read the novel several times before I realized that she was Black.

Middle class writers have been no more successful in representing class diversity. Although the early lesbian movement, particularly in 1971 and 1972, was quite militant about class divisions, later lesbian feminists tended to ignore or overlook them.[25] Picaresque novels such as *Rubyfruit Jungle* and *Who Was That Masked Woman?* have a working class "flavor" typical of the genre (the piquancy of poverty), but only *Yesterday's Lessons* and later *Folly* recreate the pain of economic deprivation and the values of working class culture. Nor have more than a few novels attended to other identity issues such as age or physical ability.[26]

The politics of publishing may well impede this diversity. Consider a few examples. In 1974, the Women's Press Collective made the political decision to publish *Yesterday's Lessons* unedited, leaving misspellings and grammatical errors intact, because to do otherwise, in their view, would impose "middle class" standards on a working class text. Had this press survived longer, it might have published more working class literature.

Later in the decade Persephone Press, founded and run by Jewish lesbians, not only published a groundbreaking anthology of writings by women of color, *This Bridge Called My Back,* but also made a special effort to seek out Jewish texts, resulting in the publication of *Nice Jewish Girls,* a collection of essays and personal narratives. But until the formation of Kitchen Table: Women of Color Press, the only means of literary production controlled by lesbians of color was the journal *Azalea,* which was not in the position to publish long works of fiction. To publish, a lesbian of color or a working class lesbian had to pass the tests established by predominantly white middle class women. Even if these women wanted to publish such texts, even if they actively solicited them, other historical realities might stand in the way. As poet and critic Linda J. Brown wrote in 1980, an author would have to overcome a long history of mistrust: "understand the politics of having to (in most cases) give up control—artistic and otherwise—of your work to someone who possibly doesn't understand what you are saying."[27]

I suspect that censorship—intended or not—is but one part of the answer. The tastes and values of publishers certainly influence what is published, but I would not automatically conclude that significant numbers of novel manuscripts by working class lesbians or lesbians of color were suppressed in the 1970s. As Virginia Woolf put it, "fiction is like a spider's web, attached ever so lightly perhaps, but still attached to life at all four corners."[28] In other words, lesbian fiction does not float free in a fantasy land of our own making. It emerges from a flawed community weighted down by the same oppressions and inequities that exist in society at large.

Lesbian fiction was defined at the beginning by white middle class women. As the hegemony of this group of women diminished, lesbian fiction changed. Change occurred first in the political discourse, and then was incorporated into the literature (which in turn furthered the ideological changes in the community). What it is possible to say, and therefore to write, is determined by the political climate. And *who* identifies with the community is also determined by, and helps to determine, how that community defines itself.

Conditions established by the larger society also inhibit or direct literary production. Audre Lorde, for example, echoes Woolf in pointing out the economic burden of cultural production: "even the form our creativity takes is often a class issue. Of all the art forms, poetry is the most economical. . . . writing a novel on tight finances, I came to appreciate the enormous differences in the material demands between poetry and prose." [29] Certainly it is evident that the *poetic* expression of lesbians of color was less inhibited during the 1970s, which Linda J. Brown attributes in part to the fact that these literary cultures draw heavily upon "oral and rhythmic traditions." Furthermore, Brown suggests, "dark" lesbians may have been inhibited by the homophobia of their communities and the simple lack of a tradition of "womon-identified material." [30] As both Woolf and Alice Walker have pointed out, "the effect of discouragement upon the mind of the artist" must be taken into account. [31] Literary genius requires nurturing if it is to flourish, and who, as critics Barbara Smith and Gloria Hull have eloquently demonstrated, has been more discouraged than the lesbian of color? [32] Finally, it may be that women who experience multiple oppressions, often with great immediacy, and who have energy, creativity, and time, are more likely to direct their attention toward political action rather than artistic endeavors, at least in the first stages of a movement. Poetry, Audre Lorde has written, is not a luxury, but neither may it be one's first priority. [33]

For some or all of these reasons, and no doubt others, only in 1979, in a special issue of *Conditions* edited by Barbara Smith and Lorraine Bethel, did Black lesbian writing become widely public. [34] Within a few years, the voices of Asian-American, American Indian, and Latina lesbians also took written form, in *Lesbian Fiction: An Anthology,* edited by Elly Bulkin, and *This Bridge Called My Back,* edited by Cherríe Moraga and Gloria Anzaldúa (both 1981). By the mid-eighties, several more novels, memoirs, and short story collections focused on racial and ethnic identity. Several factors combined to create a receptive audience for this literature. The first wave of writing by Black, Latina, and Jewish lesbians inspired more of the same. Journals and presses actively solicited manuscripts by lesbians of color, and lesbians of color established publishing institutions of their own. Also, the political discourse of the community changed so that writing by lesbians of color or working class lesbians became "fashionable." As a result, the literature of the 1980s is more diverse and cosmopolitan than it was a decade before.

The texts published since 1980 by and about lesbians of color or ethnic lesbians (I use this term to refer to white women whose ethnicity,

Jewish especially but not exclusively, is central to their identities and their stories) add a strong and subtle critique of racism to lesbian fiction. These writers do not necessarily pose an us-against-them dialectic in their texts. Ruth Geller's *Triangles* portrays the protagonist's growing awareness of anti-Semitism; Alice Bloch's *The Law of Return* focuses on the racism and classism of Israeli society. Michelle Cliff structures *Abeng* around the "colorism" in Jamaican society. Paula Gunn Allen's *The Woman Who Owned the Shadows* demonstrates both the overt racism of the nuns at the reservation school and the subtle racism of white liberals. It also makes painfully clear the dilemma of an individual of mixed origins who is not fully accepted by either society.

Since the consciousness of racism (including anti-Semitism as a form of racism) in these books comes from a member of the inside not outside group, it is complex and subtle. The member of an oppressor group, no matter how liberal and well-meaning, may not see subtleties or feel comfortable expressing them. Novels by well-intentioned white women often substitute a polemical analysis of racism and a program for over-coming it in place of storytelling. In contrast, novels and memoirs by women of color and ethnic women create an imaginative landscape steeped in ethnic particularity, or what we might call a sense of place. They are primarily about what it means to be Black (or Indian or Jewish) *and* female and lesbian. Racism is presented through the lived experi-ence of the characters.

In some novels—Dodici Azpadu's *Saturday Night in the Prime of Life,* for example, with its Sicilian family scenes—this sense of place seems to be all the writer intends. Sarah Schulman's *The Sophie Horowitz Story,* takes its hero on a picaresque journey through New York's restaurants and food shops. Sophie is an unmistakably Jewish hero. Her diet is both multinational and Jewish—a metaphor for her identity. But her Jew-ishness is an effect of her personality, not her politics. So too with her lesbianism. The reader cannot think of Sophie Horowitz as anything but a Jew and a lesbian. However, the novel ignores community debates about homophobia and anti-Semitism, and Sophie's search for her roots is entirely satirical. She finds her "place" as a Jewish lesbian by making love in the women's section of the synagogue (61). When she encounters her foremothers, it is in the shape of a mechanical Jewish grandmother at the Jewish museum. These are hardly exemplary experiences of Jewish culture and family life. Satire, to be sure, is rare in lesbian literature, and almost nonexistent around sensitive ethnic and political issues. This quality makes *The Sophie Horowitz Story* a delightful novel.

The majority of texts written in the 1980s, on the other hand, are profoundly "about" ethnic and sexual identity. Several texts published between 1982 and 1987 explore the meaning of African-American lesbian identity (*Zami, Abeng,* and Becky Birtha's collections of short stories), Chicana lesbian identity (*Borderlands* and *Loving in the War Years*), American Indian lesbian identity (*The Woman Who Owned the Shadows* and *The Mohawk Trail*) and Jewish lesbian identity (*The Law of Return* and *Triangles*). These texts are often transparently autobiographical; they also mix genres so dramatically that some can hardly be called novels and a few barely labeled narratives. They are all well-written; many are sophisticated in their use of literary and historical allusion, and thoroughly rooted in the theoretical languages of the 1980s. They are complex constructs that need to be read from a variety of perspectives; focusing on only one aspect, as I must do in this chapter, necessarily flattens them.

Reading them as lesbian feminist narratives, we can see that they develop many of the common themes and metaphors in lesbian fiction: myths of origins, homecoming, mothers and nurturance, communities of women, and the meaning of identity. While lesbian writers of the dominant culture imagine a return to Lesbos, lesbians of color and ethnic lesbians undertake a more complex search for the source and meaning of identity. All these texts incorporate the metaphor of "home," a material and spiritual location where the protagonist feels herself finally unified and whole. The manner in which these authors construct and deconstruct concepts of self and home has profoundly influenced the direction of lesbian theory and culture.

Writing from the House of Difference

Since the impact of poststructuralist and French feminist theory was first felt in American academic circles, "difference" has become a word of some consequence generating considerable controversy. *Différence* (in the French mode) refers to *sexual* difference, the way in which society and language structures oppositions between male and female.

Such a definition, and theories which derive from it, is conceptually heterosexual; it necessitates placing female in relation to male. Whether the female is defined as absence or "lack," as in Freudian or Lacanian schemes, or, in the revisions of theorists Julia Kristeva, Luce Irigaray, and Hélène Cixous, as a plenitude of *jouissance* (bodily pleasure), the basis of the theory remains the same: how woman is distinguished or differs from man.[35]

Monique Wittig, one of the few self-professed lesbians among this group, is also the only one to propose a category standing outside the male-female difference, that of the lesbian. Instead of replacing the ontological dualism of "male" and "female" with that of "gay" and "straight," she offers "lesbian" as a category outside that dualism which, in effect, breaks it down: "Lesbianism opens onto another dimension of the human (insofar as its definition is not based on the 'difference' of the sexes). Today lesbians are discovering this dimension outside what is masculine and feminine."[36] We could conclude that the lesbian is required to abolish or transform gender essentialism. Unless a position can be developed outside of that dualistic system, feminist theory may oscillate endlessly between the poles, perhaps redefining "woman" or the female principle, but not eliminating sexual difference entirely. *Lesbian* is that position, a point of exit from sexual dualism.

When lesbians speak of difference, then, we are not referring to *sexual* or *gender* difference. Nor do we refer to difference between heterosexual and homosexual, since, in general, lesbian feminist theorists postulate fluidity, or at least potential fluidity, between lesbianism and heterosexuality along a "lesbian continuum." Instead we draw attention to the differences among women or lesbians. Lesbians are asking the same question posed by theorist Gayatri Spivack: "Not merely who am I? But who is the other woman?"[37] Or, in fact, who are the other *women?.*: for it is important to note that lesbians speak more often of differenc*es*—of diversity—than of difference. By exploring multiple differences, we resist the conclusion that there are essential categories of being of any kind at all.[38]

To be sure, lesbian theorists can fail to dismantle essentialist notions of identity, and instead construct more and more narrowly defined categories of being. Political transformation within the lesbian feminist movement throughout the 1970s and 80s has been a history of splits along dualistic lines—working class vs. middle class, Black vs. white, old vs. young, and so on—that lead to more and more narrowly defined political categories. But when the splits begin to shatter individuals themselves into fragments, we are forced to rethink and reframe the politics of identity.

Audre Lorde, in *Zami,* pinpoints the consciousness of the 1980s:

> For some of us there was no one particular place, and we grabbed whatever we could from wherever we found space, comfort, quiet, a smile, non-judgment.
>
> *Being women together was not enough. We were different. Being gay-girls together was not enough. We were different. Being Black together was not enough. We were different. Being Black women together was not enough. We were different. Being Black dykes together was not enough. We were different.*
>
> Each of us had our own needs and pursuits, and many different alliances. Self-preservation warned some of us that we could not afford to settle for one easy definition, one narrow individuation of self. At the Bag, at Hunger College, uptown in Harlem, at the library, there was a piece of the real me bound in each place, and growing. (226).

In this passage Lorde eloquently articulates the difficulties inherent in identity politics. Recognizing the multiple aspects of any self, and realizing that some of these aspects carry a political significance that overarches the individual, the subject must struggle to find or create a position within various communities. The lesbian community has attempted to redefine itself so that individuals with multiple allegiances may find a home there. The challenge for both individual and community is how to accommodate such multiplicity without losing its cohesive identity.

The next four sections will explore how narratives by lesbians of color and ethnic lesbians restructure both the individual and the community through articulation of a theory based on differences. This restructuring has taken directions that both reaffirm and subvert an "essentialist" notion of identity; directions that, on the one hand, reinforce the idea that there can be a whole, unified, essential Self (to use the capitalization preferred by Mary Daly and those inspired by her), or, on the other, suggest that what we call the self is a constantly fluctuating set of positions and relations the individual adopts in response to specific situations and "homes."

THE FALL INTO FREE SPACE

As I discussed in chapter 2, many lesbians feel that an innate self or core lesbian identity existed before they took the name lesbian. Lesbians who came out more self-consciously may become "archaeologists" or "miners" (a metaphor used by Adrienne Rich, for example) digging deep for traces of a lesbian self beneath the heterosexual surface.[39] The most common metaphor for coming out is "coming home" to your real self. *True* identity is believed to be discovered, not constructed or learned. Once it is discovered, the individual feels herself to be finally whole.

For white, middle-class, christian (with a lower-case "c") lesbians, discovering such a core identity may be relatively unproblematic since "white," "middle class," and "christian" are not taken to be positive aspects of identity, but the invisible backdrop against which the real drama—coming out as a lesbian—is performed. Such is not the case for the African-American, Latina, American Indian, Jewish, or working class lesbian. Her identity cannot be so easily unified, because several core identities are in play and she may feel herself torn in several directions and asked to choose between various political and social allegiances in the outside world. Furthermore, because of her awareness of the possibility of having conflicting identities, she may discover yet other, more contingent identities such as student, poet, mother, activist. These she must integrate with her fundamental identities established at birth or through early socialization.

In order to express this decentering or fragmenting of self, writers of color, and those white women who are exploring "white" as a specific ethnicity rather than a norm, employ a number of metaphors, some quite familiar, such as falling or displacement, loss, journeys, and borders. Lesbian writers often revise the myth of the fall, for example, to signify either the fall from innocence (in prefeminist texts), the "fortunate fall" into human community (in *Desert of the Heart*), or the adolescent female's fall into femininity (in *The Woman Who Owned the Shadows* and *Abeng*). But falling may also signify the displacement of the old falsely-defined self, a falling away into free space where a new self may be imagined and constructed.

Minnie Bruce Pratt, in her autobiographical piece "Identity: Skin Blood Heart," narrates the story of her long search for a "complex self" and a notion of home and community that is no longer "culture-bound" (*Yours in Struggle*, 33, 50). Her journey begins with a fall from the comfortable niche established for her by her white, middle class, heterosexual, Christian upbringing: "I lived in a kind of vertigo: a sensation of my body having no fixed place to be: the earth having opened, I was falling through space" (35). As Biddy Martin and Chandra Talpade Mohanty note in their instructive analysis of Pratt's narrative, most feminist stories of political awakening (and, I would add, lesbian coming out stories) progress in a linear fashion toward an expected end: the triumph of the enlightened Self.[40] Pratt's does not; it is written in "fits and starts." It has no fixed direction; its movement is open and exploratory. It is characterized by the movement of free-fall, not a pilgrim's progress along a straight and narrow path.

In a similar fashion, Audre Lorde's autobiographical narrative, *Zami*, relates a mock-epic journey "up Sugar Hill" to the local comic book store in "the Harlem summers of [her] earliest days" (48–49). In these journeys toward literature (even in the form of comic books), Audre discovers the world in all its terror and excitement. Returning down the hill one day, she imagines a journey without end, a vision that prefigures her lonely travels away from home as an adult: "I shook with a sudden spasm of terror. Suppose I fell down at that crucial point? I could roll down hill after successive hill all the way back across Lenox Avenue, and if I happened to miss the bridge I could roll right on into the water" (52). Eventually, to establish a new self and a new home, she must indeed "float slowly out to sea" away from parents and sisters, neighbors and classmates—all those who impose a rigid, if safe, identity upon the free-floating, questing hero of her own life.

The writer who most thoroughly develops the metaphor of falling is Paula Gunn Allen in *The Woman Who Owned the Shadows*, the story of Ephanie, a woman weaving together the Indian, female, and lesbian strands of her life. Allen, a literary critic as well as novelist and poet, describes the protagonist's journey as a discovery of "her place within the ritual tradition of her people and her responsibility to continue it."[41]

Among the Indian legends that parallel Ephanie's life is that of The Woman Who Fell. We first see her at a moment of adolescent crisis, the first awareness of self as lesbian and lesbian as sin:

> Ephanie sat. Stunned. Mind empty. Stomach a cold cold stone. The hot sun blazed on her head. She felt sick. She felt herself shrinking within. Understood, wordlessly. . . . That they were becoming lovers. That they were in love. That their loving had to stop. To end. That she was falling. Had fallen. Would not recover from the fall, smashing, the rocks. . . . The enormity of the abyss she was falling into. The endless, endless depth of the void. (30)

The context for falling here is homophobic, and hence, limiting and destructive. Although the words resemble those used by Minnie Bruce Pratt, they suggest no possibility of growth or redemption. That comes later, as Ephanie recovers an Indian framework for falling.

Getting to that point takes the rest of Ephanie's life. She journeys "in ancient ways, and along new edges of mind and being," and at these new borders she "remembers" another adolescent fall (101). Like her alter ego, the woman who fell from the sky, Ephanie had jumped from a tree only to damage her body, after which "everything changed" (202). She became passive, fearful, "feminine"; she "sins" by forgetting and losing her self: "Had forgotten how to spin dreams, imaginings about her life, her future self, her present delights. Had cut herself off from the sweet spring of her own being" (203). As the truncated sentences indicate, these falls of her adolescence, constructed by Christian myth and morality, pinch and stifle Ephanie's growth and selfhood. But the Indian myth, retold to her by Spirit Woman, gives her a different context for falling:

> "Little sister, you have jumped. You have fallen. You have been brave, but you have misunderstood. So you have learned. How to jump. How to fall. How to learn. How to understand.
> "We are asking you to jump again. To fall into this world like the old one, the one you call Anciena, sky woman, jumped, fell, and began in a world that was new." (211)

Having jumped and fallen, Ephanie is once again able to dream. Like Minnie Bruce Pratt, Paula Gunn Allen suggests that reconstructing identity and community requires falling away from old constructs and taking risks by jumping into new ways of being.

But falling also involves loss of the old comfortable (or at least familiar) identity bestowed upon us in childhood—the "Name" (as Emily Dickinson put it) dropped upon our heads by the powerful Fathers.[42] After her initial falls, Ephanie is a lost soul—alienated, split, dispossessed, a "halfbreed" at home neither on the reservation nor in the city, comfortable in neither man's world nor woman's (3). Pratt suggests that "our fear of the losses can keep us from changing." She then asks, "what is it, exactly, that we are afraid to lose?" (*Yours in Struggle,* 39). Her answer is that we fear the loss of *home,* of our old identities, our birth families, even our new feminist community. But it is an old axiom that to gain you must first lose, to find yourself in the sunshine you must first go through the long night of the soul. For this reason, most of these narratives inscribe a story of loss, of journeying away from one's birthplace, one's family, even one's friends. All novels of development, particularly the picaresque, involve journeys away from home. But the more marginalized the protagonist—the more she must depend upon her particular culture and community—the more conflicted and painful is her journey, the more precipitous her fall, the more profound her loss.

In many of these texts, the protagonist travels between actual territories that carry symbolic weight. Audre in *Zami* journeys between New York, the home of her childhood, and Connecticut and Mexico, locations that validate her lesbian and Black identities (43). Elisheva, in *The Law of Return,* searches unsuccessfully for a home between Israel and the United States: "America is my birthplace, Israel my homeland, nowhere my home. My home is that hollow of maple, music, and flesh, remembered but lost" (11). Clare, in *Abeng,* moves between her parents' urban home and her grandmother's sanctuary in the country.

Gloria Anzaldúa, on the other hand, situates herself directly on the border between territories that are both geographic and metaphoric. The title of *Borderlands/La Frontera* refers not only to the physical territory occupied by Chicanos—a people who merge the identities of both Mexican and American—but also to a border territory of spirit, language, and culture. As the book's title assertively juxtaposes English and Spanish, its form brings together prose and poetry, expository essay and lyric memoir. This place on the borders—rather than the journey from the center of one country to another—is the terrain of *la mestiza,* a being at once historical and metaphoric. A borderland "is in a constant state of transition. The prohibited and forbidden are its inhabitants. *Los atravesados* live here: the squint-eyed, the perverse, the queer, the troublesome, the mongrel, the mulato, the half-breed, the half-dead; in short, those who cross over, pass over, or go through the confines of the 'normal'" (3). From this borderland—what Anzaldúa names elsewhere "*el Mundo Zurdo*" (the left-handed world)—lesbians of color construct a new definition of self and community.[43] This definition is inclusive not exclusive, multifaceted not unifocal, mutable not static. Its intent is complex wholeness, not monolithic identity.

THE NARRATIVE OF THE MOTHER

As writers evoke the condition of fragmentation through the language of falling and journeying, so they inscribe the search for wholeness through metaphors and myths of mothers, communities of women, female eroticism, and female power. Some of these texts—*Zami, The Woman Who Owned the Shadows, Abeng,* and *The Law of Return*—resemble what the French call *l'écriture féminine* in both form and content: they intermingle genres, are formally disjointed and circuitous rather than linear, evoke both mythical and historical images of women, and move between reality and dream language. They also "write the body," as Hélène Cixous commands, by inscribing what Audre Lorde has named the power of the erotic.[44] As is true in some texts by white lesbians, that eroticism is deeply connected to the relationship between mother and daughter. Through the working out of a matrilineal family drama, many of these protagonists "re-member" the self.

Mothers in narratives by lesbians of color and ethnic lesbians are sources of personal and collective identity; mothers connect the protagonist to her racial and sexual heritage. Since they bear their daughters in their own bodies, they provide the explicit link to the ethnic group, the origin, the root. Love for the mother also implies love of self, of one's race or ethnicity, and of women. Fathers, on the other hand, either represent patriarchal elements internalized by the nondominant culture, or belong to the dominant group itself.[45]

Ephanie, for example, is the child of an Indian mother and white father; symbolically she is "mothered" by her Indian heritage but disconnected and uprooted as a result of her father's legacy. In the Jamaica of *Abeng,* races intermarried for generations, so Clare's parents are both of mixed race. But her father is lighter-skinned and hence responsible (at least symbolically) for her own whiteness, while her mother is the source of her Black identity. Since *Abeng* reverses conventional racist hierarchies by valuing Black more than white, Clare desires her mother and resists her father.[46] In *The Law of Return* Elisheva was nurtured in the womb by her mother's music, and in Israel the songs of Yemeni women represent Jewish female culture and power. The patriarchs of ancient and modern Israel, on the other hand, dispossess Elisheva of her home. She cannot settle in Israel because it does not provide adequate mothering for women, especially lesbian women. In an autobiographical narrative, Cherríe Moraga describes the complexity of her heritage: "Maybe you'll understand this. My mother was not the queer one, but my father. . . . *But it is this queer I run from.* This white man in me" (*Loving in the War Years,* 8). Instead, Moraga runs toward her actual and symbolic mother:

> How then was I supposed to turn away from La Madre, La Chicana? If I were to build my womanhood on this self-evident truth, it is the love of the Chicana, the love of myself as a Chicana I had to embrace, no white man. Maybe this ultimately was the cutting difference between my brother and me. To be a woman fully necessitated my claiming the race of my mother. My brother's sex was white. Mine, brown. (94)

Zami, in particular, creates a matrilineal "herstory" for the protagonist. In a circular, "feminine" fashion, the text begins and ends by evoking Audre's historic and mythic foremothers, while in between it inscribes a life closely entwined with that of her biological mother. Whereas Audre's unnamed father is "distant lightning," her mother, Linda, is the source of Audre's stories, strength, and lesbianism (3). (Moraga similarly claims that "these stories my mother told me crept under my 'güera' skin. I had no choice but to enter into the life of my mother" [*Loving in the War Years,* 52].) Since *Zami* is a "biomythography," the text slides continually between a realistic representation and symbolic evocation of the mother. To the extent that Linda represents a real woman, Audre must separate from her—indeed, turn away from her in anger—in order to create an independent self. But as a *symbol*, the mother (in this and other texts) represents female power, lesbian eroticism, and, most importantly, home.

Early in *Zami*, Audre describes Linda as a powerful woman "in a time when that word-combination of *woman* and *powerful* was almost unexpressible in the white american common tongue" (15). Since neither "woman" nor "man" could adequately describe Linda, Audre searches for "the third designation," which she discovers to be the word "lesbian": "to this day I believe that there have always been Black dykes around—in the sense of powerful and women-oriented women—who would rather have died than use that name for themselves. And that includes my momma." This female-orientation may be so deeply erotic that in loving the mother, the daughter learns to look for love from other women. Mother, female power, women's bodies: all create a home for the traveler along the borderlands. In the same way that Adrienne Rich imagines it, lesbianism—the "re-membering" of primal love between women—is a cure for homesickness.

Audre finds many homes in *Zami:* Brooklyn and Connecticut, Mexico and Greenwich Village, a hint as well of the Africa that will figure so prominently in Lorde's later poetry. Audre also makes herself into "home" for many lost and forlorn, mostly white, women. But always, the book suggests, Audre is not quite at home, as a Black in white America, as one of the Branded in high school, as a girl among the middle-aged expatriate women in Mexico, as a poet in the lesbian Village, or as a lesbian anywhere. She meets other lost or maimed women along her path—Gennie, Eudora, Muriel—and struggles to make her way home, to wholeness, to the source of her Blackness, her femaleness, her lesbianism, her creativity.

That place is consistently symbolized by Carriacou, the island of Black women whose loves and friendships are sustaining and whose mythic presence inspires her poetry:

> Once *home* was a long way off, a place I had never been to but knew out of my mother's mouth. I only discovered its latitudes when Carriacou was no longer my home.

There it is said that the desire to lie with other women is a drive
from the mother's blood. (256)

This myth that embodies Linda's existence is one that Audre (and Audre
Lorde, the author) pursues in her life. It bestows its name upon the text
and eventually, as Audre "spells" her name anew, upon the protagonist
herself: "*Zami. A Carriacou name for women who work together as friends and
lovers*" (255). Linda's history belongs to this island of women who love
each other; Carriacou is the source (the home) of Audre's identity as a
Black, women-loving woman. Although the text eventually reveals its
geographical location, Carriacou exists primarily as a "magic place," a
myth of origins, conveyed to Audre through her mother's words (14).
Precisely because Carriacou cannot be pinned down to any one point on
printed maps, it remains a place of the mind, of dreams and stories: the
place of the artist, the visionary, the lesbian. Lorde offers Carriacou as the
island home for Black lesbians floating in the maternal safe sea of
women.

Although few texts ascribe this much symbolic weight to the *biological* mother, all locate power, erotic identity, and home in the *historic* or
mythic foremothers of their cultures. The title of *The Law of Return,* for
example, is derived from the premise that Israel is a homeland for all
Jews. The parallel between the situation of Jews and lesbians is interesting and, for Jewish lesbians, ironic. Israel, of course, was a more real
homeland for ancient Jews than was Lesbos for lesbians. The latter has
always functioned primarily as a symbol. But after the diaspora, the
Jews were a dispossessed people, united by history, culture, and persecution, until the reclamation of a geographical home. Theoretically, lesbians desire a similar home in Lesbian Nation. Elisheva travels to Israel
in search of her Jewish roots as she will later journey back to America to
discover her lesbian home.

But unlike the matriarchal Carriacou, Israel is a patriarchal homeland. Elisheva longs for women and for learning, as well as for validation
as a Jew, and Israel denies her both. To be a Jew and a woman is self-
abnegating. To be a Jew and a lesbian is contradictory. The Law of
Return, both literally and symbolically, does not apply to homosexuals.
To be sure, Elisheva finds communities of women in Israel—at the
mikvah (ritual bath) and in the women's section of the synagogue—and

individual female friends. But these communities are actually ghettoes (afterthoughts or leftovers for the women) and the friendships are always secondary to marriage. Israel cannot be a home for Elisheva unless she returns as the Jewish wife of a Jewish husband.

Returning to her first home, the United States, Elisheva is beckoned into another community, that of women and lesbians. In the poster for the annual Christopher Street lesbian and gay pride march, she sees her lesbian double (as, in Israel, she had once encountered a Jewish-wife-and-mother double) winking and inviting her in. She remeets Deborah (there are no journeys or meetings in *The Law of Return,* always journeys *back* and meetings *again*), who had first revealed to her a female power uninhibited by Israeli patriarchy:

> "Female power," Deborah called it. The power to work. The power to make peace, to supply nothing to war, not even our love, to keep ourselves for each other, a peace-offering of our life together. The power to return to the source. The Law of Return. We have returned to our Biblical names, to the origins of our Jewish female power. (230–31)

Elisheva does indeed return home—not to Israel or America, but to women. Alienated as a Jew in America, as a lesbian in Israel, Elisheva is at first attracted to the image of the hermit or the lonely Bedouin. She withdraws even from Deborah into a fantasy of complete exile with no companion but the self. But as the conventions of lesbian feminist literature demand, Elisheva finally acknowledges her need for community, which she and Deborah will find, presumably, with other Jewish lesbians in the United States.

As in *Zami,* Elisheva discovers a symbolic home: as Linda's stories recreate the mythic women of Carriacou, so Yardena's folk songs transmit the ancient power of Jewish women. Both texts suggest that an oral tradition maintained by women underlies patriarchal culture. In *Abeng,* that tradition is represented by the legends of Mma Alli and the Savage family. Mma Alli was a slave woman who loved only women (including Clare's own great-great-grandmother), and taught them how to "keep their bodies as their own" (35). This love of women is inherited by Clare, whose selfhood is rooted in erotic desire first for her mother and then for

Zoe. But class divisions, homophobia, and the incest taboo all prevent Clare from achieving wholeness. Since Clare's story ends with her menarche, we see only the crisis of loss and alienation (her separation from Zoe), not the "rematriation" celebrated in other texts.

The Woman Who Owned the Shadows takes the quest one step further. Theresa, Ephanie's Anglo friend, joins Ephanie on her journey through inner space (the psyche) and then leaves, allowing Ephanie to journey on alone through legends to her final home, writing. These journeys lead her to weave the threads of her self into one web. Spiderwoman, the Indian Great Mother, is thus the alter ego for the writer, the weaver of words or spinner of tales. Ephanie finally understands her past and her future as a woman, Indian, lesbian, and writer. She enters into the song of the Doublewomen, the women who defy men and love women, who hold and use female power. Ephanie grows fully into her name as the novel ends in an epiphany of self-acceptance, joy, and activity.

THE QUEST FOR WHOLENESS

In most narratives by lesbians of color and ethnic lesbians, the protagonist finds her home and her selfhood in symbolic artifacts of female power, particularly the power of the mother. Her personal power, as Audre Lorde writes in "Poetry is Not a Luxury," is located in her otherness, that is, in her femaleness and darkness. Finding her source there, in the "ancient and hidden . . . deep places," the protagonist is finally made whole.[47]

According to the poststructuralist theory with which I began this discussion, such a vision of self and home comes close to being romantic, essentialist, and ahistorical. In certain ways, these authors seem to return to the maligned humanist self—a unitary, authoritarian fiction—we have already seen to be characteristic of much white lesbian literature. Poststructuralists, in contrast, prefer a more fragmented and open-ended self shaped through multiple discourses. But we shall see that these texts actually introduce a *third* version of self and home, that is neither unitary nor fragmented, a version that meets the needs of individuals already split into pieces by the various oppressive systems of American society. Moreover, the concept of self and community imagined by lesbians of color and ethnic lesbians provides a model for achieving unity amidst difference.

In many lesbian narratives, there is nonetheless one clear element of nostalgia: the yearning for a final resting place in an imaginary Mother. Critics Janice Doane and Devon Hodges define "nostalgia" as a longing for "home" and a "golden past"—a time when men were men, and women were wives and mothers. Some feminists, ironically enough, also idealize a lost female past that a woman recovers "through a nourishing relationship to her mythical maternal origins." Feminist nostalgia can result in a glorification of sexual difference uncannily similar to the antifeminist dream of the past (as we saw so strikingly in lesbian utopian fictions). Doane and Hodges suggest that the "assertion of difference gives women something tangible to affirm, a stable referent instead of the *vertigo* that comes when identity, so long linked to sexual difference, begins to slip" (italics mine).[48]

These words bring to mind the content and language of many lesbian narratives. To be sure, lesbian writers, of all races and ethnicities, appear to deemphasize sexual difference by deliberately underplaying the role of men in their stories. But although they suppress men they emphasize women to such a degree that, like the old moon in the new moon's arms, dualism reappears in the shadows. Women are still *essentially* women, perhaps even more so since the female sphere now expands to cover the whole world. In reaction to the "vertigo" she experiences, the protagonist seizes upon the "stable referent" of the idealized, mythicized mother/woman, which then becomes the model for the "true self."

We can see this process at work in most of the texts I have been discussing, and nowhere better than in *The Woman Who Owned the Shadows*. As she reshapes her experience of falling, Ephanie "grounds" herself in Indian legends and words to counter the "fragmentation" produced by the white man's "lying tongue":

> To re learn. To re member. To put back what had been shattered. To re mind. To re think. The beginning so as to grasp the end.
> So that stories, similes, piles upon piles of slick, wet, shiny metaphors that would breathe on their own, within themselves, among themselves, had to be made. And all the fragments of all the shattered hearts gathered carefully into one place. Tenderly cared for. Would grow. That truth. The one where all the waters would come together. Shipap. The Mother's home. The place of the one good heart. (190)

At the conclusion, when Ephanie recovers the story of The Woman Who Fell, she learns that this mythic figure literally became the earth, the very ground upon which we stand. Similarly, Gloria Anzaldúa writes that, despite her loss of home, "I didn't leave all the parts of me: I kept the ground of my own being" (16). And Audre Lorde speaks of "a piece of the real me bound in each place, and growing" (226).

At first glance, these selections appear to argue that a true, essential, unified being (a "stable referent") rests outside language and history and can be re-learned and re-membered. (Indeed, this "re" prefix, introduced by Adrienne Rich in "Writing as Re-vision," is ubiquitous in this group of texts, signifying the recovery of that which has been lost.)[49] *The Woman Who Owned the Shadows* celebrates the unified whole, personifying it in the one place of origins and destinations: Shipap, the Mother's home. The emphasis these texts place on mythic sources for identity further intensifies this impression of an essential, fixed female principle existing before history and society. All lesbian literature is mythic, but these ethnic fictions draw with particular force upon myth and legend to structure the quest for identity and home.

According to Paula Gunn Allen, myth "allows a holistic image to pervade and shape consciousness, thus providing a coherent and empowering matrix for action and relationship."[50] Since myth helps heal the wounds caused by fragmentation, women of color and ethnic women draw upon their cultures' rich and distinctive mythic languages to construct a self. Elisheva is attracted to such heroines of Hebrew myth as Vashti and Lilit, and, with Deborah, to a mystical, nostalgic memory of their ancient mothers: "We have raised our arms in the arc of sacred dance. We have danced to the rhythm of the timbrel. We have sung the ancient songs and the sounds of the first language have hummed in our throats. We have wept over the crops" (231). The Savage family, in *Abeng,* constructs "a carefully contrived mythology . . . to protect their identities," which Clare then extends to her own myths of maternal power and eroticism (29). Audre finds first in her mother, then in women's bodies, and finally in tales of the West Indies and Africa a grounding for her emerging identity.

In short, these narratives express a certain degree of yearning for a return to a mythic, preexisting source and origins, a Mother who guarantees a fixed, unchanging Self. Poststructuralist feminist theorists attack this notion of identity and selfhood—"the real me, the essential matriarchal origin"—as being rigid and uncannily similar to patriarchal constructions of femininity. But having said that, I must question to what extent it really matters. Is this holistic self nevertheless *necessary* to subjects who have been denied the unified identity allowed to those who are white or male or heterosexual? Is the celebration of the mother/ woman life-affirming for groups whose roots and culture have been consistently attacked? Virtually all lesbians of color (and white lesbians as well) write that fragmentation is a sign of oppression, not liberation. Most claim that to be split between multiple "homes" or aspects of identity is alienating and disempowering.

The writings of lesbians of color in particular express what Audre Lorde calls "the fever of wanting to be whole," the need to integrate all the parts of the self and to find a community in which this unified self can be at home (*Zami,* 190). As Lorde writes in an essay collected in *Sister Outsider:*

> As a Black lesbian feminist comfortable with the many different ingredients of my identity, and a woman committed to racial and sexual freedom from oppression, I find I am constantly being encouraged to pluck out some one aspect of myself and present this as the meaningful whole, eclipsing or denying the other parts of self. But this is a destructive and fragmenting way to live. My fullest concentration of energy is available to me only when I integrate all the parts of who I am, openly, allowing power from particular sources of my living to flow back and forth freely through all my different selves, without the restrictions of externally imposed definition. Only then can I bring myself and my energies as a whole to the service of those struggles which I embrace as part of my living.[51]

Wholeness is power; wholeness is the path toward a previously denied authority.

Becky Birtha depicts the protagonist of her short story, "Ice Castle" in a manner very similar to Lorde's description of her position in the world:

> She loved giving readings—that was the one time when she felt completely visible. For all her colorfulness, for all her beads and bangles and bright batik prints, most of the time she felt that other people didn't see all of her. They saw only what mattered most to them at the time—her race, or her gender, or perhaps her age—and

then didn't bother to look any further. It was only when she was on stage, standing up among a room full of attentive listeners, that she felt all her colors leap into focus. (*Lovers' Choice*, 27)

The metaphor for the self used by this author is that of color; her hero dresses in many colors to symbolize the many aspects of her self. If any one aspect of the self takes priority over the others, it is the poet-self; reading her poetry highlights all the other aspects of her identity. No one aspect overshadows the other; together they come into focus as a canvas of colors that blend, accentuate, and perhaps even clash.

In contrast to essentialist or nostalgic writing, the notion of the holistic, unified self expressed by Lorde and Birtha is not static; the self is not a thing-in-itself reducing all variety and inconsistency beneath an emphatic and imperial Lesbian essence. Nor for that matter can race or class identity reign supreme. The self that emerges in these texts is fluid, shimmering, and mobile, because it is a self whose "place [is] the very house of difference rather than the security of any one particular difference" (*Zami*, 226).[52]

SHIFTING THE GROUND BENEATH THE SELF

At the same time that these texts affirm the condition of wholeness, however, they also adopt strategies that disturb the "ground" beneath the Self. This is necessary because the writers also imagine new ways in which to establish a multicultural women's community. Perhaps the greatest drawback to the notion of an essential Self—whether that Self successfully merges its many aspects or not—is that it is difficult to see how relationships can be established between monolithic and enclosed Selves. Instead, a concept of a *multivalent* self—one that has multiple capacities for combination and interaction—allows for both interconnectedness and change.

The lesbian community, like the lesbian self, was envisioned by white women in the 1970s as monochromatic and uniform. As that uniformity broke down, however, smaller and smaller units containing more and more narrowly defined categories of self became the rule. Eventually, it seemed, in place of Lesbian Nation, we had microscopic rooms containing one or two women apiece. Like cells, we divided and divided again; but, unlike cells, we had no instructions for how to cohere into one complex being. The notion of self that these writers favor provides an opening between the Scylla of monolithic identities and communities and the Charybdis of endlessly fragmented ones.

Narrative structure within these texts displaces the comfortable unity and stasis that their language sometimes implies. As I have said, these are unconventional narratives. *Loving in the War Years* and *Borderlands/La Frontera* are collections of short autobiographical narratives, essays, and poems. *Zami* is autobiography posing as fiction—or fiction posing as autobiography. Although *The Woman Who Owned the Shadows, The Law of Return,* and *Abeng* are more easily recognizable as novels, none has a linear plot or character development. In each, chronology is circuitous: the storyline is disrupted by dreams and digressions, and the protagonist finds and loses and then finds herself over and over again.

This nonlinear structure, combined with the protagonist's yearning for completion in a mythic mother or female spirit, leads to conflict in the endings of the texts. Typically the ending leaves the hero's life *symbolically* closed and complete, but *narratively* open and uncertain.[53] Each text suggests that no matter how uncertain of her identity the protagonist is, she carries within her what she needs to "re-member" her self. *Abeng* ends with Clare at menarche, the threshhold of adulthood, having resolved none of the complexities of her situation. But the last lines of the text point toward future integration: "She was not ready to understand her dream. She had no idea that everyone we dream about we are" (166). Clearly, it is implied, one day Clare will understand her dream. *The Law of Return* concludes with an image of women singing and dancing together as they did in the time of Miriam and Moses, but also with a contemporary acknowledgment that "as long as we are alive, we will struggle toward community. We are nowhere at home, but in talking with each other we will build a home of language, a nest of words" (248). *The Woman Who Owned the Shadows,* like *The Law of Return,* ends with a mythic image of "singing and dancing in the ancient steps of the women," but, narratively, Ephanie has just begun to move along her path toward wholeness and authenticity (213). None of these conclusions claim that the hero's journey is an easy or natural one; each seems as much a beginning as an ending.

Zami illustrates this point with particular complexity. The plot moves through Audre's relationship with a wounded white woman,

Muriel, to its dissolution, a fitting conclusion to a tragic tale of doomed lesbian lovers—the very tale that was written during the 1950s. But the story of Muriel and Audre, which leaves Audre lonely, fragmented, and adrift, is followed by a final chapter and epilogue. The last chapter takes the narrative back to a time when Audre and Muriel had attended lesbian parties together.[54] There, Audre met another Black lesbian, Kitty, whom she meets again following her break-up with Muriel. Audre and Kitty have a short and gloriously erotic affair that ends when Kitty leaves New York and Audre forever. The storyline concludes with a scene of loss and absence, rather than fulfillment and completion.

But on another level, Kitty never leaves Audre. For Kitty's real name (or the name Lorde gives her) is Afrekete, the "youngest daughter" of "the great mother of us all"—the "mischievous linguist, trickster, best-beloved, whom we must all become" (255). Throughout the narrative of their brief affair, Lorde intersperses paragraphs that mythicize her lover and their love. Kitty becomes Afrekete; their lovemaking is ritualized; their relationship confirms Audre's acceptance of her erotic self. The last sentence of the chapter, like the last sentence of *Abeng*, proclaims: "I never saw Afrekete again, but her print remains upon my life with the resonance and power of an emotional tattoo" (253). The short epilogue that follows expands that statement into a manifesto of identity and relationship: "Every woman I have ever loved has left her print upon me, where I loved some invaluable piece of myself apart from me—so different that I had to stretch and grow in order to recognize her. And in that growing, we came to separation, that place where work begins. Another meeting" (255). Lorde's auto-biography, then, is equally an other-biography. It answers the question—"who is the other woman?"—by showing that she is almost imperceptibly part of one's self. But this answer does not result in some inchoate merging of identities, but rather in "separation," a space in which new concepts of self, relationship, and community can be created. As she says, "Once *home* was a long way off, a place I had never been to but knew out of my mother's mouth. I only discovered its latitudes when Carriacou *was no longer my home*" (256; latter italics mine).

Lorde's evocation of her Caribbean foremothers and her African mythic mothers, of Carriacou and home, is by no means a nostalgic longing for a lost utopia. More profoundly, "home" is an idea that helps the writer shape her destiny and discover a nurturing community based upon difference and struggle. So empowered, she can recreate the stories she inherits in her own texts.

All these texts are acutely conscious of the complex shaping power of language. At the same time that writing provides a way to integrate the self, it also unsettles the self and propels it from home. As Cherríe Moraga says, "This is my politics. This is my writing. For as much as the two have eventually brought me back to my familia, there is no fooling myself that it is my education, my 'consciousness' that separated me from them. That forced me to leave home" (*Loving in the War Years,* ii–iii). The myths these authors rely on are chosen for literary and *political* reasons. In "An Open Letter to Mary Daly," Lorde chastises white feminists for ignoring the totality of female culture: "why doesn't Mary deal with Afrekete as an example? Why are her goddess images only white, western european, judeo-christian? Where was Afrekete, Yemanje, Oyo, and Mawulisa? Where were the warrior goddesses of the Vodun, the Dahomeian Amazons and the warrior-women of Dan?"[55] When Lorde uses Afrekete and Mawulisa as inspiring images in *Zami,* and Allen draws upon Spider Grandmother and Spirit Woman in *The Woman Who Owned the Shadows,* they offer a political correction to the ethnocentric vision of white women as well as an affirmation of their own cultural traditions.

Dispossessed of home, whether because of education or lesbianism, the lesbian of color or ethnic lesbian must construct a new community that does not eliminate any of the multiple positions from which she speaks. This is no easy task. She may feel herself drawn to a unified, closed community. But to make this choice would require shutting out all the multiple voices of difference.[56] Sometimes the protagonist—like Audre, Ephanie, Clare, or Sunny in *Triangles*—welcomes the voices of difference by pursuing a relationship with a woman of a different race, religion, or class. Yet the question of how to create a lesbian community that can be "home" to women with such varying identities—a multicultural island or cosmopolitan nation—has no easy answer. Home, as lesbians of the dominant culture have imagined it, "refers to the place where one lives within familiar, safe, protected boundaries;" but, as Bernice Reagon points out, once opened up to the "other woman"— whoever she is—home is no longer safe.[57]

Ultimately we may no longer be able to think of the lesbian community as "home" but as "the house of difference." As critics Biddy Martin and Chandra Mohanty conclude:

> The assumption of, or desire for, another safe place like "home" is challenged by the realization that "unity"—interpersonal as well as political—is itself necessarily fragmentary, itself that which is struggled for, chosen, and hence unstable by definition; it is not based on "sameness," and there is no perfect fit. But there is agency as opposed to passivity.[58]

The new version of community suggested through the writings of lesbians of color and ethnic lesbians (including white as a particular ethnicity) is not guaranteed by any shared lesbian identity or female experience. It is not a recreation of some recoverable ancient female past. It is not a gift from the Great Mother. Instead it "is the product of work, of struggle; it is inherently unstable, contextual; it has to be constantly reevaluated in relation to critical political priorities; and it is the product of interpretation."[59]

Because it is the product of work and interpretation, this notion of community cannot be fixed in language. For this reason, the texts I have discussed only hint at what community might look like. Alice Bloch, as we saw, calls it "a home of language, a nest of words." Gloria Anzaldúa writes: "I am participating in the creation of yet another culture, a new story to explain the world and our participation in it, a new value system with images and symbols that connect us to each other and to the planet" (*Borderlands,* 81). Audre Lorde states that lesbians "were probably the only Black and white women in New York City in the fifties who were making any real attempt to communicate with each other," that they "tried to build a community of sorts," by talking "endlessly about how best to create that mutual support which twenty years later was being discussed in the women's movement as a brand-new concept" (*Zami,* 179).

It is not incidental that these writers use speech, communication, and storytelling as metaphors for community-building. In one way, the women's or lesbian community is a "product of interpretation" in the sense that its definition and perimeters are constantly changing in response to experience and history. The terms that Anzaldúa uses to describe the situation of the *mestiza* refer also to the borderland community in which she resides: "Numerous possibilities leave *la mestiza* floundering in uncharted seas. In perceiving conflicting information and points of view, she is subjected to a swamping of her psychological borders. She has discovered that she can't hold concepts or ideas in rigid boundaries" (*Borderlands,* 79). But the community is also a product of interpretation (that is, of language or discourse) in that it is being *written* right in front of our eyes. It does not simply predate the texts that describe it. As these writers write new selves—as both Audre and Elisheva learn to spell their names anew—so too do they write new configurations of Lesbian Nation and help create it in the world.

The strikingly autobiographical and experimental narratives written by lesbians of color and ethnic lesbians in the mid-1980s unsettle the static and conventional notions of self and community created by the dominant mythology of white lesbian feminists. They remind us that we are creating new stories that must constantly be retold, much as bards reshaped the old epics each time they sang. The impulse to fix our stories—as writing fixed the oral tales in one and only one version—is strong within our community. But we have learned that no one version of lesbianism can ever signify the totality of our diverse and changing lives. Although lesbian literature is, of course, a written form, not an oral tradition, the multitude of texts and multiplicity of perspectives ought to assure us that we never have, nor would we want, one lesbian *Iliad* or *Song of Roland.* Still, the danger remains that our conventions and stereotypes will become so firmly entrenched that we stamp out version after version of the same lesbian tale. To avoid this, we need to keep in mind the words "work," "struggle," and "interpretation"; we might further adopt the values of instability and change over those of fixedness and home. Our Lesbian Nation can then expand beyond one class or race until lesbian heroes float free in imaginative space, occupying no one single position from which they always speak, but moving, rather, among all possible positions and communicating all possible points of view.

6 〰〰〰

"Where Do We Go from Here?"
The Present Moment

Here we are and the singing is fun
Here we are and we're loving as one
And we're feeling the answers growing more clear, so where
Where do we go from here?
—*Meg Christian, "Where Do We Go from Here"*

"I thought I was home. But I wasn't. And now, there's no more
movement, we're all scattered and all hell's breaking loose all over the
world. . . . . I couldn't find me anymore. Everything's changing and I'm
frightened."
—*Jean Swallow,* LEAVE A LIGHT ON FOR ME

The story of lesbian feminist fiction resembles the stories I explored in chapter 5, a tale told in "fits and starts." Moreover, it is impossible to draw final conclusions about a phenomenon still undergoing change and development, one that at any moment might unravel the strands that neatly tie up a thesis. Since no book that ends at "the present moment" can trim all its loose ends, this chapter must be ungainly, with bits of paper and twine sticking out at odd angles.[1] This said, I will conclude by surveying the most recently published lesbian fiction (roughly, 1986 through 1988) in order to suggest in what ways the established patterns of the genre have endured, and what new directions are emerging.

Lesbian fiction of the 1970s and early 1980s created a "mythography," an imaginative representation of what lesbian feminists believed to be true about lesbian identity, relationships, culture, and community. This fiction was idealistic, visionary, and closely connected to the community whose views it reflected and influenced. Today, the lesbian novel is sustained as much by commerce as by community. The lesbian publishing industry is more prolific than it has ever been: the trailblazing writers and publishers of the seventies created a fiercely devoted audience that sustains several commercially successful alternative presses and journals, each with its own point of view and readership. Between 1973 and 1981, an average of only five lesbian novels was published each year; between 1984 and 1987, that number had jumped to twenty-three, and recent figures indicate that the pace is quickening. Lesbian fiction has permeated the mass marketplace as well; nonlesbian feminist novels are increasingly likely to incorporate lesbian themes and characters, and certain novels that would only have appeared under the aegis of a feminist or lesbian press a decade or even a year ago are now published by mainstream companies.[2] Lesbian fiction also has established itself in countries other than the United States, especially Great Britain and Canada (both English- and French-speaking), suggesting that, as Monique Wittig once claimed, the lesbian community is an international phenomenon.

But that community has changed profoundly during the 1980s. Although vestiges of Lesbian Nation can still be found, it is a far less powerful and cohesive idea than it was a decade ago. The influence of feminism is weaker, or more diffuse, as in society at large. Consequently, lesbian fiction is less visionary and mythic, its voice less communal and more individual, even idiosyncratic. One positive result of this shift has been an overall improvement in the quality of individual texts. Although no one has written, or can write, The Great Lesbian Novel, many authors today are writing very good lesbian novels.

At the same time, however, we appear to have replaced the naive but invigorating optimism and idealism of our recent past with an uneasiness and complacency, even a cynicism, that is new and disconcerting. A literature so closely tied to a particular community of writers and readers could not possibly remain unaffected by the state of that community. Although it is premature to draw final conclusions about the lesbian feminist community in 1990, it appears less vital than it was a decade ago. The generation who fashioned its ideals, politics, and institutions has "burned out" or "grown up," depending on one's point of view, and, as with other post-sixties political movements, no new generation has stepped in to take over the struggle. Like the rest of American society, many lesbians seem primarily interested in personal and economic growth. Women who, a decade ago, might have been in the thick of the "feminist," "separatist," "downwardly-mobile" lifestyle now dismiss such terms as anachronisms, opting instead for well-paying jobs and perhaps donor insemination. With the commercial success of lesbian culture, we can buy our books and records and our long holiday weekend at a music festival without giving a second thought to the making and sustaining of an alternative lesbian vision.

Furthermore, the AIDS crisis has had a devastating effect on Lesbian Nation. Some of this devastation we share with gay men: AIDS has provided new "justification" for homophobia, temporarily derailing some of the progress made by the gay civil rights movement. Moreover, because of a combination of politics, compassion, and even guilt, many lesbians have abandoned separate lesbian institutions and struggle to build a united gay movement focused around AIDS.[3] Other politically active lesbians are directing their attention to coalition work around such concerns as nuclear energy or foreign policy rather than to exclusively lesbian activism. Fewer women-only spaces exist, and fewer women openly demand them. If it becomes unfashionable, indeed "politically incorrect," to have exclusively lesbian activities and environments, it will certainly be impossible to sustain the idea of Lesbian Nation.

The fiction of the past few years reflects these changes within the community first by giving fictional representation to the social realities of the late 1980s, such as AIDS and the so-called Moral Majority.[4] But more significantly, it reflects the general *mood* of lesbians today—whether we name it maturity or malaise—and hence has more to say about loss, compromise, and accommodation than about community and triumph. The fiction also reflects the movement of the lesbian subculture from the margins of society to a place nearer the center. After a certain point in its history, a group may lose its sense of radical opposition and desire a more comfortable place within the larger community. As a result, its members can reflect upon their similarities to and connections with other groups and individuals, not only their differences and separations.

At the same time, the dominant society manifests no noticeable acceptance of lesbians or the gay lifestyle. Indeed, the world appears more precarious than in the optimistic seventies. Moreover, public awareness of the many forms of violence directed against women has grown significantly during the eighties. As lesbian writers pay more attention to the everyday realities of their lives, they find they must attend to everyday violence. Lesbian fiction in the late 1980s, therefore, brings a new question to bear on the myths and genres developed in the 1970s: is it at all possible to find or create a refuge in our apocalyptic world? Can the "safe sea of women" be truly safe?

Reconsidering the Myths

The previous chapters have charted the representative journey of the lesbian hero, from coming out through falling in love to setting up housekeeping in Lesbian Nation. Each of these steps in the journey is being reconsidered by current lesbian writers. It is, for example, a newly established truth that we have "gone beyond" the coming out novel. We have dealt with that, the received wisdom intones, and are on to bigger and better subjects. Lesbian fiction "is finally growing up" because it no longer focuses on coming out and falling in love.[5]

Although this generalization oversimplifies past and present fiction, it is evident that lesbian writers no longer focus on the drama of coming out as a lesbian. How I came out—how I discovered my real self—no longer engages our attention. We *are* out, and it's time to get on with our lives. If a character does move from heterosexuality to lesbianism, the story typically emphasizes the establishment of a relationship rather than the exploration of the boundaries of the self. Only one post-1985 novel—*Shoulders* by Georgia Cotrell—is shaped like such classic lesbian coming out novels as *Rubyfruit Jungle, Riverfinger Women, Yesterday's Lessons,* and *Who Was That Masked Woman? Shoulders* narrates the picaresque journey of the hero along the path to lesbian selfhood, but, unlike most of her seventies predecessors, Cotrell's Bobby Crawford is totally uninterested in the *why's* of lesbianism. She recognizes and accepts herself as a lesbian on page thirteen, and having come out with hardly a *frisson* of guilt or shame, she quickly moves on to the *how's* of lesbianism: "It never occurred to me to be depressed, because suddenly there was a world of pursuable pleasure lying in wait for me" (13). Bobby's journey takes her not through layers of self-doubt and societal oppression, but from one lover to another in her search for the one true love that draws her journey to completion.

But if the coming out novel has become an endangered species in the late 1980s, the quest tale continues to be a fundamental lesbian form. The contemporary quest hero takes for granted the meaning of her lesbian existence, using it as a starting point for different types of adventures. She may be looking for a lover, so the lesbian adventure story, like the coming out novel, still leads to the lesbian romance. Some lesbian adventures borrow and reshape such popular quest genres as the western (for example, *The Long Trail, The Journey,* and *Yellowthroat*) or the spy novel (*The Pearls, Osten's Bay,* and, more loosely, *N.E.W.S.*). But the most popular adventure genre in the late 1980s continues to be the detective story. Since *Daughters* in 1977 introduced the first lesbian detective—M. F. Beal's Katarina Guerrera—Vicki McConnell, Camarin Grae, Sarah Schulman, Barbara Wilson, Katherine Forrest, Sarah Dreher, Lauren Wright Douglas, Marion Foster, Antoinette

Azolakov, Mary Wings, Diana McRae, and Claire McNab all have created more or less traditional detective novels that tell specifically lesbian
stories. Furthermore, the resolution of a mystery, if not necessarily a
crime, is incorporated into the plots of many other novels as well. The
lesbian detective novel has replaced the SF/utopian novel as the quintessential lesbian genre.

As one reviewer points out, the lesbian detective genre "is an obvious
form for expressing the search for social justice denied by the institutions
of the mainstream culture."[6] It is also an appropriate genre for exposing
what has become a central lesbian concern, the danger lurking within
the heterosexist, male-dominated world. The role of the lesbian detective, as in the mainstream American tradition, is to wade into the midst
of evil, wrestle with the monster, and bring it to bay—sometimes re-
storing a momentary semblance of stability and order but sometimes
emerging compromised and shaken by the battle. In the lesbian detective novel, that evil is typically bound up with male power, privilege,
and abusive sexuality. Although the main crime to be solved is usually
conventional murder, it may be complicated by other crimes including
incest, extortion, kidnapping, and various other betrayals of female integrity. The detective, who in the late 1980s may be a professional but is
more likely to be an amateur, must discover who is harming women,
specifically lesbians, in order to repair the fragile defenses we have built
around Lesbian Nation.

Unhappily for the reader, however, the genre has quickly developed a
constricting set of conventions and expectations. Since the point of the
undertaking is to indict patriarchy or homophobia, only a few lesbian
detective novelists construct an effective plot leading to a resolution both
surprising and inevitable. The guilty party is either immediately obvious (the nastiest man or most manipulative woman is a good bet) or
revealed in a haphazard way. Moreover, only occasionally does the lesbian detective novel set a believable cast of characters into motion
through a realistic landscape.

In fact, the most recent novels—even the adventures and pica-
resques—present a more stationary world than did their predecessors.
There is less journeying in them, less use of the metaphor of travel, less
adventuring and risk-taking. Willyce Kim's *Dancer Dawkins and the
California Kid,* for example, promises at first to be a rollicking lesbian

take-off on "buddy" adventure stories. Two odd, individualistic characters, each traveling toward San Francisco from a different direction,
literally crash together on Highway One and set up a partnership. But
once in the city, the author entangles her characters in a bizarre quasi-
mystery from which neither plot nor characters emerge intact. The protagonist of Elizabeth Dean's *As the Road Curves* sets off on a search for
Lesbian Nation (a lesbian revision of *Travels with Charley* or *Blue High-
ways*) but makes a quick detour into her own romantic past.

Sarah Schulman's three novels, published between 1984 and 1988,
provide other examples of the inward spiraling of the lesbian picaresque.
The Sophie Horowitz Story, as I have written, takes the hero on a lively
journey through several New York City boroughs. The novel is full
of energy and movement, even when it is exploring ugly secrets.
Schulman's world has shrunk considerably in *Girls, Visions and Everything*. Although her title recalls Douglas Adams' space romp, *Life, The
Universe and Everything*, its actual universe is limited to the Lower East
Side. The novel's copious references to Jack Kerouac evoke not *On the
Road*, but *The Subterraneans*. Finally, the plot of *After Delores*, combining
the murder mystery of the first novel with the romantic quest of the
second, is set in the claustrophobic world of the narrator's own despair.

Lesbian protagonists today are more likely to journey inward than
outward, and to take risks over the state of their souls rather than the
state of society. The classic coming out novel depicted the linear movement of the hero toward triumph, but today she is turning back "to see
the damage that was done"—to confront the demons of violence, abuse,
even guilt and shame.[7] Post-1985 novels are virtually obsessed with the
ways in which we heal the wounds inflicted by damaging pasts, inade-
quate relationships, and a violent society. Hence, the most notably
original form of the lesbian novel to emerge in the late 1980s is the story
of recovery from a traumatic experience or condition such as incest, child
abuse, rape, alcoholism, or eating disorders.

The novel of recovery is a variant of the mystery, since its purpose is to
investigate and resolve crimes. In the mystery, the investigation takes
place in city streets and back alleys; in the novel of recovery, it takes place
in the protagonist's psyche. But in each case the world within the novel
is marked by male violence and danger, and the investigation results in a
painful confrontation with evil and an often incomplete restoration of

social and personal order. Through therapy and support groups, forms of psychological detection, the protagonist discovers and exorcises the source of evil and restores her power and integrity. The closeness of these two forms is neatly demonstrated by Camarin Grae's *The Secret in the Bird,* in which the protagonist Rena's inward journey to the source of her psychological disturbance leads to the discovery and resolution of a crime.

Of all the damage explored in lesbian novels of recovery, incest has become particularly notable. Prior to 1986, incest in the lesbian novel took the *metaphoric* shape of love between sisters or mothers and daughters. I can only find reference to real-life father-daughter incest in *Clenched Fists, Burning Crosses* and to brother-sister incest in *Lovers in the Present Afternoon* (both 1984). But since 1986, incest—in its now-familiar form of male abuse of women—is present in a striking number of novels and short stories, among them *Sunday's Child, Leave a Light on For Me, Sisters of the Road, Unusual Company, Searching for Spring, Murder at the Nightwood Bar,* and stories in *A Letter to Harvey Milk* and *Trash.* In some of these, incest is essential to the development of plot or character. Patricia Murphy's *Searching for Spring,* for example, reads as an incest survivor's case history or a tool for therapy. But in other novels, incest is only intimated or is ultimately irrelevant to the novel, which raises the question of why it is there in the first place.

Why has incest become such a significant motif in lesbian fiction? The answer does not necessarily lie in a representational theory of literature; there is no reliable evidence that lesbians are any more likely than other women to be incest survivors, or that lesbianism is "caused" by sexual trauma. Lesbians may very well have a particular sensitivity to incest, however, that pervades the stories we tell and are willing to hear.[8] In lesbian feminist culture, incest has become the paradigm of patriarchal power, the ultimate abuse by the Father. (Writers used to personify the snake in the garden as the husband, but today the father has all but taken his place.) The most sharply delineated location of what we might call feminist/separatist anger against men and male power is found today in the incest story. Since incest occurs within what is supposed to be a place of primal safety, the nuclear family, to expose its deadliest secret is to demonstrate what lesbians have stated all along: the only safe space for women is the space women make for themselves.

If incest symbolizes the ultimate betrayal by others, alcohol and drug abuse have come to stand for the betrayal of one's self. It is hardly surprising that in the "just say no" eighties, lesbian fiction should take up the topic of addiction, since substance abuse is argued to be a more serious problem for lesbians than for other groups.[9] As a result of this belief, the community not only accepts but encourages identification with and participation in recovery programs. (Always sensitive to the needs of particular individuals, the lesbian community regularly offers chemical-free spaces similar to the way that it mandates wheelchair accessibility and sign language interpretation.) The community's attitude toward alcohol has shifted dramatically from the romanticism of *Sister Gin* to the realism (occasionally bordering on moralism) of Jean Swallow's *Leave a Light On for Me,* Lee Lynch's *Dusty's Queen of Hearts Diner,* and Patricia Murphy's *We Walk the Back of the Tiger.* Indeed, the most recent of these novels, Marion Michener's *Three Glasses of Wine,* deliberately rewrites June Arnold's liberatory sister as a burden and hindrance: "What I couldn't see was how sister wine followed me out of that house like a puppy who was sure she belonged with me" (85).

Different texts associate substance abuse with lesbianism in different ways. Bonnie Arthur's *Night Lights* is atypical in its offhand suggestion that both homosexuality and addiction are genetic and interconnected. Other novels present social rather than biological explanations. *Dusty's Queen of Hearts Diner* and *Leave a Light On for Me* both relate alcoholism to self-hatred and internalized oppression, while *We Walk the Back of the Tiger* indicts the drug culture of the seventies. *Three Glasses of Wine* makes the astute point that the lesbian and gay communities value alcohol "as an instrument of seduction and communion" (139). But not even this realistic and moving novel associates alcohol abuse with the lesbian bar, which remains a protected site of lesbian community.

No doubt recovery has become a prominent theme in current lesbian fiction in part because recovery programs of all kinds have taken an ever more central place in lesbian and gay culture. But the *literary* attention to incest, alcoholism, and other forms of abuse has as much to do with the privileged place accorded the personal narrative in women's communities and with the centrality of the metaphor of safety in lesbian fiction. As one recent critic points out: "Twelve-step programs provide at least one thing that all people—but especially socially stigmatized people—

are desperate to find: a predictably safe place in which to feel understood and accepted." [10] Recovery groups and recovery novels both function as retreats, islands, in which to heal the pain caused by misogyny and homophobia.

But a safe place is not enough to bring about true healing. For that we need the power of language. Historically, the women's liberation movement popularized the process of consciousness-raising, modeled on the revolutionary Chinese practice of "speaking bitterness" and the African-American tradition of testifying. In the telling of our individual stories, we learned that personal pain was in fact communal outrage; the result was personal and political empowerment. Although the first lesbian organizations were not necessarily structured as consciousness-raising groups, the idea of *speaking* ourselves out of oppression, of ending silence as a path toward liberation, has had a profound impact on the development of lesbian culture. The support groups that form the backbone of the recovery movement are clearly linked to the philosophy and organization of the feminist and lesbian movements. From consciousness-raising to coming out stories to twelve-step programs, the personal narrative has always held a place of honor in our community. The step from the personal narrative to the semiautobiographical novel of recovery is short and inevitable.

Turning to the second lesbian myth of origins, the lesbian couple, we find that writers have been questioning the safety and security of this seemingly unshakable unit. In the past a reader could rest assured that, no matter what went on for approximately two hundred pages, a lesbian novel would have a happy ending. Although a few early novels, like *Rubyfruit Jungle* and *Sister Gin,* criticized monogamy, over and over again lesbian lovers live happily ever after. After decades of reading pulp novels in which the lesbian couple suffered death, destruction, and dissolution, lesbian readers demanded a fair share of happy endings. Not surprisingly, then, lesbian novels rarely chronicled the end of lesbian relationships, or even their middle, only their beginning. There is still a type of lesbian novel—what cartoonist Alison Bechdel parodies as Generic Romance #423 and what others call, either affectionately or contemptuously, lesbian pulps or lesbian trash—that tells the same old story: girl meets girl, girl loses girl (maybe), girl gets girl (definitely). [11] Or, in the words of Barbara Wilson's antiromantic hero, Pam Nilsen, a "little confusion and then the happy ending, souls and bodies merging into Sapphic oneness" (*Sisters of the Road,* 174).

Even the pulps have begun to evince a certain uneasiness with the happily-ever-after formula, however. In a curious new romance convention, the protagonist's first lover dies early in the text, leaving her to be consoled by a new Princess Charming. The lesbian Harlequin itself must acknowledge that love does not bloom eternal, although death is still more acceptable than divorce. Moreover, several fine novels—among them Margaret Erhard's *Unusual Company,* Barbara Wilson's *Cows and Horses,* Sarah Schulman's *After Delores,* Jean Swallow's *Leave a Light On for Me,* and Jan Clausen's *The Prosperine Papers*—explore how relationships founder and sometimes end, what happens after a divorce, how lovers deal with grief and turn themselves back into separate selves. A decade after the searing honesty of *Sister Gin* and *Sita,* the romantic myth of eternal bliss finally has loosened its grip enough so that novelists can take up the story of pain and division.

Unusual Company, for example, takes us from the beginning of a love affair through its ending to the emergence of its protagonist as an adult ready to take her place in a world of women. The relationship between Franny and Claire is edenic, but the author's interpretation of the Garden is iconoclastic. Paradise, exemplified by their claustrophobic relationship, is an "imaginary world" contrasted to "the worlds of memory and possibility" (27, 29). Almost from its beginning moments, then, their relationship dissolves: "In my stronger moments I could see we were ending, and that this ending was the natural and inevitable one for our relationship. That two people would come together at all seemed such a miracle" (113).

Like a New World Eve, like any quest hero, Franny comes alive and free when she leaves the protective circle of home and undertakes an epic journey across America. Moving east to west (a counter-journey to Claire's, who moves spiritually from west to east), Frannie discovers women's community: "I was aware, always as if for the first time, that the world was populated by women. For a year before that, the world had been populated only by Claire" (136). Eventually she finds a new lover who brings the words "lesbian" and "dyke" into the text for the first time. But Frannie and Claire are both on journeys that reunite them in one last cathartic sexual encounter. It may be, as one reviewer claims, that the violence of this scene is out of character and intrusive.[12] It certainly contradicts all our myths of lesbian sexuality—including those of lesbian S/M advocates, since the violence has little to do with sexual arousal—and so proves very disquieting (especially since the novel is one of the few to receive attention outside the lesbian community). Despite this uncharacteristic scene, however, *Unusual Company* retains a trace of lesbian feminist optimism in Franny's concluding observation that Claire "made it easy for me now to love every woman I loved, and before she had made it impossible" (224).

Cows and Horses and *After Delores* are, to varying degrees, less optimistic. *Cows and Horses* recounts the familiar ways in which the protagonist, Bet, attempts to heal herself after the end of a long relationship. She mourns, she lashes out in anger, she tries arbitration, and, of course, she has an affair. But the novel leads her away from solutions that lie in another woman or even in other women. Ultimately she must rely on herself to rebuild her self-esteem and identity.

Bet finds her resources in what at first might seem an unlikely place, narratives of daily life during war: "Lately she had been reading about the Second World War in Europe. Not the battles, but how it was to live in Paris during the occupation, or London during the Blitz. What it was like to be an evacuee, a refugee, a bare survivor. She was interested in the everyday life of people who suffered momentous change: what they ate, what they wore, how they entertained themselves" (13). These stories of war and survival prove to be uniquely appropriate to Bet's mood and to the mood of our times. Rather than feeling like warriors and outlaws, as we did in the optimistic seventies, we now portray ourselves as refugees. To survive, the novel suggests, we need to ground ourselves in daily life. At the end, Bet concludes that she will find a "home" or safe space within herself: "I will buy a house of my own and never again stand outside looking in" (196). With this awareness, and in the last line of the novel, Bet is finally able to grieve for her loss.

If there is some sense at the end of *Cows and Horses* that Bet will heal herself, there is none at the conclusion of *After Delores*. It is the grimmest of these antiromances. Having been dumped by Delores, the unnamed protagonist wanders the nocturnal streets of the Lower East Side with a pistol in her pocket, unsure when to use it or even on whom. The novel is so drenched in violence and anger that the story of the end of an affair inexorably leads to the story of murder. The Wagnerian conjunction of love and death, hinted at throughout, is at one point made explicit: "Charlotte and Beatriz held a secret for me, but I couldn't tell if their answer lay in love or violence. Whenever one was apparent the other stirred in the shadows. I could not integrate those two feelings into my life the way they fit together so perfectly in theirs" (100). Although the narrator solves one mystery in the course of her journey, she does not solve the central one: how do love and violence fit together; why does love cause such pain? The novel ends on a note of exhaustion and ir-resolution: "There were many, many questions that remained and which I had no energy or ability to continue to try and solve. I could only ignore them. I was not a satisfied woman. I was only quiet" (154). Unlike Wilson's Bet, Schulman's narrator does not work through her grief; after all her adventures she still misses Delores.

In contrast to these pessimistic novels, most lesbian mysteries offer the detective a love relationship as a respite from violence and despair. Like other examples of the quest genre, the lesbian detective novel often modulates from adventure story to romance, providing an interesting twist to the conventions of detective fiction. Male or heterosexual female detectives may indulge in affairs, but they remain loners. But the lesbian mystery writer works within that convention *and* the conventions of lesbian fiction, one of which is the requirement of a serious romantic interlude. In virtually every lesbian mystery, the detective ends up in-volved either with her client or with a suspect.

If lesbian fiction has "gone beyond" the coming out story and the traditional romance, what has happened to the third myth of origins, that of the community, or Lesbian Nation? That powerful image, the cornerstone of lesbian literature and theory in the 1970s and early 80s, retains both a symbolic and concrete place in current fiction. Despite growing sensitivity to alcohol abuse, the lesbian bar still represents "les-bian heaven" (*Sunday's Child*, 65). The protagonist of *Shoulders* delivers a nostalgic paean to the bars: "In a woman's woman's world, even this, coming together in this noxious place, just coming here, showing up, dancing and drinking a little, is a gesture of love and bonding. Not so territorial as a touch, not the deep soft immersion of kisses, but a kind of love, tribal love, nonetheless. We have this bond" (166). In *The Bar Stories,* Nisa Donnelly weaves lesbian lives together at Babe's, yet an-other idealized bar that serves as a microcosm of Lesbian Nation. Novels like *Shoulders* also show community growing in a very traditional way: by the weaving of connections between lovers and ex-lovers (what we call the lesbian daisy chain). Camarin Grae, in *The Secret in the Bird* and *Edgewise,* and Pat Emmerson, in *Raging Mother Mountain,* give fictional form to these utopian leanings with their inventions of utopian lesbian communities. And a symbolic community of women is created in *Sisters of the Road,* Barbara Wilson's second Pam Nilsen mystery, when a network of women forms to protect an endangered child prostitute.

Like Wilson, Jan Clausen creates both symbolic and actual communities of women in *The Prosperine Papers.* Dale McNab is an antihero stumbling along a particularly rocky stretch of road. In the process of losing both job and lover, she leaves her lesbian "home" to heal her wounds in the circle of her birth family. There, she extends her lesbian- and women-identification back through the years, creating a sense of community first with her still-living grandmother and then with a long-dead heroic figure, Prosperine Munkers, who is revealed to her through her grandmother's stories and Prosperine's own fragmentary writings. Like a detective, Dale begins a quest to uncover the story of Prosperine's life, and in the process comes to better understand her grandmother and herself. Community between these women is hard-won, however; it is impeded by the "lies, secrets, and silence" that obscure Prosperine's story and by the everyday realities of homophobia and racism. Finally, while the novel holds out the *ideal* of an historically-grounded lesbian community in Prosperine's all-too-perfect diary (the document every feminist scholar dreams of), in *reality* Prosperine's diary goes up in smoke. The diary symbolizes the way in which, in the absence of hard evidence, contemporary lesbians create a common lesbian past through dreams and fictions. In this way, Clausen's quest hero endures and wrenches meaning out of the gaps: "Sometimes in the clear evening stillness, when birds swoop and dart all along the river bank, I feel an irremediable kinship with the dead, the lost of this continent. Then silence is an ocean, many-layered. Meanings swim up in it" (260).

Other texts contrast the dream of Lesbian Nation with a more prosaic reality. Lee Lynch, for example, creates Dusty's Queen of Hearts Diner as the "heart" of first the local gay community and then, somewhat idealistically, the entire neighborhood. Yet Lynch also undercuts the very symbolism that has been central to all her fiction and, in so doing, indicates how lesbian writers are questioning assumptions of security and separation: "The Queen of Hearts, as long as she was still a dream, was an island of safety too: my own business. The closer she gets, though, the easier it is to see that there is no safety. No matter how many sets of rules you learn, and learn to break, you're always jumping in feet first, free-falling" (33). The safe sea of women can only truly be found in dreams, like the vision of Jewish women dancing together in "a huge circle, big enough to wrap around the universe" (Lesléa Newman, *A Letter to Harvey Milk,* 168).

It is striking how many of the romances, mysteries, and recovery novels use metaphors of isolation and claustrophobia. An extreme example is the quasi-SF/quasi-romance novel, *To the Lightning,* in which two women, transported back to prehistoric times, reinvent everything, including lesbian love, in total isolation. Many other love stories, as we saw in *Unusual Company,* place the couple not within a nurturing community of women, but rather alone in enclosed rooms.

Moreover, as a number of critics have recently pointed out, the movement of the lesbian hero toward Lesbian Nation that used to characterize the lesbian feminist novel of development is no longer a foregone conclusion.[13] The detective, for example, may discover a lover as well as a solution to the mystery, but she doesn't necessarily find a lesbian community.[14] Indeed, the shift in popularity from SF to the mystery is indicative of the shift from the collective to the individual, since the detective is by convention a loner, while the utopian novel rests upon the assumption of community.

Lesbian fiction, particularly in the 1970s, managed to articulate a collective voice through the texts of individual writers. This communal perspective may have stifled or delayed individual creativity, but it also stimulated the interweaving of ideas and imaginations. The waning of community standards has resulted in the strengthening of the individual, but the loss of collective imagination. To find that optimistic voice of Lesbian Nation, the reader may need to turn to sources other than the novel. Literary journals, particularly *Common Lives, Lesbian Lives* and *Sinister Wisdom,* project a collective though not monolithic voice of lesbians still devoted to strongly radical, countercultural, predominantly separatist versions of lesbian feminism. Although the individual stories range in quality from the exquisite to the amateurish, together they create an inclusive picture of lesbian culture in the late 1980s.

An equally important example of a collective lesbian voice is the newsletter *Lesbian Connection,* which subtitles itself *A National Forum of News and Ideas For, By, and About Lesbians.* This patchwork quilt of announcements, letters, responses, advertisements, directories, and storytelling can be read as an alternative literary format, a nonlinear, collective "biomythography" of Lesbian Nation. Its pages carry debates over current values and issues: holistic medicine, vegetarianism, and roleplaying in one issue; music festivals, insemination, and recovery groups in the next. The topics and attitudes that may very well become the subject of a novel a year or two hence are discussed. Through *Lesbian Connection* and other journals and newsletters, this community maintains and extends its sense of itself as a group with its own identity and culture, precisely the role identified by one of its reader/contributors: "reading your magazine keeps up my hope that we do, in fact, have an (inter)national lesbian culture, despite signs to the contrary." [15] Lesbian Nation survives best in these non-novelistic forms because they foster a democratic, multivocal literary culture closely linked to the lives of women who do not necessarily identify themselves as professional novelists. At the same time, the writer who does so identify herself can draw upon, as Woolf imagined at the end of *A Room of One's Own,* "the common life which is the real life" in her own work. [16]

The literary journals, including *Conditions,* with its ethnically diverse editorial collective, are also virtually alone in preserving a multicultural literary community. After the flurry of texts by lesbians of color published in the early 1980s, few others have appeared. Along with *Borderlands/La Frontera, Compañeras,* an anthology consisting primarily of poems and personal narratives, is a source of Latina lesbian voices, but the only recent fictional works by lesbians of color are *The Threshing Floor,* a collection of short fiction by British Black author Barbara Burford; two novels by Willyce Kim; and Michelle Cliff's continuation of Clare Savage's story, *No Telephone to Heaven.* However Cliff's novel has barely any lesbian content, while Kim's lesbian protagonists are apparently anglos (although a secondary character is of Korean descent). Moreover, only Lesléa Newman's *Good Enough to Eat* and *A Letter to*

Harvey Milk and Rachel deVries's *Tender Warriors* are written from the perspective of the ethnic white woman. Dorothy Allison's collection of short stories, *Trash,* creates the strongest fictional voice of white working class women since *Yesterday's Lessons.* But the preponderance of lesbian fiction, outside the literary journals, indicates no deep sensitivity to the diversity of women's identities and positions. After an initial attempt to create a multiethnic literary community, we seem to have arrived at an impasse in terms of both multiplicity and community.

Several political and literary factors—the internal questioning of our own myths and conventions, the waning of lesbian separatism, the debates over difference and diversity, the AIDS crisis, the conservatism of the 1980s—have led to diminishing optimism over the possibility of lesbian community. In *Cows and Horses,* a young and idealistic character cries out that we "can't let our vision of an Amazon reality be overthrown just because some women are petty and shallow and cruel," but the novel ends with Bet grieving alone nonetheless (192). In the late 1980s, it appears to be increasingly difficult to connect the vision of Lesbian Nation to the everyday realities of lesbian lives.

Retreat and Reversals

It would appear, then, that the lesbian community, as manifested in lesbian fiction, is in retreat, both in the sense that it is pulling back from some of its most radical analyses and in the sense that it is pausing to reflect upon its situation and heal its wounds. Many characters, like the one who utters the quotation that heads this chapter, long for the safety and security of "home" only to discover that the "safe sea" is no longer safe. To use a traditional western metaphor, we might conclude that the lesbian hero is going through a long night of the soul, the stage along the journey at which success seems impossible and danger and despair lurk in every shadow. The purpose and goal of the journey once seemed clear and inevitable; with the conviction of the born-again, we lesbian feminists marched confidently toward our promised land. But having taken some unexpected turns, and lost our compass, we travel back to question the journey and the goal itself.

I do not want to become a victim of conventional religious metaphors, nor trapped in the articulation of loss and despair. Nevertheless, it is notable how thoroughly recent texts are imbued with the themes and metaphors of violence, recovery, inward searching, and closed spaces; how absent is that optimism and unbounded energy of the recent past. For a decade or more we whirled in a lively dance of politics and passion and then the music stopped and we settled down—some of us into careers and a comfortable bourgeois lifestyle, others into therapy and the recovery lifestyle, and still others into the daily struggle for survival that is no "lifestyle" at all. One way or another, as the detective-hero of *She Came Too Late* puts it, "the days of flash are over" (17).

In apparent response, some novelists, as we have seen, have moved inward, into literary versions of the twelve-step program, and although these novels can be very useful for women going through the recovery process, like the television docudramas they resemble, they are limited as creative works. Others continue to produce "luppie" romances about well-dressed and well-heeled doctors, lawyers, and real estate agents, women who are invariably beautiful, athletic, thin, and white. It is as if the feminist critique of "looksism" and its analysis of class and race had never occurred. In one of these romances—Evelyn Kennedy's *Cherished Love*—two characters (destined to be lovers, of course) casually discuss the advisability of tripling rents and developing land without the slightest ethical qualm. Artemis Oakgrove's *The Throne Trilogy* is even more disconcerting in its deliberate use of race, class, and gender oppression to evoke sexual titillation. Moreover, we no longer find a clear-cut image of lesbians as outlaws, rebels, and adventurers. Sarah Schulman's Lila Futuransky, for example, "always knew she was an outlaw, but she could never figure out which one" (*Girls, Visions and Everything,* 3). Virtually the only self-proclaimed outlaws left in Lesbian Nation are the sexual outlaws—the advocates of sadomasochism and of roleplaying—who rebel as much against lesbian feminist orthodoxy as against patriarchal society.

I cannot do justice here to these controversial topics; "sadomasochism" and "butch-femme" are fighting words, and little tolerance or understanding exists whenever these issues are debated. As I discussed in chapter three the myths and metaphors of lesbian sexuality established during the 1970s became so rigid and formulaic that rebellion against them was inevitable. We see this rebellion both in the S/M literature, which is primarily published by Oakgrove's Lace Publications, or in such journals as *On Our Backs* and *Bad Attitudes,* and in more conventional lesbian novels with their abundant amounts of sexual description. But my criticism of lesbian sexual writing remains the same. Regardless of the flavor of the sex—vanilla or rocky road—it is almost always inscribed in formulas and cliches. The S/M contingent has developed its set of formulas; the vanilla lesbians have theirs.

Moreover, in a particularly unhappy development, sex scenes unconnected to plot, theme, or character have become a staple of virtually all lesbian novels, whether they are romances, adventures, or political tales. Far too many novels have adopted a structure of four chapters plot, one chapter sex, and so on. The sex may be the soft and liquid kind, or it may be violent and kinky, but the purpose is obviously the same: sexual arousal, not storytelling.[17] To put it another way, the stories have become an excuse for sex. Lesbians certainly deserve an erotic literature of our own, but novels need not have graphic sexual description to be lesbian. Nor should sexuality be cut off from the rest of feeling and behavior. Unless intended solely for titillation, sexual writing needs to be consistent with a novel's particular context and point of view, which may mean that sexual activity should be suggested, not described in long and intrusive detail. Interestingly, *Shoulders,* a sexual picaresque, articulates this very point: "There is a power in such moments that words cannot wholly evoke. And maybe they shouldn't anyway" (38). With a few welcome exceptions—such as Barbara Wilson in *Cows and Horses* and Dorothy Allison in *Trash*—lesbian writers insist on confining that power within increasingly empty words.

The renewed popularity of butch-femme roles in recent years raises different questions, although it also reverses the lesbian feminist myths of the 1970s. Feminism, of course, rests in part upon the rejection of the polarity of masculine and feminine, arguing that this polarity arbitrarily assigns certain characteristics to men and others to women, and then marks the former as positive and the latter as negative. As feminism began to influence lesbian discourse in the early 1970s, the traditional roles of butch and femme were argued to be imitations of patriarchal gender roles. The lesbian feminist ideal was closer to androgyny, or at least to the eschewal of any characteristics markedly masculine or feminine. Whatever we actually did at home, our public ideal was one of absolute equality (or sameness) between lovers.

One result of this feminist orthodoxy was the rejection of many women who had come out prior to the feminist movement and whose identities as lesbians were profoundly connected with butch and femme roles. As lesbians have increasingly reclaimed our "herstory," however, we have come to understand better the values and choices of our fore-mothers.[18] The feminists of the seventies may have failed to explore in depth the actual dynamics of relationships: the flow between pursuing and being pursued, controlling and yielding, protecting and nurturing. As we pay closer attention to the realities of lesbian relationships, not just our myths, some women find "butch" and "femme" to be meaningful metaphors.

However, butch and femme roles also revive the notion that gender identities are innate components of the self. In some recent writing, butch or femme seems less a *role*—a pose or a metaphor—that one adopts, than an *essence* that one simply is. As a character in Barbara Wilson's *Cows and Horses* tries to explain in a deliberately awkward metaphor, "oranges" always look for "apples" and apples always seek out oranges (71). Wilson's character speaks of oranges and apples (and the author herself suggests "cows" and "horses") in order to get away from the idea that these differences have anything to do with traditional definitions of masculinity and femininity. Oranges and apples, cows and horses, are not necessarily polar opposites as are masculine and feminine. Occasionally a writer, like Jess Wells, raises gender opposition in order to deflate it: "Only as a lesbian, I think: one minute covered in lace and nearly coming in a dressing room, the next minute charging down the street towards the punching bag" (*The Dress,* 7).

Most portrayals of butch and femme, however, end up being both dualistic and essentialist. Butches are "born" lesbians who reject women's clothing and women's ways; femmes are more likely to be women's movement types who pass in the world for straight. Butches like to be in control; femmes like to take care of them. Butches initiate sex and femmes respond. Joan Nestle criticizes those who label such thinking "patriarchal," and yet her own erotic writing bears an uncanny resemblance to conventional patriarchal works. Consider this sentence from "The Three," one of Nestle's short stories in which a butch and two femmes go to Fire Island: "They followed the butch as she walked into the water, her chiseled body entering the sea without a halt, while they flirted with the small waves and slowly let the coldness take them" (*A Restricted Country*, 140). Had I come upon such a description in a man's story about heterosexuals, I would criticize its blatant use of gender-role stereotypes. Does changing the context to a lesbian story make a difference?

Whether or not the reader is personally enamored of "luppie" romances, sadomasochism, or butch-femme roleplaying, the presence of such a variety of literary styles and subjects demonstrates, first, that the genre of lesbian fiction is extensive enough to target specific audiences, and second, that the community itself has made room for competing and interacting discourses. The one serious absence, which cannot be over-emphasized, is fiction by lesbians of color, and, to some extent, overtly political fiction. Otherwise, the lesbian reader today does not have to take what she can get; she can get what she wants. The debates within our communities, reproduced within novels like *Cows and Horses, The Dog Collar Murders* and *Cass and the Stone Butch,* keep us questioning whether what we want is good for us and for other lesbians. It begins to appear as if the straightjacket of political correctness is genuinely loosening.

Of course this also means that the center of Lesbian Nation no longer holds; nor is it clear where its boundaries lie. Like Lee Lynch's Dusty, or the protagonists of the texts I discussed in chapter five, we are in collective free-fall, an aspect of the journey that is both perilous and exhilarating. Although I am nostalgic for the visionary, optimistic novels of our recent past—works like *Riverfinger Women, Lover, The Wanderground, Toothpick House,* even *The Cruise*—that inscribed a collective dream and myth of origins, at the same time I see a new individuality and variety in lesbian fiction.

Lesbian Fiction at a Crossroads

Where will our journey take us? I must reiterate the impossibility of offering a simple formula or prescription for what lesbian literature can or should be. But it is always an author's privilege to make a few last points for the reader's consideration. I will conclude, then, by suggesting that, like the worshippers of the goddess Trivia, lesbian writers stand at a crossroads from which three paths branch out.

In some quest tales, particularly the picaresque, the hero returns after his (no generic intended) travels to consolidate all he has learned, integrate his new self into his old society, and take the reins of power and authority into his own hands. Along these lines, one direction for lesbian fiction would be a general accommodation to the dominant culture, which would signify not the abandoning of lesbianism (as in the pre-feminist novel of development) but the *domestication* of the lesbian novel. We can already see this process at work in the conventional "girl-meets-girl" romances that Bertha Harris mocked in 1977.[19] We can also see it in the tendency toward normalizing lesbianism, the insistence that lesbians are no different from other women, except for the "incidental" fact of whom we choose to sleep with. As I mentioned in chapter one, instead of the feminist politicization of lesbianism some recent authors are returning to the more traditional definition of lesbians as women who have sexual relationships with other women, and nothing more. Occasionally, a novel—such as Diana McRae's detective story, *All the Muscle You Need,* or Cecil Dawkins' love story, *Charleyhorse,* both stylishly written—succeeds in destigmatizing lesbianism so thoroughly that, were the sex of the protagonist's love interest changed it would make virtually no difference to the story.

But the resurgence of homophobia in the late 1980s, which should remind us that the liberal seventies may have been a momentary aberration, makes the choice of accommodation and domestication difficult and perhaps moot. I myself question how desirable a choice it is. This path takes us no further than escapist fiction with which we may while away a Sunday afternoon. Lacking complexity or provocation, its purpose is to soothe and pacify (or sexually titillate), not to challenge the reader to attend to either content or style. On a practical level, of course, most lesbians want to be left alone to get on with our lives, without having to deal constantly with both petty and serious obstacles put in our way by fear and prejudice. And, like heterosexuals, we sometimes want to read entertaining novels. But the attempt to normalize lesbian fiction cannot be an exclusive strategy, for it produces little more than the tame and superficial romances that currently dominate lesbian publishing.

Returning to the conventions of the quest, a second strategy for lesbian fiction would be to keep the hero in the magic forest, the "wild zone," and to refuse the accommodation with society symbolized by the return to the patriarchal city. This strategy would maintain lesbian literature as a truly oppositional genre, one that continually questions all conventions and all myths, that experiments with both content and form. It would continue to inscribe "the condition of marginality" and remain staunchly critical of any movement toward the center.[20] It would necessarily be a separatist literature consciously opposed to and subversive of patriarchal values. Such a literature would also restore the image of the lesbian as outlaw, breaker of codes. What might be most notable about these texts would be their formal experimentation: a disruptive, nonlinear strategy, like that of Francophone writers such as Monique Wittig or Jovette Marchessault, that challenges our commonsense notions of reality and realism and our comfortable assumptions of a fixed, unified, unchanging lesbian identity and community.

A few texts suggest how writers perceive the wild zone today. Some resemble the futuristic, utopian/dystopian fictions I discussed in chapter four. In two political British novels (British writers are particularly adept in their use of overtly political discourse) the dystopian present all but overwhelms the vague intimation of a utopian future.[21] Anna Wilson's *Altogether Elsewhere* juxtaposes the exploits of women urban vigilantes with scenes that take place "Elsewhere," the location of a superior, otherworldly being named only "A" who holds out the promise of a new society: "If you come with me now, I will teach you everything. . . . The point of this is power, A continues, don't you want to take a hand in the world? Come back with me, and then you may use it as you see fit. I won't interfere" (135). In Anna Livia's *Bulldozer Rising,* a convincing glimpse of an ominous near-future, youth reigns supreme. Like Wilson's vigilantes, or like the Shirley Temples of *Sister Gin,* "old-women" fight back until they are forced to flee the city for a wild zone across the mountains where mysterious crones have created an alternative reality in deep and hidden caverns.

The few American novels to follow this path evoke the wild zone primarily through fantasy. In speculative fictions such as those collected in a 1988 issue of *Sinister Wisdom* devoted to "Lesbian Visions, Fantasy, SciFi," the wild zone is that place across the river or over the mountains where women live free of men and their culture of violence.[22] Particularities of time and space are unimportant: in fantasy, lesbians move freely across chronological barriers and pay little attention to the landscape of ordinary life. Judy Grahn's *Mundane's World*, a different kind of example, employs incantatory, repetitive, nonlinear prose to imagine an original women-centered (although not lesbian) civilization before the patriarchal takeover. And in Andrea Carlisle's *The Riverhouse Stories*, two innocent lovers living on a magical houseboat pursue adventures in a fairy tale world.

But overall, the conventions of mythmaking and SF have given way to spirituality and mysticism (not unlike the shift in popularity in the mainstream from science fiction to sword-and-sorcery fantasies). Given the popularity of new age consciousness, the psychic detective-hero of Sandy Bayer's *The Crystal Curtain* may mark the beginning of a trend. Artemis Oakgrove's S/M fiction is also imbued, somewhat oddly, with romantic fantasy and magic. Whether or not this literature can be designated oppositional, however, depends upon the reader's point of view. While "sexual outlaws" certainly reject mainstream society in personal style, their stated views on power and violence seem to me to be firmly rooted in a patriarchal paradigm.[23] The ambiguous position of S/M literature is yet one more indication that, with the boundaries of Lesbian Nation in question, we can no longer say with any assurance who is in or out—or who "we" are at all.

To push this point one step further, it is highly questionable whether any representation can truly exist outside the established boundaries of language and literature. As we have seen, even the most experimental and speculative texts to some extent rewrite the literature of the dominant culture. We may have no choice but to write with "the master's tools."[24] Hence, lesbian fictions may combine elements of both of the above strategies into a third way. The hero will return to the city, but only to transform it through the knowledge she has gained from her experiences along the way.[25] She will walk the middle way of ordinary human life, but keep her memories of heaven and of hell.

Such a journey is imagined in Monique Wittig's most recent novel, *Across the Acheron*, a loose retelling of Dante's *Commedia*. Dante's masterpiece articulates the perspective of an orderly, hierarchical society with a clearly-marked, linear path through the circles and levels of hell, purgatory, and paradise. But the journey undertaken by the main character, named Wittig, is circuitous and constantly interrupted. With her guide, Manastabal, she crosses and recrosses the River Acheron, the boundary between the real world and the surreal; she moves back and forth incessantly between limbo, hell, and paradise. The boundaries are no longer defined: "What is she [Manastabal] waiting for? Is she going to take me on her shoulders to make the crossing? But what crossing? There's no river here. There's no sea" (8). It is not necessary to enter or leave the wild zone because it exists within the quest hero herself. Her journeys into hell function as an allegory for her confrontations with the heterosexual world, as her sojourns in paradise celebrate the lesbian alternative: "There's nothing where we are going, Wittig, at least nothing you don't know already. We're certainly entering another world, as you imagine, but the sun shines on it just as it shines on the world we are leaving" (8).

In novels that follow this third path, then, lesbianism serves as an opening to the world around us. Lesbianism is neither the totality of the author's vision, nor incidental to it. An example of this kind of novel is Jeanette Winterson's *Oranges Are Not the Only Fruit* (published first in Britain in 1985 and then in the United States in 1987). This impressive autobiographical *bildungsroman* follows its protagonist, Jeanette, from her childhood in a working class Pentecostal family to her lesbian adulthood—a journey from Genesis to the book of Ruth. Jeanette's coming out story, her understanding of difference, and her experience of maternal power—all themes characteristic of lesbian novels—are placed within the context created by her particular class and religious culture, not divorced from it. Jeanette travels through a vivid and concrete external reality and an internal world of dreams and myths. Just as the character crosses the borders of religious belief and sexuality, the author effectively crosses boundaries of genre and style.

Fictions such as *Oranges Are Not the Only Fruit* express general experiences and ideas through the particular "slant" given by a lesbian point of view.[26] As Wittig puts it, a writer "must assume both a particular *and* a universal point of view, at least to be part of literature. That is, one must work to reach the general, even while starting from an individual or from a specific point of view."[27] Wittig's tone may be overly prescriptive, but her point is important. The majority of lesbian novels of the past twenty years have been about the local experience of being a lesbian. They have focused on coming out, falling in love, and moving to Lesbian Nation. At the same time, the mythic quality of so many lesbian fictions softened the rough edges and diluted the individuality of their representations of daily life. The majority of lesbian novels (and this includes most of the popular romances published today) have been both too particular and not particular enough.

We have needed these stories, and we continue to need them. But we also need stories that tell about those aspects of our lives that we share with all other lives—without, however, minimizing or marginalizing the particular slant that lesbianism gives to our point of view. We also need to think about what parts of the forest we fear entering. There have always been taboo subjects in lesbian writing. Some of these have been removed, but many still remain: violence in lesbian relationships, controversy within the lesbian community, internalized homophobia, and unhappy endings, to name just a few. The dilemma, or challenge, facing lesbian writers (and the community as a whole) is how to preserve the specificity of lesbian identity and experience while recognizing and embracing both the differences within our ranks and our similarities with others.

Such novels have been written over the past two decades, as I hope this book has demonstrated. And our dissatisfaction, or boredom, with conventional coming out stories and romances can be the impetus to more and even better novels. Already, in the novels and stories I have discussed in this chapter, we see a careful attention both to the particular details of everyday lesbian life and to the social and philosophical concerns that characterize significant works of fiction. These writers lavish loving care on the fundamentals of fiction—plot, narration, imagery, characterization—and place their tales within wide historical, philosophical, and sociopolitical contexts. The novels are increasingly "thicker," that is, complex, resonant, and layered in perspective and expression. We can look back to a literary heritage sprinkled with a small number of fine, creative, and visionary novels that began to travel the third path I have suggested. Since 1986, novels and short story collections like *Cows and Horses, Unusual Company, Memory Board, Cass and the Stone Butch, Oranges*

Are Not the Only Fruit, The Prosperine Papers, Trash, Leave a Light on for Me, A Letter to Harvey Milk, The Bar Stories, and *Three Glasses of Wine* have continued their work. But the future is, quite literally, an open book.

I have reached the end of my own journey. As I was taught, and as I teach my students, what is left is to restate my thesis and then open up my own special aperture to the world around me. My thesis is a simple one: For two decades, fiction has provided a way for writers to shape the fantasies, politics, and everyday experiences of the lesbian community. We write (and read) to reflect our reality, but also to create new realities. We lesbians are intensely idealistic and self-critical, and so our fiction continually sets up a version of reality and then pulls it down again. We write, and rewrite, and rewrite once more the stories and myths of the dominant culture and our own alternative lesbian culture. The result is a complex and contradictory literary genre. At the same time, however, like virtually all marginal groups, we cling to a center— a fixed point that guarantees our identity and our place within a recognizable and definable community. The history of the lesbian movement, and the fiction that belongs to it, has been marked by a tense dialectic between openness and closedness, inclusion and exclusion, flexibility and rigidity.

It may always remain that way. We simply cannot define where the boundaries of the community lie, nor of the self, nor of the literature— much as we continue to try. Personally, I find this shapelessness both necessary and disconcerting. Living as I do both near the center of the dominant culture and at its edge (for I am white and economically comfortable, yet still female, Jewish, and lesbian), I feel how strong the pull toward recentering can be. For me, that center—the position from which I evaluate everything that comes within my view—is provided by feminism and the myth of Lesbian Nation. For other women, the center may be "altogether elsewhere." So the metaphors of center and margin make very little sense at all. And yet, how can one live without boundaries, definitions, and centers of being? I do not know the answer, but I do know that I will continue to look to lesbian fiction to give me some clues.

Notes

Preface

1. Gene Damon [Barbara Grier] and Lee Stuart, *The Lesbian in Literature: A Bibliography* (San Francisco: The Ladder, 1967).
2. Alma Routsong, "Writing and Publishing *Patience and Sarah,*" in *Gay American History: Lesbians and Gay Men in the U.S.A.,* ed. Jonathan Katz (New York: Thomas Y. Crowell Co., 1976; New York: Avon Books, 1978), 652–65.
3. All page references to primary sources are to the editions listed in the bibliography, and will appear in the text.
4. Michal Brody, *Are We There Yet?: A Continuing History of Lavender Woman* (Iowa City: Aunt Lute Book Company, 1985), 3.
5. Virginia Woolf, *The Common Reader,* First and Second Series (New York: Harcourt, Brace & Co., 1948).
6. Adrienne Rich, "Notes toward a Politics of Location," in *Blood, Bread, and Poetry: Selected Prose 1979–1985* (New York: W. W. Norton & Company, 1986), 224.

Chapter One

1. Lesbian writing, fictional and otherwise, has been published by Daughters Inc., The Women's Press Collective, Diana Press, and Persephone Press, all of which are currently defunct. Many other novels were self-published and, consequently, lost to us unless they were later reprinted by successful publishing houses. In 1989, the most prolific publishers of lesbian fiction include The Naiad Press (the giant by anyone's reckoning), Firebrand Books, The Crossing Press, Spinsters/Aunt Lute, Alyson Publications, The Seal Press, New Victoria Publishers, Banned Books, and Lace

233

Publications (specializing in sadomasochistic literature). Some writers continue to publish under their own imprint. In Great Britain, lesbian fiction is most often published by Onlywomen Press and The Women's Press. (Canada also has a press of that name.) In the first half of the 1970s, when feminism and lesbianism were "hot" topics, mainstream presses published works by Monique Wittig, Ann Allen Shockley, Isabel Miller, Rita Mae Brown, Kate Millet, and Jane Rule. But once the glamour, and selling-power, of lesbianism wore off, so too did the interest of commercial publishers. In the past two or three years, there has been a renewal of interest in lesbian fiction. Whether this is a fad or a trend remains to be seen. *New Lesbian Literature 1980—88,* ed. Miriam Saphira (Auckland, New Zealand: Papers Inc., 1988) is a useful reference, although it unfortunately contains many errors and doubtful attributions.

2. Bertha Harris, "Lesbian Literature: An Introduction," in *Our Right to Love,* ed. Ginny Vida (Englewood Cliffs, N.J.: Prentice-Hall, 1978), 257.

3. On Bieris de Romans, see Meg Bogin, *The Women Troubadours* (New York and London: W. W. Norton & Company, 1976); on Aphra Behn, see Maureen Duffy, *The Passionate Shepherdess* (New York: Avon Books, 1977); on Wu Tsao, see Kenneth Rexroth and Ling Chung, trans. and ed., *The Orchid Boat: Women Poets of China* (New York: The Seabury Press, 1972). For an exhaustive overview of lesbian themes and images in literature, see Jeannette H. Foster, *Sex Variant Women in History* (Tallahassee: The Naiad Press, 1985 [1956]).

4. Lillian Faderman, *Surpassing the Love of Men: Romantic Friendship and Love Between Women from the Renaissance to the Present* (New York: William Morrow and Company, 1981).

5. The brief historical overview that follows is taken largely from Faderman, *Surpassing the Love of Men;* John D'Emilio and Estelle B. Freedman, *Intimate Matters: A History of Sexuality in America* (New York: Harper & Row, 1988); Jonathan Katz, *Gay American History* (New York: Thomas Crowell, 1976) and *Gay/Lesbian Almanac* (New York: Harper & Row, 1983); Barry D. Adam, *The Rise of a Gay and Lesbian Movement* (Boston: Twayne Publishers [Twayne's Social Movements Series], 1987); Jeffrey Weeks, *Coming Out: Homosexual Politics in Britain from the Nineteenth Century to the Present* (London: Quartet Books, 1977); Martha Vicinus, *Independent Women: Work and Community for Single Women 1850—1920* (Chicago and London: The University of Chicago Press, 1985); Leila J. Rupp, "'Imagine My Surprise': Women's Relationships in Historical Perspective," *Frontiers* 5 (3) (Fall 1980): 61—70; Lillian Faderman and Brigitte Eriksson, ed. and trans., *Lesbian-Feminism in Turn-of-the-Century Germany* (Weatherby Lake,

Mo.: The Naiad Press, 1980); and John Lauritsen and David Thorstad, *The Early Homosexual Rights Movement (1864–1935)* (New York: Times Change Press, 1974).

6. Vicinus, among others, discusses the prevalence of intense love between girls or women at boarding schools and colleges in the late nineteenth and early twentieth centuries. The girls' school (or dormitory) remains one of the most prominent motifs in lesbian literature throughout the twentieth century. See Bonnie Zimmerman, "Exiting from Patriarchy: The Lesbian Novel of Development," in *The Voyage In: Fictions of Female Development,* ed. Elizabeth Langland, Marianne Hirsch, and Elizabeth Abel (Hanover and London: University Press of New England, 1983), 244–257.

7. Faderman, "The Morbidification of Love Between Women by 19th-Century Sexologists," *Journal of Homosexuality* 4 (1) (Fall 1978): 73–90.

8. Sylvia Stevenson, *Surplus* (Tallahassee: The Naiad Press, 1986 [1924]), 225. Chapter XIX of this novel movingly illustrates the protagonist's realization of her difference and inferiority in society's eyes. See also Christina Simmons, "Companionate Marriage and the Lesbian Threat," *Frontiers* 4 (3) (Fall 1979), 54–59.

9. The femme fatale has been written about extensively; for an overview, see Sandra M. Gilbert and Susan Gubar, *No Man's Land: The Place of the Woman Writer in the Twentieth Century,* vol. 1, *The War of the Words* (New Haven and London: Yale University Press, 1988), and vol. 2, *Sexchanges* (New Haven and London: Yale University Press, 1989). For more on this stereotype, see Faderman, *Surpassing the Love of Men,* especially the chapters "Lesbian Evil" and "Fiction as a Weapon"; also Faderman, "Love Between Women in 1928: Why Progressivism Is Not Always Progress," in *Historical, Literary, and Erotic Aspects of Lesbianism,* ed. Monika Kehoe (New York and London: Harrington Park Press, 1986), 23–42.

10. Consider for example Frank Marcus's play and film, *The Killing of Sister George* (1965). The three lesbian characters conform exactly to these stereotypes.

11. See Gilbert and Gubar, *Sexchanges,* particularly section III, "Reinventing Gender."

12. On Barney and Vivien, see Sheri Benstock, *Women of the Left Bank* (Austin: University of Texas Press, 1986); Karla Jay, *The Amazon and the Page: Natalie Clifford Barney and Renée Vivien* (Bloomington and Indianapolis: Indiana University Press, 1988); and Elyse Blankley, "Return to Mytilene: Renée Vivien and the City of Women," in *Women Writers and the City,* ed. Susan Squier (Knoxville: University of Tennessee Press, 1984), 45–67. This was not an exclusively western phenomenon. At roughly the same

time in Japan, a small circle of women poets, including the great Yosano Akiko, were writing lesbian love poetry. See Kenneth Rexroth and Ikuko Atsumi, trans, and ed., *The Burning Heart: Women Poets of Japan* (New York: The Seabury Press, 1977).

13. The reference is to novels like Ann Bannon's *Women in the Shadows* (1959), Miriam Gardner's (pseudonym for Marion Zimmer Bradley) *Twilight Lovers* (1964), and Paula Christian's *Edge of Twilight* (1959). On lesbian circles during the 1950s and early 1960s, see Adam, *The Rise of a Gay and Lesbian Movement;* also, Del Martin and Phyllis Lyon, *Lesbian/Woman* (San Francisco: Glide Publications, 1972; New York: Bantam Books, 1972); Sidney Abbott and Barbara Love, *Sappho Was a Right-On Woman* (New York: Stein and Day, 1972); Ruth Simpson, *From the Closet to the Courts: The Lesbian Transition* (New York: Penguin Books, 1977); Andrea Weiss and Greta Schiller, *Before Stonewall: The Making of a Gay and Lesbian Community* (Tallahassee: The Naiad Press, 1988); John D'Emilio, *Sexual Politics, Sexual Communities: The Making of a Homosexual Minority in the United States, 1940–1970* (Chicago: University of Chicago Press, 1983).

14. The Naiad Press has reprinted the novels of Bannon and Taylor under its Volute imprint. Bannon's novels are *Odd Girl Out* (1957), *I Am a Woman* (1959), *Women in the Shadows* (1959), *Journey to a Woman* (1960), and *Beebo Brinker* (1962)—all reprinted in 1983. Taylor's wonderful titles are *A World without Men* (1963), *Return to Lesbos* (1963), and *Journey to Fulfillment* (1964)—all reprinted in 1982. Taylor has recently published a conclusion to the Erika Frohmann series, *Ripening* (Austin: Banned Books, 1988). On this genre, see Barbara Grier, *Lesbiana: Book Reviews from the Ladder, 1966–1972* (Reno: The Naiad Press, 1976); Fran Koski and Maida Tilchen, "Some Pulp Sappho," in *Lavender Culture,* ed. Karla Jay and Allen Young (New York: Jove/HBJ, 1978), 262–274.; Julia Penelope Stanley, "Uninhabited Angels," *Margins* 23 (August 1975): 7–10. *The Lesbian in Literature* bibliography, especially the 1967 edition, contains an extensive list of pulp paperbacks.

15. Catharine R. Stimpson, "Zero Degree Deviancy: The Lesbian Novel in English," *Critical Inquiry* 8 (2) (Winter 1981), 373–74. On lesbian images in twentieth-century literature, see also Jane Rule, *Lesbian Images* (Garden City, N.Y.: Doubleday & Company, 1975).

16. On the use of "lesbian" as metaphor, see Marilyn R. Farwell, "Toward a Definition of the Lesbian Literary Imagination," *Signs: Journal of Women in Culture and Society* 14 (1) (Autumn 1988): 100–118; Radicalesbians, "The Woman Identified Woman," in *Radical Feminism,* ed. Anne Koedt, Ellen

Levine, and Anita Rapone (New York: Quadrangle/The New York Times Book Company, 1973), 240; Monique Wittig, "Paradigm," in *Homosexualities and French Literature,* ed. George Stambolian and Elaine Marks (Ithaca: Cornell University Press, 1979), 117; Bertha Harris, "*What we mean to say:* Notes toward Defining the Nature of Lesbian Literature," *Heresies* 3 (1977): 5–8. See also, Harriet Desmoines, "Notes for a Magazine I," *Sinister Wisdom* 1 (1) (July 1976): 3–4; Mary Carruthers, "The Re-Vision of the Muse: Adrienne Rich, Audre Lorde, Judy Grahn, Olga Broumas," *The Hudson Review* 36 (2) (Summer 1983): 294–295.

17. I wish to be very clear here. The lesbian feminist culture and community I delineate was and is not the only lesbian culture and community to exist in the 1970s and 80s. Many women remain tangentially connected or entirely unconnected to it. The various communities can misunderstand and mistrust each other. Furthermore, "the lesbian community" is a concept more than an entity. Each lesbian may refer to something different when she uses the term. Nevertheless, it is fair to say that the lesbian feminist community, amorphous as it may be, is the source of most lesbian literature, art, and music. As we shall see, the hegemony of lesbian feminism breaks down in the 1980s. But the splits and factionalization taking place are between groups continuing to talk to (or yell at) each other— which still defines a community. Recognizing that more precision might be necessary in a different context, here I will use the terms "lesbian community" and "lesbian feminist community" interchangeably.

18. Billie Wahlstrom and Caren Deming, "Chasing the Popular Arts through the Critical Forest," *Journal of Popular Culture* 13 (3) (Spring 1980): 412.

19. Adrienne Rich, *On Lies, Secrets, and Silence: Selected Prose 1966–1978* (New York: W. W. Norton & Company, 1979).

20. Wittig, "Paradigm," 117.

21. I have deliberately chosen to use conventional spelling rather than such feminist revisions as *womon* and *wimmin, herstory,* or *hera.* While these revisions have an important consciousness-raising effect, when used routinely in a book this length they create an impediment to smooth reading. However, I employ the word *hero* rather than the feminine diminutive *heroine.* As Rachel M. Brownstein defines her, a heroine is a woman who achieves selfhood within a heterosexual context. The word hero is more appropriate to the lesbian protagonist. See *Becoming a Heroine: Reading about Women in Novels* (New York: Viking Press, 1982).

22. For a feminist approach to "the death of the author," see Nancy K.

Miller, "Changing the Subject: Authorship, Writing, and the Reader," in *Feminist Studies/Critical Studies,* ed. Teresa de Lauretis (Bloomington: Indiana University Press, 1986), 102–120.

23. For this reason I have not included novels like Doris Grumbach's *Chamber Music,* Rosa Guy's *Ruby,* Alice Walker's *The Color Purple,* or Gloria Naylor's *The Women of Brewster Place* in my analysis. I do think, however, that some of these and other novels have been influenced by the lesbian myths I will discuss.

24. Julia Penelope Stanley and Susan J. Wolfe, introduction to *The Coming Out Stories* (Watertown, Mass.: Persephone Press, 1980), xxi.

25. See Harris, "Notes toward Defining"; Barbara Smith, "Toward a Black Feminist Criticism," *The New Feminist Criticism: Essays on Women, Literature & Theory,* ed. Elaine Showalter (New York: Pantheon Books, 1985), 168–185; Susan J. Wolfe, "Stylistic Experimentation in Millett, Johnston, and Wittig," unpublished paper presented at the annual meeting of the Modern Language Association, New York, December 1978.

26. Virginia Woolf, *A Room of One's Own* (New York and London: Harcourt, Brace & World, 1929), 79–80.

27. June Arnold, "Lesbians in Literature," *Sinister Wisdom* 1 (2) (Fall 1976): 29. For a similar analysis, see Annis Pratt, *Archetypal Patterns in Women's Literature* (Bloomington: Indiana University Press, 1981), 107; Elly Bulkin, "A Look at Lesbian Short Fiction," introduction to *Lesbian Fiction: An Anthology* (Watertown, Mass.: Persephone Press, 1981), xxvii; Mab Segrest, *My Mama's Dead Squirrel: Lesbian Essays on Southern Culture,* with an introduction by Adrienne Rich (Ithaca: Firebrand Books, 1985), 126.

28. Two other novels deserve mention here: Lynn Strongin's *Bones and Kim* (1980) and Alesia Kunz's *Shangrila and Linda* (1981). Both books have been out of print for years. My generalization applies most particularly to American fiction. British and French-Canadian authors are more likely to employ nonrepresentational modes of writing.

29. Julia Penelope, "True Confessions," review of *Confessions of a Failed Southern Lady* by Florence King and *My Mama's Dead Squirrel* by Mab Segrest, in *The Women's Review of Books* 3 (7) (April 1986): 8. Joanna Russ, letter, in *The Women's Review of Books* 3 (11) (August 1986): 6. In addition to published expressions of displeasure, I offer my own anecdotal evidence: over and over again, the first question asked me about this book has been, "are you going to point out how bad this literature is?" For an enlightening discussion of "literary value," see Terry Eagleton, *Literary Theory: An Intro-*

duction (Minneapolis: University of Minnesota Press, 1983), particularly "Conclusion: Political Criticism."

30. Collective Lesbian International Terrors, "First C.L.I.T. Statement," *off our backs* 4 (6) (May 1974): 16.

31. See Jane Rule, "Notes on Autobiography," in *A Hot-Eyed Moderate* (Tallahassee: The Naiad Press, 1985), 31–36.

32. Joanna Russ, "Listen, there's a Story for You . . . ," review of *Retreat! As It Was, Sinister Wisdom* 12 (Winter 1980): 89–92. Marion Zimmer Bradley and Susanna J. Sturgis, "Response: A Few Comments on the Gentle Art of Reviewing in the Feminist Press," *Sinister Wisdom* 14 (1980): 99–102.

33. See Valerie Miner, interview by Alice Henry and Lorraine Sorrel, *off our backs* 13 (1) (January 1983): 16.

34. Janice Radway, *Reading the Romance* (Chapel Hill: University of North Carolina Press, 1984), 190.

35. We shall see that in the 1980s, mainstream popular genres such as the mystery and the romance have come to dominate alternative lesbian publishing.

36. Review of *The Cook and the Carpenter, The Treasure, Nerves,* and *Early Losses,* in *off our backs* 4 (3) (February 1974): 14.

37. Stimpson, "Zero Degree Deviancy," 376.

38. Stanley and Wolfe, *The Coming Out Stories,* xxi.

39. Nancy Toder, interview by Janis Kelly, *off our backs* 10 (11) (December 1980): 16.

40. Mircea Eliade, *Myth and Reality* (New York: Harper & Row, 1963), 6; Northrop Frye, *The Secular Scripture* (Cambridge: Harvard University Press, 1976), 6. See also Bonislaw Malinowski, *Sex, Culture, and Myth* (New York: Harcourt, Brace & World, 1962).

41. Stanley, "Uninhabited Angels," 8.

42. Fran Moira, review of *The Lesbian Body,* by Monique Wittig, *off our backs* 6 (6) (April 1976): 16.

43. This is the vision that Adrienne Rich, in her foreword to *The Coming Out Stories,* deliberately evokes (204).

44. Paula Gunn Allen, *The Sacred Hoop: Recovering the Feminine in American Indian Traditions* (Boston: Beacon Press, 1986), 103. See also Marks, "Lesbian Intertextuality."

45. Audre Lorde, interview by Claudia Tate, *Black Women Writers at Work,* ed. Claudia Tate (New York: Continuum, 1983), 115. Lorde goes on to reject the narrow generic term "novel," however.

46. Alison Hennegan, introduction to *Girls Next Door: Lesbian Feminist Stories,* ed. Jan Bradshaw and Mary Hemming (London: The Women's Press, 1985), 2–3.

47. On "expressive realism," see Catherine Belsey, *Critical Practice* (London and New York: Methuen, 1980).

48. For an exposition of this poststructuralist position, see Alice Jardine, *Gynesis: Configurations of Women and Modernity* (Ithaca: Cornell University Press, 1985); Toril Moi, *Sexual/Textual Politics: Feminist Literary Theory* (London and New York: Methuen, 1985).

49. Wahlstrom and Deming, "Chasing the Popular Arts," refer to what I am calling "good" myths as "monomyths"—James Joyce's term—and the "bad" ones as "culture-specific myths" (413). Lesbian fiction differs from heterosexual feminist writing in that few authors rewrite *specific* myths and legends. Wittig, for one, rewrites such stories as the golden fleece, and Harris, the lives of the saints. Most other lesbian writers avoid particular patriarchal myths in favor of the general, core myths of western civilization. See also Estella Lauter, *Women as Mythmakers: Poetry and Visual Art by Twentieth-Century Women* (Bloomington: Indiana University Press, 1984); Alicia Ostriker, "The Thieves of Language: Women Poets and Revisionist Mythmaking," in *New Feminist Criticism,* 314–38.

50. Arnold, 28. Almost a decade ago, I used this phrase to title an article on lesbian criticism ("What Has Never Been: An Overview of Lesbian Feminist Criticism," in *New Feminist Criticism,* 200–24). I still think that the notion of virgin birth is an empowering myth, but not an accurate description of how literature or criticism works.

51. Judy Grahn is probably the leading exponent of the idea of a recoverable women's or lesbian tradition. See *The Highest Apple: Sappho and the Lesbian Poetic Tradition* (San Francisco: Spinsters Ink, 1985). Although we identify similar images and myths in lesbian literature, I am inclined to see these as parts of a wider cultural tradition and modified by the dynamics of a particular historical era.

52. Patricia Yeager, "'Because a Fire Was in My Head': Eudora Welty and the Dialogic Imagination," *PMLA* 99 (5) (October 1984): 955.

53. Northrop Frye, *The Secular Scripture,* suggests that "it is a certain quality of importance or authority for the community that marks the myth, not truth as such" (p. 16). This is quite pertinent to lesbian fiction. See also Stimpson, "Zero Degree Deviancy," on "romanticism" and "realism" in the classic (prefeminist) lesbian novel, 372–73.

54. My discussion of myths of origin is taken largely from Eliade. See also Benstock, *Women of the Left Bank,* on Djuna Barnes's *The Ladies Almanack* as

a "lesbian creation myth" (p. 247) and Grahn, *The Highest Apple,* on "a new or restored creation myth" (p. 130).

55. See Helen Diner, *Mothers and Amazons: The First Feminine History of Culture,* with an introduction by Brigitte Berger (New York: Doubleday Anchor, 1973 [1965]); Elizabeth Gould Davis, *The First Sex* (Baltimore: Penguin Books, 1972).

56. Barbara Hill Rigney, *Lilith's Daughters: Women and Religion in Contemporary Fiction* (Madison: University of Wisconsin Press, 1982), 9. See also Carruthers, "The Re-Vision of the Muse," 295.

57. Stimpson, "Zero Degree Deviancy," 377.

58. Stimpson, "Zero Degree Deviancy," 377.

Chapter Two

1. Karla Jay, "Coming Out As Process," in *Our Right to Love,* 28.

2. Recent collections of personal narratives or individual autobiographies often incorporate metaphors of travel and territory in their titles: for example, *The Coming Out Stories, The Lesbian Path, Lesbian Crossroads, This Bridge Called My Back, The Mohawk Trail,* and *Borderlands/La Frontera.* So too do the titles of many lesbian novels and short story collections such as *The Wanderground, Anna's Country, Movement, To the Cleveland Station, Walking on the Moon, Spring Forward, Fall Back, The Journey, The Long Trail,* and *Sisters of the Road.*

3. See Zimmerman, "Exiting from Patriarchy."

4. Rich, foreword to *The Coming Out Stories,* xiii.

5. Rule has continued to write, of course, although she has always maintained an intellectual and artistic distance from the movement as such. Ironically her novel has recently achieved new popularity through its adaptation as the cult film, *Desert Hearts.*

6. Susan J. Rosowski, "The Novel of Awakening," in *The Voyage In,* 49–68.

7. See Stuart Miller, *The Picaresque Novel* (Cleveland: The Press of Case Western Reserve University, 1967).

8. Jerome Buckley, *Season of Youth: The Bildungsroman from Dickens to Golding* (Cambridge: Harvard University Press, 1974), 20.

9. Phyllis Birkby, Bertha Harris, Jill Johnston, Esther Newton, and Jane O'Wyatt, eds., *Amazon Expedition: A Lesbian Feminist Anthology* (New York: Times Change Press, 1973).

10. Janet Cooper, "Coming Out" in *The Coming Out Stories,* 53. See further Stanley and Wolfe, introduction, xvix.

11. Stimpson, "Zero Degree Deviancy," 364.

12. Stanley and Wolfe, *The Coming Out Stories*, xxii.

13. As an interesting side note: Moyano is one of the women who wrote the C.L.I.T. manifesto. Here we see a real-life example of the transformations I am describing. See Sarah Lucia Hoagland and Julia Penelope, *For Lesbians Only: A Separatist Anthology* (London: Onlywomen Press, 1988), 583.

14. Stimpson, "Zero Degree Deviancy," 371.

15. For example, *Lesbian Connection* 5 (1) (September 1980): 6; *Lesbian Connection* 7 (3) (August/September 1984): 7.

16. [Djuna Barnes], *The Ladies Almanack,* written and illustrated by a Lady of Fashion (New York: Harper & Row, Publishers, 1972 [1928]), 26.

17. Barbara Ponse, *Identities in the Lesbian World* (Westport, Conn.: Greenwood Press, 1976), 99–100.

18. See Lee Zevy with Sahli A. Cavallaro, "Invisibility, Fantasy, and Intimacy: Princess Charming Is Not a Prince," in *Lesbian Psychologies: Explorations and Challenges,* ed. the Boston Lesbian Psychologies Collective (Urbana and Chicago: University of Illinois Press, 1987), 83–94.

19. Joseph Campbell, *The Hero with a Thousand Faces,* Bollingen Series XVII (Princeton: Princeton University Press, 1949), 37–38, 319–334.

20. In *Confessions of Cherubino,* Bertha Harris writes "when there's no more of a family left to be born, then its women begin to live forever" (109).

21. See Marilyn Frye, *The Politics of Reality: Essays in Feminist Theory* (Trumansburg, N.Y.: The Crossing Press, 1983), 20.

22. See Carroll Smith-Rosenberg, "The Female World of Love and Ritual: Relations Between Women in Nineteenth-Century America," in *A Heritage of Her Own,* ed. Nancy F. Cott and Elizabeth H. Pleck (New York: Simon and Schuster, 1979), 311–342; Lillian Faderman, *Surpassing the Love of Men;* Nancy Sahli, "Smashing: Women's Relationships Before the Fall," *Chrysalis* 8 (Summer 1979): 17–27; Blanche Wiesen Cook, "Female Support Networks and Political Activism: Lillian Wald, Crystal Eastman, Emma Goldman," in Cott, 412–444.

23. Zevy, "Invisibility, Fantasy, and Intimacy," 84–88.

24. In contrast to Esther Newton's analysis of Radclyffe Hall and early twentieth-century conceptualizations of the lesbian, I have seen no evidence in lesbian feminist fiction of the 1970s and 1980s that masculinity is associated with sexuality. See Newton, "The Mythic Mannish Lesbian: Radclyffe Hall and the New Woman," *Signs* 9 (4) (Summer 1984): 557–575.

25. For a discussion of "common sense" as a discourse, see Belsey, *Critical Practice,* 1–7.

26. On Christianity and homosexuality, see John Boswell, *Christianity, Social Tolerance, and Homosexuality: Gay People in Western Europe from the Beginning of the Christian Era to the Fourteenth Century* (Chicago and London: The University of Chicago Press, 1980). Karl Heinrich Ulrichs, a nineteenth-century German homosexual, popularized the notion of homosexuality as a congenital condition. Richard von Krafft-Ebing adopted Ulrich's ideas in his influential *Psychopathia Sexualis*. On inversion theories, see Faderman, "The Morbidification of Love Between Women"; and Lauritsen and Thorstad, *The Early Homosexual Rights Movement*. On existentialism, see Simone de Beauvoir, "The Lesbian," in *The Second Sex,* trans. and ed. H. M. Parshley (New York: Alfred A. Knopf, 1953; New York: Bantam Books, 1961), 379–399. (To be sure, de Beauvoir's discussion is tinged with the Freudianism of her day.) The revised congenital theory can be found everywhere in contemporary gay journals and newspapers. In 1988 the organization Parents and Friends of Lesbians and Gays included in its mailing a newspaper editorial stating, without any qualification, that sexual orientation is "a matter of biological roulette" (Robert A. Bernstein, "My Daughter is a Lesbian," *New York Times,* 24 February 1988). See also Christine Browning, "Changing Theories of Lesbianism: Challenging the Stereotypes," in *Women-Identified Women,* ed. Trudy Darty and Sandee Potter, with a foreword by Judith Schwarz (Palo Alto: Mayfield Publishing Company, 1984), 11–30; and Celia Kitzinger, *The Social Construction of Lesbianism* (London: SAGE Publications, 1987).

27. For example, Maricla Moyano, *BeginningBook;* Sandy Boucher, "Mountain Radio" and "Retaining Walls" in *Assaults and Rituals;* Elana Nachmann, *Riverfinger Women;* Nancy Toder, *Choices;* Noretta Koertge, *Who Was That Masked Woman?;* Barbara Wilson, "Walking on the Moon" in *Walking on the Moon:* Sheila Ortiz Taylor, *Spring Forward, Fall Back.*

28. Segrest, *My Mama's Dead Squirrel,* 126. On autobiographical narratives, see also Daphne Patai, "Constructing a Self: A Brazilian Life Story," *Feminist Studies* 14, 1 (Spring 1988): 143–166; Joanne Frye, *Living Stories, Telling Lives: Women and the Novel in Contemporary Experience* (Ann Arbor: The University of Michigan Press, 1986).

29. Ponse, 159–160.

30. Rich, "Compulsory Heterosexuality and Lesbian Existence," in *Blood, Bread, and Poetry,* 23–75.

31. Alix Dobkin, "View from Gay Head," *Lavender Jane Loves Women* (1975). Stereo recording, Women's Wax Works, A001.

32. See Gay Revolution Party Women's Caucus, "Realesbians and Politi-

calesbians," in *Out of the Closets: Voices of Gay Liberation,* ed. Karla Jay and Allen Young (New York: Jove/HBJ, 1972), 177–81; and Deborah Goleman Wolf, *The Lesbian Community* (Berkeley: University of California Press, 1979), 81–82.

33. Camarin Grae gives a psychological twist to these lesbian feminist myths in her 1984 fantasy-thriller, *Paz.* When the protagonist gains the power to change minds, she discovers that men's emotional limitations prevent her from loving them in the way she loves women. She comes out as a result of recognizing women's superiority to men.

34. Unfortunately, Carol Anne Douglas does not treat Brenda's story with the irony and self-criticism that this moment in feminist history sorely needs.

35. Julia Penelope Stanley, "My Life as a Lesbian," in *The Coming Out Stories,* 195.

36. However, in Norwegian author Gerd Brantenberg's delightful coming out novel, *What Comes Naturally*—first published in Norwegian in 1973, and published in English translation in 1986—the protagonist states simply, "I was *born* a lesbian" (London: The Women's Press), 66.

37. See, for example, Nancy Chodorow, *The Reproduction of Mothering: Psychoanalysis and the Sociology of Gender* (Berkeley: University of California Press, 1978); Adrienne Rich, *Of Woman Born: Motherhood as Experience and Institution,* esp. chapter IX, "Motherhood and Daughterhood" (New York: W. W. Norton, 1976; New York: Bantam Books, 1977).

38. Rich, "Transcendental Etude," *The Dream of a Common Language,* 75.

39. Jill Johnston, *Lesbian Nation: The Feminist Solution* (New York: Simon and Schuster, 1973), 266.

40. Marilyn Frye, review of *The Coming Out Stories* ed. by Julia Penelope Stanley and Susan J. Wolfe, *Sinister Wisdom* 14 (1980): 98.

41. Jo Nesbitt, "The Causes of Lesbianism," *off our backs* 10 (11) (December 1980): 17.

42. For example: Joyce Bright, *Sunday's Child;* Judith Alguire, *All Out;* Elizabeth Dean, *As the Road Curves.* On the lesbian sports community, see Yvonne Zipter, *Diamonds Are a Dyke's Best Friend* (Ithaca: Firebrand Books, 1988).

43. Rich, *Twenty-One Love Poems,* "XIII," in *The Dream of a Common Language,* 31.

44. See Bonnie Zimmerman, "Daughters of Darkness: Lesbian Vampires," *Jump Cut* 24–25 (March 1981): 23–24.

45. Jewelle Gomez, "No Day Too Long," in *Lesbian Fiction,* 219–25. See

also Gomez, "Writing Vampire Fiction," *Hot Wire* (November 1987): 42—43.

46. Bob Dylan, "Absolutely Sweet Marie," in *Lyrics, 1962—1985* (New York: Alfred A. Knopf, 1985), 233. Chris Williamson repeats the line in "Bandit Queen," *Live Dream,* Olivia Records (1977).

47. Frye, *The Politics of Reality,* 159.

48. Harris, "Notes toward Defining," 8.

49. See in *Lesbianism and the Women's Movement,* ed. Nancy Myron and Charlotte Bunch (Baltimore: Diana Press, 1975).

50. In some lesbian detective novels, like *Murder in the Collective* and *The Sophie Horowitz Story,* the search for the solution to a crime is tied to the search for personal identity. For an expansion of this point, see Sally Munt, "The Inverstigators: Lesbian Crime Fiction," in *Sweet Dreams: Sexuality, Gender and Popular Fiction,* ed. Susannah Radstone (London: Lawrence and Wishart, 1988), 91—119.

51. Nyla Wade appears in Vicki McConnell's *Mrs. Porter's Letter, The Burnton Widows,* and *Double Daughter.* Stoner McTavish is the protagonist of Sarah Dreher's *Stoner McTavish, Something Shady,* and *Grey Magic.* Kate Delafield is the hero of Katherine Forrest's *Amateur City* and *Murder at the Nightwood Bar.*

52. Rich, "It Is the Lesbian in Us . . . ," in *On Lies, Secrets, and Silence,* 201.

53. See Laura Lederer, ed., *Take Back the Night: Women on Pornography* (New York: William Morrow & Co., 1980).

54. Audre Lorde, "Dahomey," "125th Street and Abomey," and "The Women of Dan," in *The Black Unicorn* (New York: W. W. Norton, 1978), 10—15; see also Carolyn Gage's dramatic monologue, "The Second Coming of Joan of Arc," *Sinister Wisdom* 35 (Summer/Fall 1988): 95—116.

55. See also Jeffner Allen's use of "amazon" in *Lesbian Philosophy: Explorations* (Palo Alto: Institute of Lesbian Studies, 1986).

56. For example, Jewelle Gomez, "A Cultural Legacy Denied and Discovered: Black Lesbians in Fiction by Women," in *Home Girls: A Black Feminist Anthology,* ed. Barbara Smith (New York: Kitchen Table: Women of Color Press, 1983), 111—112.

57. See Sandra M. Gilbert and Susan Gubar, *The Madwoman in the Attic* (New Haven: Yale University Press, 1979); Barbara Hill Rigney, *Madness and Sexual Politics in the Feminist Novel: Studies in Bronte, Woolf, Lessing, and Atwood* (Madison: University of Wisconsin Press, 1978).

58. See "WITCH Documents," in *Sisterhood Is Powerful: An Anthology of*

Writings from the Women's Liberation Movement, ed. Robin Morgan (New York: Vintage Books, 1970), 538–53.

59. For example, Dale Hoak, "The Great European Witch Hunts: A Historical Perspective," *American Journal of Sociology* 88 (May 1983): 1270–74; Richard A. Horsley, "Who Were the Witches: The Social Roles of the Accused in the European Witch Trials," *Journal of Interdisciplinary History* 9 (Spring 1979): 689–715; Carolyn Matalene, "Women As Witches," *International Journal of Women's Studies* 1 (November-December 1978): 573–87.

60. Other novels that draw upon the figure of the witch include Sally Gearhart, *The Wanderground;* Rochelle Singer, *The Demeter Flower;* Sandi Hall, *The Godmothers;* Alice Bloch, *The Law of Return;* and Michelle Cliff, *Abeng.*

61. Feminists who have popularized inflated figures include Mary Daly, *Gyn/Ecology: The Metaethics of Radical Feminism* (Boston: Beacon Press, 1978), 183; Andrea Dworkin, *Woman Hating* (New York: E. P. Dutton, 1974), 130; Barbara Ehrenreich and Deirdre English, *Witches, Midwives and Nurses: A History of Women Healers* (Old Westbury, N.Y.: The Feminist Press, 1973), 7–8.

62. My discussion of the patterner is inspired by two speculative/fantasy novels: Octavia Butler, *Patternmaster* (New York: Doubleday & Company, 1976) and Elizabeth A. Lynn, *The Dancers of Arun* (New York: Berkley Books, 1979).

63. Sally Gearhart and Susan Rennie, *A Feminist Tarot: A Guide to Intrapersonal Communication* (Watertown: Mass.: Persephone Press, 1977), 4.

64. Frye, *The Politics of Reality,* 170.

65. Judy Grahn, *Another Mother Tongue: Gay Words, Gay Worlds* (Boston: Beacon Press, 1984), 269.

66. See the special issue on androgyny of *Women's Studies* 2 (2) (1974).

67. Johnston, *Lesbian Nation,* 182ff.

68. The preference for a unified and unambiguous self may also be part of the reason why lesbians are so mistrustful of bisexuality.

69. Joan Nestle, "Sexual Courage in the Fifties," in *A Restricted Country* (Ithaca: Firebrand Books, 1987), 100–101.

70. See Grace Stewart, *A New Mythos: The Novel of the Artist as Heroine* (Montreal: Eden Press, 1981).

71. See Claudia Stillman Franks, "Stephen Gordon, Novelist: A Reevaluation of Radclyffe Hall's *The Well of Loneliness,*" *Tulsa Studies in Women's Literature* 1 (2) (Fall 1982): 125–139.

72. Gilbert and Gubar, *The Madwoman in the Attic,* 45.

73. Lee Lynch, "Fruitstand II: Honeydew Moon," in *Old Dyke Tales,* 141–157.

74. Rich, "Natural Resources," in *The Dream of a Common Language,* 67. See Julia Penelope Stanley and others, "The Transformation of Silence into Language and Action" (The Lesbians and Literature Panel of the annual meetings of the Modern Language Association, Chicago, December 1977), *Sinister Wisdom* 6 (Summer 1978): 4–25; Adrienne Rich, "Women and Honor: Some Notes on Lying," in *On Lies, Secrets and Silence,* 185–194; Michelle Cliff, "Notes on Speechlessness," *Sinister Wisdom* 5 (Winter 1978): 5–9. Of course, this is also one of the ways in which feminists define women's oppression. Throughout lesbian writing, a close connection exists between lesbian feminist and radical feminist ideas.

75. The term "wild zone" comes from Elaine Showalter, "Feminist Criticism in the Wilderness," in *New Feminist Criticism,* 262.

Chapter Three

1. For example, David Hamilton and Alain Robbe-Grillet, *Sisters* (New York: William Morrow & Co., 1973).

2. Denis de Rougemont, *Love in the Western World* (New York: Harcourt, Brace, and Co., 1940), 1.

3. See Laurence Lerner, *Love and Marriage: Literature and Its Social Context* (New York: St. Martin's Press, 1979).

4. Adrienne Rich, *Twenty-One Love Poems,* "XVII," in *The Dream of a Common Language,* 33.

5. Annis Pratt, *Archetypal Patterns in Women's Literature,* 17.

6. de Rougemont, *Love in the Western World* 52; Plato, *The Symposium,* trans. Suzy Q. Groden (Amherst: University of Massachusetts Press, 1970), 67.

7. Jean-Paul Sartre, *No Exit,* in *No Exit and The Flies,* trans. Stuart Gilbert (New York: Alfred A. Knopf, 1965).

8. The reference is to Sappho, "Lament for a Maidenhead," in *Sappho: A New Translation,* trans. Mary Barnard (Berkeley: University of California Press, 1958) 34. Judy Grahn uses the same image as the inspiration for *The Highest Apple.*

9. See Benstock, *Women of the Left Bank,* 301; Jay, *The Amazon and the Page,* 24.

10. Marny Hall, "Lesbians, Limerence and Longterm Relationships," in *Lesbian Sex,* by JoAnn Loulan (San Francisco: Spinsters Ink, 1984), 143.

11. Donna Tanner, *The Lesbian Couple* (Lexington, Mass.: Lexington

Books, 1978), 91.

12. Doris Grumbach, interview, *Belles Lettres* (1) (1985): 11.

13. It should be noted that beds figure as a tantalizing if ambiguous symbol of sexuality and insularity in the letters and diaries of other women who were, in the most conservative interpretation, involved in romantic friendships, or who may be described as lesbians. In addition to the Ladies of Llangollen, consider the cases of Susan B. Anthony and Jane Addams. See Katz, *Gay American History,* 973; Cook, "Female Support Networks," 419.

14. Emily Dickinson, *The Complete Poems of Emily Dickinson,* ed. Thomas H. Johnson (Boston: Little, Brown, 1960), 214–15.

15. Katherine Philips, "To My Excellent Lucasia, on Our Friendship," in *The Norton Anthology of Literature by Women,* ed. Sandra M. Gilbert and Susan Gubar (New York: W. W. Norton & Company, 1985), 81.

16. On feminist theories of boundaries see Elizabeth Abel, "(E)Merging Identities: The Dynamics of Female Friendship in Contemporary Fiction by Women," *Signs* 6 (3) (Spring 1981): 413–35; Judith Kegan Gardiner, "The (US)es of (I)dentity: A Response to Abel on '(E)Merging Identities,'" *Signs* 6 (3) (Spring 1981): 436–42; Gardiner, "On Female Identity and Writing by Women," *Critical Inquiry* 8 (2) (Winter 1981): 347–61.

17. Letitia Ann Peplau and others, "Loving Women: Attachment and Autonomy in Lesbian Relationships," *The Journal of Social Issues* 34 (3) (1978): 7–27.

18. Irene Yarrow, "Woman Becoming," in *The Lesbian Reader,* ed. Gina Covina and Laurel Galana (Guerneville, Calif.: Amazon Press, 1975), 8.

19. Although the lovers are reunited in the third Pam Nilsen mystery, *The Dog Collar Murders* (1989), they continue to struggle over autonomy and monogamy.

20. For a fictional recreation of the debate over monogamy, see Becky Birtha, "A Monogamy Story" in *For Nights Like This One,* 49–60. See also D. Merilee Clunis and G. Dorsey Green, *Lesbian Couples* (Seattle: The Seal Press, 1988), 80–94.

21. See, for example, Judith Fetterley, "Writes of Passing," in *Gossip: A Journal of Lesbian Feminist Ethics,* (5) (n.d.): 21–28.

22. Woolf, *A Room of One's Own,* 51.

23. In describing their marriage, Jane says "We talk, I believe, all day long: to talk to each other is but a more animated and an audible thinking." Charlotte Brontë, *Jane Eyre,* ed. Q. D. Leavis (Harmondsworth: Penguin Books, 1966), 476.

24. Katz, "Smash Phallic Imperialism," in *Out of the Closets* 260.

25. A. prilfool [pseud.], "Shocking Finding," *off our backs* 17 (5) (May 1987): 15; *Lesbian Connection* 10 (1) (July/August 1987): 2.

26. Leslie Lawrence, "Bodily Fictions," *The Women's Review of Books* 4 (10–11) (July-August 1987): 8–9.

27. Psychotherapist Margaret Nichols uses the same example to illustrate her theory that sexual arousal is related to a necessary barrier, or "disequilibrium" between lovers. See "Lesbian Sexuality: Issues and Developing Theory," in *Lesbian Psychologies,* 106, 112.

28. Kathy Hruby, "Rolling in the Mouth," in *The Lesbian Reader,* 81.

29. Sappho, "Prayer to my lady of Paphos," 38.

30. Ann Snitow, "The Front Line: Notes on Sex in Novels by Women," *Signs* 5 (4) (Summer 1980): 710.

31. See, for example, Samois, ed., *Coming to Power: Writings and Graphics on Lesbian S/M* (Boston: Alyson Publications, 1982). Some readers may feel that I have not paid adequate attention to sadomasochistic fiction, especially since the issue has been so divisive within the lesbian feminist community, and the literature has proliferated in the second half of the 1980s. I believe that this literature needs a serious and dispassionate study of its own, one that would place it within the historical tradition of libertine and pornographic literature, as well as lesbian literature, and that would take on the difficult question of differentiating between pornography and erotica. This is not the place for such a study.

32. This is one justification of S/M offered by its feminist adherents; see Samois, *Coming to Power.* Many others argue that, in reality, S/M becomes an end in itself. See, for example, Robin Ruth Linden and others, eds., *Against Sadomasochism: A Radical Feminist Analysis* (East Palo Alto: Frog In the Well, 1982).

33. Joan Nestle, "Butch-Femme Relationships: Sexual Courage in the 1950s," in *A Restricted Country* (Ithaca: Firebrand Books, 1987), 100.

34. See also many of Becky Birtha's short stories in *For Nights Like This One* and *Lover's Choice.*

35. Barbara Christian raises this point in "Trajectories of Self-Definition: Placing Contemporary Afro-American Women's Fiction," in *Black Feminist Criticism: Perspectives on Black Women Writers* (New York: Pergamon Press, 1985), 184. The same volume contains her essay, "No More Buried Lives: The Theme of Lesbianism in Audre Lorde's *Zami,* Gloria Naylor's *The Women of Brewster Place,* Ntozake Shange's *Sassafras, Cypress and Indigo,* and Alice Walker's *The Color Purple.*"

36. Audre Lorde, *Zami,* 226.

Chapter Four

1. Johnston first referred to "lesbian nation" in "Anybody Dying of Love," *The Village Voice,* 14 October 1971: 23.
2. Susan Krieger, "Lesbian Identity and Community: Recent Social Science Literature," *Signs* 8 (1) (Autumn 1982): 92.
3. Sasha Gregory Lewis, *Sunday's Women: A Report on Lesbian Life Today* (Boston: Beacon Press, 1979), 56.
4. Rich, "Transcendental Etude," in *The Dream of a Common Language,* 76.
5. See, in particular, Marks, "Lesbian Intertextuality," 353–377.
6. Blankley, "Return to Mytilene," 46, 51.
7. Blankley, "Return to Mytilene," 61.
8. Jay, *The Amazon and the Page,* 67.
9. Lynch, "The Isles of Lesbos," in *The Amazon Trail* (Tallahassee: The Naiad Press, 1988), 61.
10. Grahn, *The Highest Apple,* 5–7.
11. Emily Dickinson, "I dwell in Possibility," (no. 657), p. 327.
12. Namascar Shaktini, "Displacing the Phallic Subject: Wittig's Lesbian Writing," *Signs* 8 (1) (Autumn 1982): 40–41.
13. Henry Handel Richardson, "Two Hanged Women," in *New Lesbian Writing: An Anthology,* ed. Margaret Cruikshank (San Francisco: Grey Fox Press, 1984), 79–83; Rich, "Natural Resources," in *The Dream of A Common Language,* 67.
14. Pamela Allen, "Free Space," in *Radical Feminism,* 271–79.
15. See in particular Myron and Bunch, *Lesbianism and the Women's Movement.* The politics and principles of lesbian separatism were defined (roughly between 1971 and 1974) primarily through newspapers and manifestos put out by collectives around the country: *Ain't I a Woman?* in Iowa City, *Spectre* in Ann Arbor, and *Lesbian Separatism: An Amazon Analysis* from Seattle, as well as *The Furies* in Washington, D.C.
16. Frye, *The Politics of Reality,* 95–109. Separatist theory developed in complexity and sophistication in the 1980s. See *For Lesbians Only;* also *Lesbian Ethics* 3 (2) (Fall 1988).
17. Alix Dobkin, "Lavender Jane loves . . . ," interview by Fran Moira and Anne Williams, *off our backs* 4 (5) (April 1974): 6.
18. Rich, "Compulsory Heterosexuality and Lesbian Existence," in *Blood, Bread, and Poetry,* 51.
19. See Nina Baym, "Melodramas of Beset Manhood: How Theories of American Fiction Exclude Women Authors," in *New Feminist Criticism,* 71–72. For this reason, perhaps, *Rubyfruit Jungle* was one of the few lesbian

novels originally published by an alternative press to be purchased later by a commercial publishing house.

20. Lois Gould, "Creating a Women's World," *New York Times Magazine,* 2 January 1977, 11.

21. See, for example, Piercy's *Small Changes* (Greenwich, Conn.: Fawcett Crest, 1972); Schulman's *Burning Questions* (New York: Alfred A. Knopf, 1978); and Geller's *Seed of a Woman* (Buffalo: Imp Press, 1979).

22. It is unclear whether or not Shockley can actually be called a lesbian writer. See SDiane Bogus, review of *Loving Her, The Black and White of It,* and *Say Jesus and Come to Me,* in *Sinister Wisdom* 35 (Summer/Fall 1988): 130. Nevertheless, her fiction clearly meets several of the criteria I established in chapter one.

23. Anne Bradstreet, "The Prologue," in *The Norton Anthology of Literature by Women,* 62. See Elaine Hedges, "The Nineteenth-Century Diarist and Her Quilts," *Feminist Studies* 8 (Summer 1982): 293–99; Elaine Showalter, "Piecing and Writing," in *The Poetics of Gender,* ed. Nancy K. Miller (New York: Columbia University Press, 1986), 222–247; Nancy K. Miller, "Arachnologies: The Woman, The Text, and the Critic," in *The Poetics of Gender,* 270–295.

24. Janice Raymond, *A Passion for Friends: Toward a Philosophy of Female Affection* (Boston: Beacon Press, 1986), 3; Rich, "Natural Resources," in *A Dream of a Common Language,* 61.

25. Johnston, *Gullible's Travels* (New York: Links Books, 1974); Kate Millett, "All Spruced Up," *Ms,* May 1988: 30. See also Joyce Cheney, ed., *Lesbian Land* (Minneapolis: Word Weavers, 1985).

26. Not surprisingly, given the politics of most lesbian feminist writers, there are few examples of the military as Lesbian Nation. Sharon in *Yesterday's Lessons* meets her first lover in boot camp, and Tretona in *Who Was that Masked Woman?* is almost seduced into believing she can be all that she can be in the army. Moreover, coeducation appears to have eliminated another of the classic locations of lesbian community, the girls' school or women's college.

27. Tony Tanner, *Adultery in the Novel: Contract and Transgression* (Baltimore: The Johns Hopkins University Press, 1979), 18–23. See also Raymond Williams, *The Country and the City* (New York: Oxford University Press, 1973).

28. See D. H. Lawrence, *Studies in Classic American Literature* (New York: T. Seltzer, 1923); Leslie Fiedler, *Love and Death in the American Novel* (New York: Stein and Day, 1966).

29. On The Family of Woman, see *Are We There Yet?,* ed. Michal Brady, 8

and 63–64; Steichen, *The Family of Man: The Greatest Photographic Exhibition of All Time* (New York: Museum of Modern Art, 1955).

30. Joan Nestle, "Lesbian Artists," *Heresies* 3 (1977): 41. See also Stimpson, "Zero Degree Deviancy," 371.

31. For a fascinating, although non-lesbian, treatment of the alien/alienation theme, see James Tiptree Jr. [Alice Sheldon], "The Women Men Don't See," *The New Women of Wonder,* ed. Pamela Sargent (New York: Vintage, 1978), 176–217.

32. On feminist and lesbian utopian fiction and SF, see Ruby Rohrlich and Elaine Hoffman Baruch, *Women in Search of Utopia* (New York: Schocken Books, 1984); Jean Pfaelzer, *The Utopian Novel in America 1886–1896* (Pittsburgh: University of Pittsburgh Press, 1984); Natalie Rosinsky, *Feminist Futures: Contemporary Women's Speculative Fiction* (Ann Arbor: UMI Research Press, 1984); Marleen Barr, ed., *Women and Utopia: Critical Interpretations* (Lanham, Md.: University Press of America, 1983); Thelma J. Shinn, *Worlds Within Women: Myth and Mythmaking in Fantastic Literature by Women* (New York: Greenwood Press, 1986).

33. See Jane Gurko and Sally Gearhart, "The Sword and the Vessel Versus the Lake on the Lake: A Lesbian Model of Nonviolent Rhetoric," unpublished paper presented at the annual meeting of the Modern Language Association, San Francisco, December, 1979.

34. "Bridging" can also represent the creation of community, as I used it in the previous chapter, or as Cherríe Moraga and Gloria Anzaldúa used it in *This Bridge Called My Back Writings by Radical Women of Color* (Watertown, Mass.: Persephone Press, 1981). Context is all-important.

35. Natalie Rosinsky makes the same point in *Feminist Futures,* 89.

36. Compare to Walter M. Miller, Jr.'s *A Canticle for Leibowitz* (New York: J. B. Lippincott Company, 1959) and Suzy McKee Charnas's *Walk to the End of the World* (New York: Ballantine Books, 1974).

37. Tucker Farley, "Realities and Fictions: Lesbian Visions of Utopia," in Rohrlich, *Women in Search of Utopia,* 241.

38. Krieger, *The Mirror Dance: Identity in a Women's Community* (Philadelphia: Temple University Press, 1983), 168.

39. Sarah Pearlman, "The Saga of Continuing Clash in Lesbian Community, or Will an Army of Ex-Lovers Fail?," in *Lesbian Psychologies,* 314.

40. Pearlman, "The Saga of Continuing Clash," in *Lesbian Psychologies,* 316.

41. See Frye, *The Politics of Reality,* 128–151.

42. Marilyn R. Schuster, "Strategies for Survival: The Subtle Subversion of Jane Rule," *Feminist Studies* 7 (3) (Fall 1981): 443.

Chapter Five

1. Frances M. Beal, "Double Jeopardy: To Be Black and Female," in Robin Morgan, ed., *Sisterhood is Powerful,* 340–353.
2. "Redstockings Manifesto," Robin Morgan, ed., *Sisterhood is Powerful,* 535.
3. For discussions of "the personal is the political," see Sara Evans, *Personal Politics: The Roots of Women's Liberation in the Civil Rights Movement & the New Left* (New York: Random House, 1979); Bonnie Zimmerman, "The Politics of Transliteration: Lesbian First-Person Narratives," *Signs* 9 (4) (Summer 1984): 663–682.
4. See, for example, Zillah R. Eisenstein, ed., *Capitalist Patriarchy and the Case for Socialist Feminism* (New York and London: Monthly Review Press, 1979).
5. Zimmerman, "The Phantom of Camilla Hall," in *Are We There Yet?,* ed. Michal Brody, 113.
6. Desmoines, "There Goes the Revolution . . . ," *Sinister Wisdom* 9 (Spring 1979): 21.
7. Alice Echols discusses cultural feminism in "The Taming of the Id: Feminist Sexual Politics 1968–83," in *Pleasure and Danger: Exploring Female Sexuality,* ed. Carole S. Vance (Boston: Routledge & Kegan Paul, 1984), 50–72.
8. For an historical account of the Alpert/Saxe/SLA debates, the reader can do no better than to read issues of *off our backs* during the years 1974 through 1976.
9. Woolf, *Three Guineas* (New York: Harcourt, Brace & World, 1938), 109; Rich, "Notes toward a Politics of Location," in *Blood, Bread, and Poetry,* 212.
10. Combahee River Collective, "A Black Feminist Statement," in *This Bridge Called My Back,* ed. Moraga and Anzaldúa, 212.
11. Barbara Smith, "Between a Rock and a Hard Place: Relationships Between Black and Jewish Women," in *Yours in Struggle: Three Feminist Perspectives on Anti-Semitism and Racism,* Elly Bulkin, Minnie Bruce Pratt, and Barbara Smith (Brooklyn: Long Haul Press, 1984), 84. Julia Penelope writes a powerful separatist response to Smith in "The Mystery of Lesbians," in *Lesbian Separatism,* 506–547.
12. See for example, Adrienne Rich, "Notes for a Magazine: What does Separatism Mean?," *Sinister Wisdom* 18 (1981), 83–91; Lois Anne Addison, "Separatism Revisited," *Sinister Wisdom* 21 (1982), 29–34; Cathy

McCandless, "Some Thoughts about Racism, Classism and Separatism," in *Top Ranking: A Collection of Articles on Racism and Classism in the Lesbian Community,* compiled by Joan Gibbs and Sara Bennett (New York: February 3rd Press, n.d.).

13. Alison Colbert, aka/Sarahgold, "The 'All Women's Interests are the Same' Line: A Trap for Non-Privileged Women?," in *Top Ranking,* ed. Gibbs and Bennett, 51.

14. Charoula, "Prison Work and the Lesbian Issue: A Personal Statement," in *Top Ranking,* ed. Gibbs and Bennett, 47.

15. Bernice Johnson Reagon, "Coalition Politics: Turning the Century," in *Home Girls,* ed. Barbara Smith, 358–359.

16. Here is the "political problem" of pronouns raised by Adrienne Rich to which I referred in my preface.

17. Sally Gearhart, in conversation at the annual meetings of the Modern Language Association, Houston, December 1980. See Gearhart's own reconsideration in "Future Visions: Today's Politics: Feminist Utopias in Review," in *Women in Search of Utopia,* ed. Rohrlich, 307.

18. Lorde, *Zami,* 226. The House of Women was the title of a conference on women's culture held at California State University at Long Beach, November 1984. Judy Grahn uses "the house of women" extensively as a symbol in *The Highest Apple.*

19. Smith, *Yours in Struggle,* 71.

20. Unidentified author and article, quoted in Gwendolyn!!, "Righteous Anger in 3 Parts: Racism in the Lesbian Community—One Black Lesbian's Perspective," in *Top Ranking,* ed. Gibbs and Bennett, 75.

21. On racism and literature, see Bulkin, "Racism and Writing: Some Implications for White Lesbian Critics," *Sinister Wisdom* 13 (Spring 1980), 3–22.

22. For a different perspective, see Jane Marcus, "Afterword" to June Arnold, *Sister Gin* (New York: The Feminist Press, 1989), 217–236.

23. See, in particular, *Lesbian Fiction,* ed. Bulkin.

24. On southern lesbian writing, see Mab Segrest, *My Mama's Dead Squirrel.*

25. See, for example, the Iowa City newspaper *Ain't I a Woman?* and the articles from *The Furies* reprinted as *Class and Feminism,* ed. Charlotte Bunch and Nancy Myron (Baltimore: Diana Press, 1974). The lesbian approach to class supports my contention that we conceptualize differences in personal, not political, terms. Whereas Marxist or socialist feminists define class traditionally, as one's relation to the means of production, lesbian

feminists tend to focus on the personal or lifestyle consequences of that relation, such as attitudes toward money or anger.

26. On aging, see *Sister Gin* and *Prism;* on disability, the sole example seems to be Lynn Strongin's experimental *Bones and Kim,* a novel that has been unavailable for several years.

27. Linda J. Brown, "Dark Horse: A View of Writing and Publishing by Dark Lesbians," *Sinister Wisdom* 13 (Spring 1980): 47. See also Jewelle Gomez, "Imagine a Lesbian . . . A Black Lesbian . . . ," *Trivia: A Journal of Ideas* 12 (Spring 1988): 45–60.

28. Woolf, *Room,* 43.

29. Lorde, "Age, Race, Class, and Sex: Women Redefining Difference," in *Sister Outsider,* 116.

30. Brown, "Dark Horse," 46 and 47.

31. Woolf, *Room,* 55. See also Alice Walker, *In Search of Our Mothers' Gardens* (New York: Harvest/HBJ, 1984).

32. Smith, "Toward a Black Feminist Criticism"; Gloria T. Hull, "'Under the Days': The Buried Life and Poetry of Angelina Weld Grimke," *Conditions: Five* 2 (2) (Autumn 1979): 17–25.

33. Lorde, "Poetry Is Not a Luxury," in *Sister Outsider* 36–39.

34. *Conditions Five: The Black Women's Issue* 2 (2) (Autumn 1979).

35. On sexual difference and poststructuralist theory, see Jardine, *Gynesis,* and Moi, *Sexual/Textual Politics.*

36. Wittig, "Paradigm," 117.

37. Gayatri Chakravorty Spivack, "French Feminism in an International Frame," in *In Other Worlds: Essays in Cultural Politics* (New York and London: Methuen, 1987), 150. See also Jane Gallop, "Annie Leclerc Writing a Letter, with Vermeer," in *The Poetics of Gender,* ed. Nancy K. Miller, 137–156.

38. See Leslie Wahl Rabine, "A Feminist Politics of Non-Identity," *Feminist Studies* 14 (1) (Spring 1988): 27.

39. See Rich, "Power" and "Natural Resources," in *The Dream of a Common Language.*

40. Biddy Martin and Chandra Talpade Mohanty, "Feminist Politics: What's Home Got to Do with It?," in *Feminist Studies/Critical Studies,* ed. Teresa de Lauretis, 196.

41. Allen, *The Sacred Hoop,* 100.

42. Emily Dickinson, "I'm ceded—I've stopped being Theirs," *The Complete Poems of Emily Dickinson,* ed. Thomas H. Johnson, 247.

43. Anzaldúa, "La Prieta," in *This Bridge Called My Back,* ed. Moraga and Anzaldúa, 208.

44. Hélène Cixous, "The Laugh of the Medusa," *Signs* 1 (4) (Summer 1976): 875–93; Lorde, "Uses of the Erotic: The Erotic as Power," in *Sister Outsider*, 53–59.

45. Occasionally a narrative does not conform to this pattern. In Beth Brant's autobiographical *Mohawk Trail*, her father is Indian and her mother white.

46. Class is less neatly structured in the novel: it is through her mother and grandmother that Clare is propertied and thus socially superior to her poor, darker-skinned friend, Zoe.

47. Lorde, "Poetry Is Not a Luxury," in *Sister Outsider*, 36.

48. Janice Doane and Devon Hodges, *Nostalgia and Sexual Difference* (New York and London: Methuen, 1987), 3, 92, 140.

49. Rich, "When We Dead Awaken: Writing As Re-Vision," in *On Lies, Secrets, and Silence*, 33–49.

50. Allen, *The Sacred Hoop*, 104–105.

51. Lorde, "Age, Race, Class, and Sex," *Sister Outsider*, 120–121.

52. See also the conclusions of Linda Alcoff in "Cultural Feminism versus Post-Structuralism: The Identity Crisis in Feminist Theory," *Signs* 13 (3) (Spring 1988): 412.

53. Since Doane and Hodges note that nostalgic writers "never leave any ending open" (p. 42), we might conclude that lesbians of color and ethnic lesbians both are and are not nostalgic.

54. Chapter 31 was previously published as a story titled "Tar Beach," in *Conditions: Five:* 34–47.

55. Lorde, "An Open Letter to Mary Daly," *Sister Outsider*, 67.

56. See Elana Dykewomon [Nachmann], "The Fourth Daughter's Four Hundred Questions," in *Nice Jewish Girls: A Lesbian Anthology*, ed. Evelyn Torton Beck (Watertown, Mass.: Persephone Press, 1982), 148–160.

57. Martin and Mohanty, "Feminist Politics," 196.

58. Martin and Mohanty, "Feminist Politics," 208–209.

59. Martin and Mohanty, "Feminist Politics," 210.

Chapter Six

1. The phrase is from Virginia Woolf, *Orlando* (New York: Harcourt Brace Jovanovich, 1928), 298.

2. Consider, for example, the novels published by E. P. Dutton since 1987: Margaret Erhart's *Unusual Company*, Sarah Schulman's *After Dolores*, and Michelle Cliff's *No Telephone to Heaven*.

3. See Jackie Winnow, "Lesbians Working on AIDS: Assessing the Impact on Health Care for Women," *Out/Look* 2, 1 (Summer 1989), 10–18.

4. In *Leave a Light On for Me, Memory Board* and "Something Shiny" in *A Letter to Harvey Milk,* for example, the lesbian characters must come to terms with the loss of a gay male friend to AIDS. In *Dusty's Queen of Hearts Diner* and *Night Lights,* a united community of women and men draws together to protect itself against gay-bashing. Although *Leave a Light On for Me* concludes with a scene (recalling *Valley of the Amazons* or *The Burnton Widows*) in which virtually all the characters, female and male, gather together for the Gay Pride Parade, none of these novels actually shows a gay community forming on the basis of a collective vision rather than a defense against oppression.

5. Adrian Oktenberg, "The End of the Affair," review of *Unusual Company* by Margaret Erhart and *Cows and Horses* by Barbara Wilson, in *The Women's Review of Books,* 5 (9) (June 1988): 15. See also Bonnie Zimmerman, "Out and About," review of *Other Women* by Lisa Alther, *Triangles* by Ruth Geller, *The Sophie Horowitz Story* by Sarah Schulman, and *Valley of the Amazons* by Noretta Koertge, in *The Women's Review of Books* 2 (6) (March 1985): 14–15.

6. Sherri Paris, "In a World They Never Made," review of *Cass and the Stone Butch* by Antoinette Azolakov, *The Always Anonymous Beast* by Lauren Wright Douglas, *Sisters of the Road* by Barbara Wilson, and *She Came Too Late* by Mary Wings, in *The Women's Review of Books* 5 (10–11) (July 1988): 20.

7. Rich, "Diving Into the Wreck," in *Diving into the Wreck: Poems 1971–1972* (New York: W. W. Norton, 1973), 23.

8. Toni A. H. McNaron and Yarrow Morgan, eds., *Voices in the Night: Women Speaking about Incest* (Minneapolis: Cleis Press, 1982).

9. See Jean Swallow, ed., *Out from Under: Sober Dykes and Our Friends* (San Francisco: Spinsters Ink, 1983); Lee K. Nicoloff and Eloise A. Stiglitz, "Lesbian Alcoholism: Etiology, Treatment, and Recovery," in *Lesbian Psychologies,* 283–293.

10. Ellen Herman, "Getting to Serenity: Do Addiction Programs Sap Our Political Vitality?" *Out/Look* 1 (2) (Summer 1988): 14.

11. Alison Bechdel, "Theory and Practice," *off our backs* 18 (6) (June 1988): 19.

12. Oktenberg, 15–16. See also June Thomas, "Promoting Lesbian Writing," *off our backs* 18 (10) (November 1988): 3.

13. Yvonne M. Klein, "Myth and Community in Recent Lesbian Autobio-

graphical Fiction," in *Radical Revisions,* ed. Karla Jay and Joanne Glasgow (New York: New York University Press, forthcoming); Marilee Lindemann, "Natal Attractions: Politics, Art, and Eroticism in the Contemporary Lesbian Novel," unpublished paper presented at the annual meeting of the Modern Language Association, San Francisco, December 1987.

14. Mary Wings's *She Came Too Late* and Antoinette Azolakov's Cass Milam novels (*Cass and the Stone Butch* and *Skiptrace*) do create realistic scenes of local lesbian communities.

15. Letter in *Lesbian Connection* 10 (5) (March/April 1987): 6.

16. Woolf, *A Room of One's Own,* 117.

17. In a 1988 advertising flyer, The Naiad Press identified the three "most often asked about" categories that its books fell into. There were two titles or authors listed in the "humor" category, six in the "romance" category, and fifteen in the category labeled "erotic books (hot sex too)."

18. See, for example, Madeline Davis and Elizabeth Lapovsky Kennedy, "Oral History and the Study of Sexuality in the Lesbian Community: Buffalo, New York, 1940–1960; *Feminist Studies* 12 (1) (Spring 1986): 7–26.

19. Harris, "Notes toward Defining": 6.

20. David Lloyd, *Nationalism and Minor Literature* (Berkeley: University of California Press, 1987), 24.

21. Anna Livia's biographical note in *Sinister Wisdom* 34 (Spring 1988) states: "She is finding it harder and harder to write the end of *Bulldozer Rising* as happy endings get scarcer and scarcer" (120).

22. *Sinister Wisdom* 34 (Spring 1988). Five of the eleven short narratives are identified as belonging to novels-in-progress.

23. For example, S/M fiction, such as Pat Califia's short story collection *Macho Sluts,* has a close affinity to male libertine or pornographic literature.

24. Audre Lorde, "The Master's Tools Will Never Dismantle the Master's House," in *Sister Outsider,* 110–113.

25. See Campbell, *The Hero With a Thousand Faces.* The hero's final task "is to return then to us, transfigured, and teach the lesson he has learned of life renewed" (20).

26. The reference is to Emily Dickinson's familiar poem #1129, "Tell all the Truth, but tell it slant." Interestingly enough, one dictionary definition of "slant" is "to turn or lie in a direction that is not straight up and down or straight across."

27. Wittig, "The Point of View: Universal or Particular?" *Feminist Issues* 3 (2) (Fall 1983): 68.

Select Bibliography

Primary Sources Mentioned in Text

Alguire, Judith. *All Out*. Norwich, Vt.: New Victoria Publishers, 1988.

Allard, Jeannine. *Légende*. Boston: Alyson Publications, 1984.

Allen, Paula Gunn. *The Woman Who Owned the Shadows*. San Francisco: Spinsters Ink, 1983.

Allison, Dorothy. *Trash*. Ithaca: Firebrand Books, 1988.

Alther, Lisa. *Other Women*. New York: Alfred A. Knopf, 1984.

Anzaldúa, Gloria. *Borderlands/La Frontera*. San Francisco: Spinsters/Aunt Lute, 1987.

Arnold, June. *The Cook and the Carpenter*. Plainfield, Vt.: Daughters Inc., 1973.

———. *Sister Gin*. Plainfield, Vt.: Daughters Inc., 1975; reprint, New York: The Feminist Press, 1989.

Arnold, Madelyn. *Bird-Eyes*. Seattle: The Seal Press, 1988.

Arobateau, Red Jordan. *The Bars across Heaven*. Self-published, 1975.

Arthur, Bonnie S. *Night Lights*. Racine, Wisc.: Mother Courage Press, 1987.

Azolakov, Antoinette. *Cass and the Stone Butch*. Austin, Tex.: Banned Books, 1987.

———. *Skiptrace*. Austin, Tex.: Banned Books, 1988.

Azpadu, Dodici. *Saturday Night in the Prime of Life*. Iowa City: Aunt Lute Book Company, 1983.

———. *Goat Song*. Iowa City: Aunt Lute Book Company, 1984.

Bayer, Sandy. *The Crystal Curtain*. Boston: Alyson Publications, 1988.

Beal, M. F. *Angel Dance*. New York: Daughters Inc., 1977.

Birtha, Becky. *For Nights Like This One*. East Palo Alto, Calif.: Frog in the Well, 1983.

————. *Lovers Choice.* Seattle: The Seal Press, 1987.

Bloch, Alice. *The Law of Return.* Boston: Alyson Publications, 1983.

Boucher, Sandy. *Assaults and Rituals.* Oakland: Mama's Press, 1975.

————. *The Notebooks of Leni Clare.* Trumansburg, N.Y.: The Crossing Press, 1982.

Bradshaw, Jan & Mary Hemming. *Girls Next Door: Lesbian Feminist Stories.* With an introduction by Alison Hennegan. London: The Women's Press, 1985.

Brady, Maureen. *Folly.* Trumansburg, N.Y.: The Crossing Press, 1982.

————. *The Question She Put to Herself.* Freedom, Calif.: The Crossing Press, 1987.

Brant, Beth. *The Mohawk Trail.* Ithaca: Firebrand Books, 1985.

Brantenberg, Gerd. *What Comes Naturally.* Translated and revised by the author. London: The Women's Press, 1986 [1973].

Bright, Joyce. *Sunday's Child.* Tallahassee: The Naiad Press, 1988.

Brown, Rita Mae. *Rubyfruit Jungle.* Plainfield, Vt.: Daughters,Inc., 1973; reprint, New York: Bantam Books, 1977.

————. *In Her Day.* Plainfield, Vt.: Daughters, Inc., 1976; reprint, New York: Bantam Books, 1988.

————. *Six of One.* New York: Bantam Books, 1978.

Bulkin, Elly, ed. *Lesbian Fiction: An Anthology.* Watertown, Mass.: Persephone Press, 1981.

Burford, Barbara. *The Threshing Floor.* London: Sheba Feminist Publishers, 1986; reprint, Ithaca: Firebrand Books.

Califia, Pat. *Macho Sluts.* Boston: Alyson Publications, 1988.

Cameron, Anne. *The Journey.* San Francisco: Spinsters/Aunt Lute, 1986.

Carlisle, Andrea. *The Riverhouse Stories.* Corvallis, Oreg.: Calyx Books, 1986.

Chambers, Jane. *Burning.* New York: JH Press, 1978.

Christian, Paula. *The Cruise.* New York: Timely Books, 1982.

Clausen, Jan. *Sinking, Stealing.* Trumansburg, N.Y.: The Crossing Press, 1985.

————. *The Prosperine Papers.* Freedom, Calif.: The Crossing Press, 1988.

Cliff, Michelle. *Abeng.* Trumansburg, N.Y.: The Crossing Press, 1984.

————. *No Telephone to Heaven.* New York: E. P. Dutton, 1987.

Conrad, Heather. *N.E.W.S.* Racine, Wisc.: Mother Courage Press, 1987.

Cotrell, Georgia. *Shoulders.* Ithaca: Firebrand Books, 1987.

Covina, Gina. *The City of Hermits.* Berkeley: Barn Owl, 1983.

Covina, Gina, and Laurel Galana. *The Lesbian Reader.* Guerneville, Calif.: Amazon Press, 1975.

Dawkins, Cecil. *Charleyhorse.* Contemporary American Fiction. New York: Viking Penguin Inc., 1985.

Dean, Elizabeth. *As the Road Curves.* Norwich, Vt.: New Victoria Publishers, 1988.

deVries, Rachel Guido. *Tender Warriors.* Ithaca: Firebrand Books, 1986.

Donnelly, Nisa. *The Bar Stories: A Novel After All.* New York: St. Martin's Press, 1989.

Douglas, Carol Anne. *To the Cleveland Station.* Tallahassee: The Naiad Press, 1982.

Douglas, Lauren Wright. *The Always Anonymous Beast.* Tallahassee: The Naiad Press, 1987.

Dreher, Sarah. *Stoner McTavish.* Norwich, Vt.: New Victoria Publishers, 1985.

———. *Something Shady.* Norwich, Vt.: New Victoria Publishers, 1986.

———. *Grey Magic.* Norwich, Vt.: New Victoria Publishers, 1987.

Due, Linnea. *Give Me Time.* New York: William Morrow, 1985.

Emmerson, Pat. *Raging Mother Mountain.* Tallahassee: The Naiad Press, 1989.

Ennis, Catherine. *To the Lightning.* Tallahassee: The Naiad Press, 1988.

Erhart, Margaret. *Unusual Company.* New York: E. P. Dutton, 1987.

Fleming, Kathleen. *Lovers in the Present Afternoon.* Tallahassee: The Naiad Press, 1984.

Forrest, Katherine. *Curious Wine.* Tallahassee: The Naiad Press, 1983.

———. *Amateur City.* Tallahassee: The Naiad Press, 1984.

———. *Daughters of a Coral Dawn.* Tallahassee: The Naiad Press, 1984.

———. *An Emergence of Green.* Tallahassee: The Naiad Press, 1986.

———. *Murder at the Nightwood Bar.* Tallahassee: The Naiad Press, 1987.

Foster, Marion. *The Monarchs are Flying.* Ithaca: Firebrand Books, 1987.

Frye, Ellen. *Look under the Hawthorne.* Norwich, Vt.: New Victoria Publishers, 1987.

Galford, Ellen. *Moll Cutpurse.* Ithaca: Firebrand Books, 1985.

Gearhart, Sally. *The Wanderground.* Watertown, Mass.: Persephone Press, 1978; reprint, Boston: Alyson Publications, 1984.

Geller, Ruth. *Triangles.* Trumansburg, N.Y.: The Crossing Press, 1984.

Grae, Camarin. *The Winged Dancer.* Chicago: Blazon Books, 1983.

———. *Paz.* Chicago: Blazon Books, 1984.

———. *Soul Snatcher.* Chicago: Blazon Books, 1985.

———. *The Secret in the Bird.* Tallahassee: The Naiad Press, 1988.

———. *Edgewise.* Tallahassee: The Naiad Press, 1989.

Grahn, Judy. *Mundane's World.* Freedom, Calif.: The Crossing Press, 1988.

————, ed. *True to Life Adventure Stories Volume One.* Oakland: Diana Press, 1978.

————, ed. *True to Life Adventure Stories Volume Two.* Trumansburg, N.Y.: The Crossing Press and Oakland: Diana Press, 1981.

Grumbach, Doris. *The Ladies.* New York: E. P. Dutton, 1984.

Hall, Radclyffe. *The Well of Loneliness.* New York: Pocket Books, 1950 [1928].

Hall, Sandi. *The Godmothers.* London: The Women's Press, Ltd., 1982.

Hanscombe, Gillian. *Between Friends.* Boston: Alyson Publications, 1982.

Harris, Bertha. *Confessions of Cherubino.* New York: Harcourt Brace Jovanovich, 1972; reprint, New York: Daughters Inc., 1978.

————. *Lover.* Plainfield, Vt.: Daughters Inc., 1976.

Hayes, Penny. *The Long Trail.* Tallahassee: The Naiad Press, 1986.

————. *Yellowthroat.* Tallahassee: The Naiad Press, 1988.

Isabell, Sharon. *Yesterday's Lessons.* Oakland: The Women's Press Collective, 1974.

Kennedy, Evelyn. *Cherished Love.* Tallahassee: The Naiad Press, 1988.

Kim, Willyce. *Dancer Dawkins and the California Kid.* Boston: Alyson Publications, 1985.

————. *Dead Heat.* Boston: Alyson Publications, 1988.

Koertge, Noretta. *Who Was That Masked Woman?* New York: St. Martin's Press, 1981.

————. *Valley of the Amazons.* New York: St. Martin's Press, 1984.

Kunz, Alesia. *Shangrila and Linda.* Prickly Pear Press, 1981.

Lang, Elizabeth. *Anna's Country.* Tallahassee: The Naiad Press, 1981.

Livia, Anna. *Relatively Norma.* London: Onlywomen Press, n.d.

————. *Bulldozer Rising.* London: Onlywomen Press, n.d. [1988].

Loewenstein, Andrea. *This Place.* London: Routledge & Kegan Paul, 1984; London: Pandora Press, 1985.

Lorde, Audre. *Zami: A New Spelling of My Name.* Watertown, Mass.: Persephone Press, 1982; reprint, Freedom, Calif.: The Crossing Press, 1983.

Lynch, Lee. *Toothpick House.* Tallahassee: The Naiad Press, 1983.

————. *Old Dyke Tales.* Tallahassee: The Naiad Press, 1984.

————. *The Swashbuckler.* Tallahassee: The Naiad Press, 1985.

————. *Home in Your Hands.* Tallahassee: The Naiad Press, 1986.

————. *Dusty's Queen of Hearts Diner.* Tallahassee: The Naiad Press, 1987.

March, Caeia. *Three Ply Yarn.* London: The Women's Press, 1986.

Marchessault, Jovette. *Lesbian Triptych.* Translated by Yvonne M. Klein. Toronto: The Women's Press, 1985 [1980].

McConnell, Vicki. *Mrs. Porter's Letter.* Tallahassee: The Naiad Press, 1982.

———. *The Burnton Widows.* Tallahassee: The Naiad Press, 1984.

———. *Double Daughter.* Tallahassee: The Naiad Press, 1988.

McNab, Claire. *Lessons in Murder.* Tallahassee: The Naiad Press, 1988.

McRae, Diana. *All the Muscle You Need.* San Francisco: Spinsters/Aunt Lute, 1988.

Michener, Marian. *Three Glasses of Wine Have Been Removed from This Story.* Seattle: Silverleaf Press, 1988.

Miller, Isabel. *Patience and Sarah.* Greenwich, Conn.: Fawcett Publications, Inc. 1973. Originally published as *A Place for Us,* 1969.

Millett, Kate. *Sita.* New York: Farrar, Straus and Giroux, 1976; New York: Ballantine Books, 1978.

Miner, Valerie. *Blood Sisters.* London: The Women's Press, 1981.

———. *Movement.* Trumansburg, N.Y.: The Crossing Press, 1982.

Moraga, Cherríe. *Loving in the War Years.* Boston: South End Press, 1983.

Moyano, Maricla. *BeginningBook.* New York: Print Center, 1973.

Murphy, Patricia. *Searching for Spring.* Tallahassee: The Naiad Press, 1987.

———. *We Walk the Back of the Tiger.* Tallahassee: The Naiad Press, 1988.

Nachmann, Elana. *Riverfinger Women.* Plainfield, Vt.: Daughters Inc., 1974.

Newman, Lesléa. *Good Enough to Eat.* Ithaca: Firebrand Books, 1986.

———. *A Letter to Harvey Milk.* Ithaca: Firebrand Books, 1988.

Oakgrove, Artemis. *The Raging Peace* (volume 1 of the Throne Trilogy). Denver: Lace Publications, Inc., 1984.

———. *Dreams of Vengeance* (volume 2 of the Throne Trilogy). Denver: Lace Publications, Inc., 1985.

———. *Throne of Council* (volume 3 of the Throne Trilogy). Denver: Lace Publications, Inc., 1986.

Ramos, Juanita, ed. *Compañeras: Latina Lesbians (An Anthology).* New York: Latina Lesbian History Project, 1987.

Rule, Jane. *Desert of the Heart.* Tallahassee: The Naiad Press, 1987 [1964].

———. *Contract with the World.* Tallahassee: The Naiad Press, 1980.

———. *Memory Board.* Tallahassee: The Naiad Press, 1987.

———. *After the Fire.* Tallahassee: The Naiad Press, 1989.

Russ, Joanna. *The Female Man.* New York: Bantam Books, 1975.

———. *On Strike Against God.* New York: Out & Out Books, 1980.

Schulman, Sarah. *The Sophie Horowitz Story.* Tallahassee: The Naiad Press, 1984.

———. *Girls, Visions, and Everything.* Seattle: The Seal Press, 1986.

———. *After Delores.* New York: E. P. Dutton, 1988.

Shockley, Ann Allen. *Loving Her*. Tallahassee: The Naiad Press, 1987 [1974].

———. *The Black and White of It*. Tallahassee: The Naiad Press, 1987 [1980].

———. *Say Jesus and Come to Me*. Tallahassee: The Naiad Press, 1987 [1982].

Singer, Rochelle. *The Demeter Flower*. New York: St. Martin's Press, 1980.

Smith, Shelley. *The Pearls*. Tallahassee: The Naiad Press, 1987.

South, Chris. *Clenched Fists, Burning Crosses*. Trumansburg, N.Y.: The Crossing Press, 1984.

Stefan, Verena. *Shedding*. Plainfield, Vt.: Daughters, Inc., 1978 [1975].

Strongin, Lynn. *Bones and Kim*. Argyle, N.Y.: Spinsters Ink, 1980.

Swallow, Jean. *Leave a Light On for Me*. San Francisco: Spinsters/Aunt Lute, 1986.

Taylor, Sheila Ortiz. *Faultline*. Tallahassee: The Naiad Press, 1982.

———. *Spring Forward, Fall Back*. Tallahassee: The Naiad Press, 1985.

Taylor, Valerie. *Prism*. Tallahassee: The Naiad Press, 1981.

Toder, Nancy. *Choices*. Watertown, Mass.: Persephone Press, 1980; reprint, Boston: Alyson Publications, 1984.

Van Deurs, Kay [Kady]. *The Notebooks That Emma Gave Me: The Autobiography of a Lesbian*. Self-published, 1978.

Veto, Janine. *Iris*. Boston: Alyson Publications, 1984.

Vole, Zenobia N. *Osten's Bay*. Tallahassee: The Naiad Press, 1988.

Weathers, Brenda. *The House at Pelham Falls*. Tallahassee: The Naiad Press, 1986.

Wells, Jess. *The Dress and the Sharda Stories*. San Francisco: Library B Productions, 1986.

Wilson, Anna. *Altogether Elsewhere*. London: Onlywomen Press, 1985.

Wilson, Barbara. *Ambitious Women*. Seattle: The Seal Press, 1982.

———. *Walking on the Moon*. Seattle: The Seal Press, 1983.

———. *Murder in the Collective*. Seattle: The Seal Press, 1984.

———. *Sisters of the Road*. Seattle: The Seal Press, 1986.

———. *Cows and Horses*. Portland, Oreg.: The Eighth Mountain Press, 1988.

———. *The Dog Collar Murders*. Seattle: The Seal Press, 1989.

Wings, Mary. *She Came Too Late*. Freedom, Calif.: The Crossing Press, 1987.

Winterson, Jeanette. *Oranges Are Not the Only Fruit*. New York: The Atlantic Monthly Press, 1987 [1985].

Wittig, Monique. *The Opoponax*. Plainfield, Vt.: Daughters Inc. [1966].

———. *Les Guérillères*. New York: Viking Press, 1971 [1969]; reprint, Boston: Beacon Press, 1985.

———. *The Lesbian Body*. New York: Avon Books, 1975 [1973]; reprint, Boston: Beacon Press, 1986.

———. *Across the Acheron*. London: Peter Owen, 1987 [1985].

Wittig, Monique, and Sande Zweig. *Lesbian Peoples: Materials for a Dictionary*. New York: Avon Books, 1976.

Young, Donna. *Retreat! As It Was*. Tallahassee: The Naiad Press, 1979.

Secondary Sources

Abbott, Sidney, and Barbara Love. *Sappho Was a Right-On Woman*. New York: Stein and Day, 1972; Day Books, 1978.

Abel, Elizabeth, Marianne Hirsch, and Elizabeth Langland, eds. *The Voyage In: Fictions of Female Development*. Hanover and London: University Press of New England, 1983.

Alcoff, Linda. "Cultural Feminism versus Post-Structuralism: The Identity Crisis in Feminist Theory." *Signs: Journal of Women in Culture and Society* 13 (3) (Spring 1988): 405–36.

Allen, Jeffner. *Lesbian Philosophy: Explorations*. Palo Alto: Institute of Lesbian Studies, 1986.

Allen, Paula Gunn. *The Sacred Hoop: Recovering the Feminine in American Indian Traditions*. Boston: Beacon Press, 1986.

Arnold, June. "Lesbians and Literature" (A Seminar at the Modern Language Association, San Francisco, December 1975). *Sinister Wisdom* 1 (2) (Fall 1976): 28–30.

Beck, Evelyn Torton, ed. *Nice Jewish Girls: A Lesbian Anthology*. Watertown, Mass.: Persephone Press, 1982; revised edition, Boston: Beacon Press, 1989.

Belsey, Catherine. *Critical Practice*. London and New York: Methuen, 1980.

Benstock, Sheri. *Women of the Left Bank*. Austin: University of Texas Press, 1986.

Birkby, Phyllis, Bertha Harris, Jill Johnston, Esther Newton, and Jan O'Wyatt. *Amazon Expedition: A Lesbian Feminist Anthology*. New York: Times Change Press, 1973.

Boston Lesbian Psychologies Collective, eds. *Lesbian Psychologies*. Urbana and Chicago: University of Illinois Press, 1987.

Boswell, John. *Christianity, Social Tolerance, and Homosexuality: Gay People in Western Europe from the Beginning of the Christian Era to the Fourteenth Century,* Chicago and London: University of Chicago Press, 1980.

Brody, Michal, ed. *Are We There Yet?: A Continuing History of Lavender Woman*. Iowa City: Aunt Lute Book Company, 1985.

Brown, Linda J. "Dark Horse: A View of Writing and Publishing by Dark Lesbians." *Sinister Wisdom* 13 (Spring 1980): 45–50.

Buckley, Jerome. *Season of Youth: The Bildungsroman from Dickens to Golding*. Cambridge: Harvard University Press, 1974.

Bulkin, Elly. "Racism and Writing: Some Implications for White Lesbian Critics." *Sinister Wisdom* 13 (Spring 1980): 3–22.

Bulkin, Elly, Minnie Bruce Pratt, and Barbara Smith. *Yours in Struggle: Three Feminist Perspectives on Anti-Semitism and Racism*. Brooklyn: Long Haul Press, 1984.

Bunch, Charlotte. *Passionate Politics: Feminist Theory in Action*. New York: St. Martin's Press, 1987.

Bunch, Charlotte, and Nancy Myron, eds. *Class and Feminism*. Baltimore: Diana Press, 1974.

Campbell, Joseph. *The Hero with a Thousand Faces*. Bollingen Series XVII. Princeton: Princeton University Press, 1949.

Carruthers, Mary. "The Re-Vision of the Muse: Adrienne Rich, Audre Lorde, Judy Grahn, Olga Broumas." *The Hudson Review* 36 (2) (Summer 1983): 293–322.

Cheney, Joyce, ed. *Lesbian Land*. Minneapolis: Word Weavers, 1985.

Chodorow, Nancy. *The Reproduction of Mothering: Psychoanalysis and the Sociology of Gender*. Berkeley: University of California Press, 1978.

Christian, Barbara. *Black Feminist Criticism: Perspectives on Black Women Writers*. The Athene Series. New York: Pergamon Press, 1985.

Cixous, Hélène. "The Laugh of the Medusa." *Signs* 1 (4) (Summer 1976): 875–893.

Clunis, D. Merilee, and G. Dorsey Green. *Lesbian Couples*. Seattle: The Seal Press, 1988.

Cott, Nancy F., and Elizabeth H. Pleck, eds. *A Heritage of Her Own*. New York: Simon and Schuster, Touchstone, 1979.

Daly, Mary. *Gyn/Ecology: The Metaethics of Radical Feminism*. Boston: Beacon Press, 1978.

Damon, Gene [Barbara Grier], and Lee Stuart. *The Lesbian in Literature: A Bibliography*. San Francisco: The Ladder, 1967.

Darty, Trudy, and Sandee Potter, eds. *Women-Identified Women*. With a foreword by Judith Schwarz. Palo Alto: Mayfield Publishing Co., 1984.

Davis, Elizabeth Gould. *The First Sex*. Baltimore: Penguin Books, 1972.

de Beauvoir, Simone. *The Second Sex*. Translated and edited by H. M. Parshley. New York: Alfred A. Knopf, 1952; New York: Bantam Books, 1961.

de Lauretis, Teresa, ed. *Feminist Studies/Critical Studies.* Bloomington and Indianapolis: Indiana University Press, 1986.

de Rougemont, Denis. *Love in the Western World.* New York: Harcourt, Brace, and Co., 1940.

Desmoines, Harriet. "Notes for a Magazine I." *Sinister Wisdom* 1 (1) (July 1976): 3–4.

Diner, Helen. *Mothers and Amazons: The First Feminine History of Culture,* with an introduction by Brigitte Berger. New York: Doubleday Anchor, 1973 [1965].

Doane, Janice, and Devon Hodges. *Nostalgia and Sexual Difference.* New York and London: Methuen, 1987.

Eagleton, Terry. *Literary Theory: An Introduction.* Minneapolis: University of Minnesota Press, 1983.

Eliade, Mircea. *Myth and Reality.* New York: Harper & Row, 1963.

Evans, Sara. *Personal Politics: The Roots of Women's Liberation in the Civil Rights Movement and the New Left.* New York: Random House, 1979.

Faderman, Lillian. "The Morbidification of Love between Women by Nineteenth-Century Sexologists." *Journal of Homosexuality* 4 (1) (Fall 1978): 73–90.

———. *Surpassing the Love of Men: Romantic Friendship and Love between Women from the Renaissance to the Present.* New York: William Morrow & Co., 1981.

Farwell, Marilyn R. "Toward a Definition of the Lesbian Literary Imagination." *Signs: Journal of Women in Culture and Society* 14 (1) (Autumn 1988): 100–118.

Fetterley, Judith. "Writes of Passing." *Gossip: A Journal of Lesbian Feminist Ethics* 5 (n.d.): 21–28.

Foster, Jeannette. *Sex Variant Women in Literature.* Tallahassee: The Naiad Press, 1985 [1956].

Frye, Joanne. *Living Stories, Telling Lives: Women and the Novel in Contemporary Experience.* Ann Arbor: The University of Michigan Press, 1986.

Frye, Marilyn. *The Politics of Reality: Essays in Feminist Theory.* Trumansburg, N.Y.: The Crossing Press, 1983.

Frye, Northrop. *The Secular Scripture.* Cambridge: Harvard University Press, 1976.

Gibbs, Joan, and Sara Bennett, eds. *Top Ranking: A Collection of Articles on Racism and Classism in the Lesbian Community.* New York: February 3rd Press, n.d.

Gilbert, Sandra M., and Susan Gubar. *The Madwoman in the Attic.* New Haven: Yale University Press, 1979.

————. *No Man's Land: The Place of the Woman Writer in the Twentieth Century.* Vol. 1, *The War of the Words.* New Haven and London: Yale University Press, 1988. Vol. 2, *Sexchanges.* New Haven and London: Yale University Press, 1989.

Gilligan, Carol. *In a Different Voice: Psychological Theory and Women's Development.* Cambridge: Harvard University Press, 1982.

Gomez, Jewelle. "Imagine a Lesbian . . . A Black Lesbian . . ." *Trivia: A Journal of Ideas,* 12 (Spring 1988): 45–60.

Grahn, Judy. *Another Mother Tongue: Gay Words, Gay Worlds.* Boston: Beacon Press, 1984.

————. *The Highest Apple: Sappho and the Lesbian Poetic Tradition.* San Francisco: Spinsters Ink, 1985.

Harris, Bertha. "*What we mean to say:* Notes toward Defining the Nature of Lesbian Literature." *Heresies* 3 (1977): 5–8.

Herman, Ellen. "Getting to Serenity: Do Addiction Programs Sap Our Political Vitality?" *Out/Look* 1 (2) (Summer 1988): 10–21.

Hoagland, Sarah Lucia. *Lesbian Ethics: Toward New Value.* Palo Alto: Institute of Lesbian Studies, 1988.

Hoagland, Sarah Lucia, and Julia Penelope, eds. *For Lesbians Only: A Separatist Anthology.* London: Onlywomen Press, 1988.

Hull, Gloria T. "'Under the Days': The Buried Life and Poetry of Angelina Weld Grimke." *Conditions: Five* 2 (2) (Autumn 1979): 17–25.

Jardine, Alice. *Gynesis: Configurations of Women and Modernity.* Ithaca: Cornell University Press, 1985.

Jay, Karla. *The Amazon and the Page: Natalie Clifford Barney and Renée Vivien.* Bloomington and Indianapolis: Indiana University Press, 1988.

Jay, Karla, and Allen Young. *Out of the Closets: Voices of Gay Liberation.* New York: Jove/HBJ, 1977 [1972].

Johnston, Jill. *Lesbian Nation: The Feminist Solution.* New York: Simon and Schuster, 1973.

————. *Gullible's Travels.* New York: Links Books, 1974.

Katz, Jonathan. *Gay American History: Lesbians and Gay Men in the U.S.A..* New York: Thomas Y. Crowell Co., 1976; New York: Avon Books, 1978.

Kitzinger, Celia. *The Social Construction of Lesbianism.* Inquiries in Social Construction Series. London: SAGE Publications, 1987.

Koedt, Anne, Ellen Levine, and Anita Rapone, eds. *Radical Feminism.* New York: Quadrangle/The New York Times Book Co., 1973.

Krieger, Susan. "Lesbian Identity and Community: Recent Social Science Literature." *Signs* 8 (1) (Autumn 1982): 91–108.

———. *The Mirror Dance: Identity in a Women's Community.* Philadelphia: Temple University Press, 1983.

Lauter, Estella. *Women as Mythmakers: Poetry and Visual Art by Twentieth-Century Women.* Bloomington: Indiana University Press, 1984.

Lawrence, Leslie. "Bodily Fictions." *The Women's Review of Books,* 4 (10–11) (July-August 1987): 8–9.

Lerner, Laurence. *Love and Marriage: Literature and Its Social Context.* New York: St. Martin's Press, 1979.

Lewis, Sasha Gregory. *Sunday's Women: A Report on Lesbian Life Today.* Boston: Beacon Press, 1979.

Linden, Robin Ruth, Darlene R. Pagano, Diana E. H. Russell, Susan Leigh Star, eds. *Against Sadomasochism: A Radical Feminist Analysis.* East Palo Alto: Frog In the Well, 1982.

Lloyd, David. *Nationalism and Minor Literature.* Berkeley: University of California Press, 1987.

Lorde, Audre. *Sister Outsider: Essays and Speeches.* Trumansburg, N.Y.: The Crossing Press, 1984.

Loulan, Joann. *Lesbian Sex.* San Francisco: Spinsters Ink, 1984.

Lynch, Lee. *The Amazon Trail.* Tallahassee: The Naiad Press, 1988.

Malinowski, Bronislaw. *Sex, Culture, and Myth.* New York: Harcourt, Brace, & World, 1962.

Martin, Del, and Phyllis Lyon. *Lesbian/Woman.* San Francisco: Glide Publications, 1972; New York: Bantam, 1972.

Miller, Nancy K., ed. *The Poetics of Gender.* New York: Columbia University Press, 1986.

Miller, Stuart. *The Picaresque Novel.* Cleveland: The Press of Case Western Reserve University, 1967.

Moi, Toril. *Sexual/Textual Politics: Feminist Literary Theory.* London and New York: Methuen, 1985.

Moraga, Cherríe, and Gloria Anzaldúa, eds. *This Bridge Called My Back: Writings by Radical Women of Color.* With a foreword by Toni Cade Bambera. Watertown, Mass.: Persephone Press, 1981; reprint, Kitchen Table: Women of Color Press, 1983.

Morgan, Robin, ed. *Sisterhood is Powerful: An Anthology of Writings from the Women's Liberation Movement.* New York: Vintage Books, 1970.

Myron, Nancy, and Charlotte Bunch, eds. *Lesbianism and the Women's Movement.* Baltimore: Diana Press, 1975.

Nestle, Joan. *A Restricted Country.* Ithaca: Firebrand Books, 1987.

Newton, Esther. "The Mythic Mannish Lesbian: Radclyffe Hall and the New Woman." *Signs* 9 (4) (Summer 1984): 557–575.

Oktenberg, Adrian. "The End of the Affair," review of *Unusual Company* by Margaret Erhart and *Cows and Horses* by Barbara Wilson. In *The Women's Review of Books* 5 (9) (June 1988): 15–16.

Paris, Sherri. "In a World They Never Made," review of *Cass and the Stone Butch* by Antoinette Azolakov, *The Always Anonymous Beast* by Lauren Wright Douglas, *Sisters of the Road* by Barbara Wilson, and *She Came Too Late* by Mary Wings. In *The Women's Review of Books* 5 (10–11) (July 1988): 20.

Patai, Daphne. "Constructing a Self: A Brazilian Life Story." *Feminist Studies* 14 (1) (Spring 1988): 143–166.

Penelope, Julia [Stanley]. "True Confessions," review of *Confessions of a Failed Southern Lady* by Florence King and *My Mama's Dead Squirrel* by Mab Segrest. In *The Women's Review of Books* 3 (7) (April 1986): 8–9.

Peplau, Letitia Anne, Susan Cochran, Karen Rook, and Christine Padesky. "Loving Women: Attachment and Autonomy in Lesbian Relationships." *The Journal of Social Issues* 34 (3) (1978): 7–27.

Plato. *The Symposium.* Translated by Suzy Q. Groden. Amherst: University of Massachusetts Press, 1970.

Ponse, Barbara. *Identities in the Lesbian World.* Westport, Conn.: Greenwood Press, 1978.

Pratt, Annis. *Archetypal Patterns in Women's Fiction.* Bloomington: Indiana University Press, 1981.

Rabine, Leslie Wahl. "A Feminist Politics of Non-Identity." *Feminist Studies* 14 (1) (Spring 1988): 11–31.

Radway, Janice. *Reading the Romance.* Chapel Hill: University of North Carolina Press, 1984.

Raymond, Janice. *A Passion for Friends: Toward a Philosophy of Female Affection.* Boston: Beacon Press, 1986.

Rich, Adrienne. *Blood, Bread, and Poetry: Selected Prose 1979–1985.* New York: W. W. Norton & Co., 1986.

———. *Of Woman Born: Motherhood as Experience and Institution.* New York: W. W. Norton, 1976; New York: Bantam Books, 1977.

———. *On Lies, Secrets and Silence.* New York: W. W. Norton, 1979.

———. *The Dream of a Common Language.* New York: W. W. Norton, 1978.

Rigney, Barbara Hill. *Lilith's Daughters: Women and Religion in Contemporary Fiction.* Madison: University of Wisconsin Press, 1982.

Rohrlich, Ruby, and Elaine Hoffman Baruch. *Women in Search of Utopia.* New York: Schocken Books, 1984.

Rosinsky, Natalie. *Feminist Futures: Contemporary Women's Speculative Fiction.* Ann Arbor: UMI Research Press, 1984.

Ruddick, Sara. "Maternal Thinking." *Feminist Studies* 6 (2) (Summer 1980): 342–367.

Rule, Jane. *Lesbian Images.* Garden City, N.J.: Doubleday & Co., 1975.

———. *A Hot-Eyed Moderate.* Tallahassee: The Naiad Press, 1985.

Samois, ed. *Coming to Power: Writings and Graphics on Lesbian S/M,* 2d ed. Boston: Alyson Publications, 1982.

Saphira, Miriam, ed. *New Lesbian Literature 1980–88.* Auckland, New Zealand: Papers Inc., 1988.

Schuster, Marilyn. "Strategies for Survival: The Subtle Subversion of Jane Rule." *Feminist Studies* 7 (3) (Fall 1981): 431–450.

Segrest, Mab. *My Mama's Dead Squirrel: Lesbian Essays on Southern Culture,* with an introduction by Adrienne Rich. Ithaca: Firebrand Books, 1985.

Shaktini, Namascar. "Displacing the Phallic Subject: Wittig's Lesbian Writing." *Signs* 8 (1) (Autumn 1982): 29–44.

Showalter, Elaine, ed. *The New Feminist Criticism: Essays on Women, Literature and Theory.* New York: Pantheon Books, 1985.

Smith, Barbara, ed. *Home Girls: A Black Feminist Anthology.* New York: Kitchen Table: Women of Color Press, 1983.

Snitow, Ann. "The Front Line: Notes on Sex in Novels by Women." *Signs* 5 (4) (Summer 1980): 702–718.

Spivack, Gayatri Chakravorty. *In Other Worlds: Essays in Cultural Politics.* New York and London: Methuen, 1987.

Squier, Susan, ed. *Women Writers and the City.* Knoxville: University of Tennessee Press, 1984.

Stambolian, George, and Elaine Marks, eds. *Homosexualities and French Literature.* Ithaca: Cornell University Press, 1979.

Stanley, Julia Penelope. "Uninhabited Angels." *Margins* 23 (August 1975): 7–10.

Stanley, Julia Penelope, and Susan J. Wolfe, eds. *The Coming Out Stories.* With a foreword by Adrienne Rich. Watertown, Mass.: Persephone Press, 1980.

Stewart, Grace. *A New Mythos: The Novel of the Artist as Heroine.* Montreal: Eden Press, 1981.

Stimpson, Catharine. "Zero Degree Deviancy: The Lesbian Novel in English." *Critical Inquiry* 8 (2) (Winter 1981): 363–379.

Tanner, Donna. *The Lesbian Couple.* Lexington, Mass.: Lexington Books, 1978.

Tanner, Tony. *Adultery in the Novel: Contract and Transgression.* Baltimore: The Johns Hopkins University Press, 1979.

Tate, Claudia. *Black Women Writers at Work.* New York: Continuum, 1983.

Vance, Carole S., ed. *Pleasure and Danger: Exploring Female Sexuality.* Boston: Routledge & Kegan Paul, 1984.

Vida, Ginny. *Our Right to Love.* Englewood Cliffs, N.J.: Prentice-Hall, 1978.

Wahlstrom, Billie, and Caren Deming. "Chasing the Popular Arts through the Critical Forest." *Journal of Popular Culture* 13 (3) (Spring 1980): 412–426.

Weiss, Andrea, and Greta Schiller. *Before Stonewall: The Making of a Gay and Lesbian Community.* Tallahassee: The Naiad Press, 1988.

Williams, Raymond. *The Country and the City.* New York: Oxford University Press, 1973.

Winnow, Jackie. "Lesbians Working on AIDS: Assessing the Impact on Health Care for Women." *Out/Look* 2 (1) (Summer 1989): 10–18.

Wittig, Monique. "The Mark of Gender." *Feminist Issues* 5 (2) (Fall 1985): 3–12.

———. "The Point of View: Universal or Particular?" *Feminist Issues* 3 (2) (Fall 1983): 63–69.

Wolf, Deborah Goleman. *The Lesbian Community.* Berkeley: University of California Press, 1979.

Woolf, Virginia. *A Room of One's Own.* New York and London: Harcourt, Brace, & World, 1929.

———. *Three Guineas.* New York: Harcourt, Brace & World, 1938.

Yaeger, Patricia S. "'Because a Fire Was in My Head': Eudora Welty and the Dialogic Imagination." *PMLA* 99 (5) (October 1984): 955–973.

Zimmerman, Bonnie. "Daughters of Darkness: Lesbian Vampires." *Jump Cut* 24–25 (March 1981): 23–24.

———. "The Politics of Transliteration: Lesbian First-Person Narratives." *Signs: Journal of Women in Culture and Society* 9 (4) (Summer 1984): 663–682.

Index